EBURY PRESS

KUNDALINI YOGA FOR ALL

Kamini Bobde is a Kundalini practitioner and spiritual aspirant who follows the Swami Satyananda tradition of yoga. She has conducted yoga and Kundalini workshops in Germany, Tanzania, Vapi and Kund in the Himalayas. People practising with her have not only experienced relief from depression, migraine, PCOD and cancer, but have reported an overall feeling of joy, love and better productivity. The author herself is a good example of the spirituality that can be practised even as you go about your daily life. A former journalist, she travelled with erstwhile prime minister Narasimha Rao when he visited the US in 1994. She taught media research for over a decade at Xavier Institute of Communications, Mumbai, and now has her own business. She has a YouTube channel on yoga and writes a blog, *Yogabhakti*.

ADVANCE PRAISE FOR THE BOOK

'I've been doing yoga for forty years and always thought Kundalini was not for householders or the worldly. Kamini has exploded this myth and claims that all can and must awaken their Kundalini, and she explains very well what is Kundalini and how to awaken it. I recommend this book for exploring your highest potential with equanimity and bliss'—Neena Gupta

Kundalini Yoga for All

Unlock the Power of Your Body and Brain

KAMINI BOBDE

EBURY
PRESS

An imprint of Penguin Random House

EBURY PRESS

USA | Canada | UK | Ireland | Australia
New Zealand | India | South Africa | China

Ebury Press is part of the Penguin Random House group of companies
whose addresses can be found at global.penguinrandomhouse.com

Published by Penguin Random House India Pvt. Ltd
4th Floor, Capital Tower 1, MG Road,
Gurugram 122 002, Haryana, India

Penguin
Random House
India

First published in Ebury Press by Penguin Random House India 2022

Copyright © Kamini Bobde 2022
Illustration copyright © Kamini Bobde 2022

Illustrations by The Magic Beans

All rights reserved

10 9 8 7 6 5 4 3 2

The views and opinions expressed in this book are the author's own and the
facts are as reported by her which have been verified to the extent possible,
and the publishers are not in any way liable for the same.

ISBN 9780143451181

Typeset in Sabon by Manipal Technologies Limited, Manipal
Printed at Replika Press Pvt. Ltd, India

www.penguin.co.in

*With reverence and humility placed at the lotus feet of
Paramhansa Swami Satyananda Saraswati*

CONTENTS

INTRODUCTION

Can Kundalini Yoga be for 'all'? Isn't it a secret practise? Isn't it to be feared because of its explosive nature? Shouldn't it be practised *only* under the expert guidance of a Guru? Won't it affect anyone adversely if practised in a wrong way?

If you have all these trepidations, then this book holds all the answers for you.

In fact, all your fears can be allayed by just one sentence: Kundalini Yoga is for all because Kundalini Shakti resides in all.

Kundalini, the primordial energy, is present in everyone. In most people, it is sleeping; in some, it is partially awakened. Scriptures say your past lives karma, your prarabdha karma, determine how awakened will be the state of Kundalini Shakti in you.

Kundalini Yoga deals with the primordial energy present in all but many either do not know it or are simply too lazy to explore. For those willing to dive into the depths of their inner being to awaken this sleeping Shakti, this book will prove to be an exciting exploration into yourself that will unravel your highest potential.

Know for sure that you are taking up a challenge because you will be discovering the fundamentals of creation itself, of which you are a part. It is about experiencing energy and consciousness which powers every aspect of this universe. Yes, experience is the key word. No intellectual arm-chair faffing around here. Kundalini is about the play of the energy and consciousness that exists within us.

Simply put, it is understanding what powers understanding itself.

Locked within the everyday process of cognition and action is the secret of all that powers our evolution as a human race. Any form of yoga is finally a journey into oneself, into unlocking one's own secret hidden behind a veil of innocence and ignorance.

The book is divided into two major sections: the theory of Kundalini and the practise of it. You may either first digest the theory and then launch into the practise or read the theory and do the practise simultaneously. The choice is yours. But if either part of this book is neglected, you will not succeed at awakening your inner Kundalini. Theory will not succeed at awakening your inner Kundalini because mere theory without practise will remain an intellectual exercise and practise without understanding the theory will not fructify into an awakened Kundalini.

My Experiences

I started practising Kundalini Yoga with profound experiences twelve years ago. First came the almost magical disappearance of some chronic niggling health problems which I had previously thought were hereditary. How could something that I have suffered for decades disappear within a fortnight of practising yoga? I did not know then that these almost magical, therapeutic results were the first level of *siddhi* (powers that you experience in yoga). It was much later that I discovered that using any form of yoga for therapeutic benefits is like using an elephant to kill an ant.

I intensified my daily practise and dived into books on Kundalini Yoga, the Upanishads, the Puranas and the Samhitas. I had grown up reading western philosophers like Socrates, Aristotle, Spinoza, Schopenhauer, Nietzsche and C.G. Jung, and realized that yoga was something that not only theorized but also showed how we could practise and experience the theory as a part of our daily lives. Sure enough, one experienced what one read. It is an awesome feeling. In many ways, it was like the physics and chemistry experiments one did in laboratories to establish the theory one read in the classroom.

The only difference being that in yoga the experiences are random and unexpected. Science likes to find an average value which then becomes fundamental for all under all situations. Yoga and Indian philosophy rely on the principle that every phenomenon is impacted by the observer until they know the truth at which point it goes beyond the scope of language and description. God knew that if he didn't do this, then humans would market Truth too. It is this core principle of yoga which engenders as many experiences as there are unique fingerprints and snowflake patterns in the world.

In the initial stages, I could not connect my experiences to my practise because they were a little out of the ordinary. Hence, it was not surprising that I started having experiences which I could not fathom and was too embarrassed to discuss with anyone. Sometimes during the practise my body would convulse with uncontrollable sobbing, without warning or due to any ostensible reason. But at the end of it, I would feel serene and energetic. Fortunately, this happened mostly towards the end of my early morning practise when I would do the japa after the asanas, pranayama and kriyas, were over. It would be at this point in my practise that an intense desire to know God would engulf me.

And so it was that I had organized a Kundalini Workshop for ten days by my Yoga Guru in Vapi, Gujarat. It was a beautiful location by the river Daman Ganga. There was a vast green lawn where we practised our morning yoga and a hall where we chanted our morning and evening mantras.

There were around twenty participants from all over the country. Every morning at 5 a.m., we assembled in the hall for chanting the Gayatri Mantra 108 times. Group chanting of mantras is always an exhilarating experience. One day, as we came to the end of the chanting, an intense desire bubbled up from my depths, 'God, when will I know you?' With this, a big sob escaped from within and my whole being shook with uncontrollable sobbing. Thus, sobbing, I walked out and sat down on the steps leading to the hall. The crying had turned into howling; I felt as if my whole being would burst forth at that very moment. In front of me, beyond the green lawn, was the Daman Ganga shedding its ink-blue into the dawn and turning into a shimmering azure blue. A flock of white birds were gracefully flying across the sky, like a scene from some ethereal, silent film. The whole scene was so utterly beautiful that it wrung my heart. The crying continued, unabated.

I went to my room to collect myself, aware that people were getting concerned about me. Some were even horrified. But this mix of feeling, jubilant from the inside and tearful on the outside, continued despite the fact that a part of me was aware of the scene it was creating and the concern it was arousing. This continued till 11 a.m. Then slowly, it subsided of its own accord.

At other times of the day, I would go into fits of uncontrollable laughter. The laughter would take over me at any time. Something funny was always the trigger but the proportion of my reaction to the situation itself was skewed.

I don't know when and how, but these instances slowly tapered off. I noticed subtle changes in my personality too; from a meek, feeble person, I had become someone who was able to overcome her deep-seated fears and inhibitions. I had an irrational fear of ghosts as a child that I had not been able to shake off even in adult life. After three years of reciting the Das Mahavidya every evening, this illogical fear had disappeared. I've shared this experience while discussing the Antahkarna (on page 40) and how mantras help clean up your deep-seated fears and complexes.

Finally, it was in Hamburg where I was assisting my yoga Guru in a spiritual workshop when I experienced the existence of another reality.

I had just sat down with my yoga Guru for a one-on-one Chakra meditation session. We were hardly a few minutes into it, when he instructed me to take my awareness to my Mooladhara Chakra. I did as he instructed and suddenly heard a loud hissing sound coming from within me and saw a black snake uncoil and raise itself to its full height. It was beautiful. It kept swaying. In that moment, nothing else existed. Not even me. Gradually, it disappeared, and any hint of its presence dissolved into a beautiful golden, glittering light. I wish I could describe the state I was in. There was nothing except a feeling of great joy. But I don't know who was experiencing it, because honestly, in that moment, I did not exist. There was only pure bliss.

I don't know how much time passed. I felt someone tugging at my hand. Calling out to me. 'Please, please don't do this', I thought as I was dragged from that state of dissolution into that golden light. It was my yoga Guru trying to call me back to this world. Later my Guru said that if I had stayed in that state for too long, it would have sapped me of all energy and might have rendered me listless for days.

It is after much internal debate that I have decided to share these experiences with the world, for it is something I have so far desisted from talking about. Your experiences can either be believed by others or make you look like a fool. But I decided to let this book be an open and honest connection between us, as we launch into the search of an ancient system designed for exploring and experiencing the ultimate Truth.

You must also know that during my research, I found that such an experience is called Pranotthana, which should not be mistaken with Kundalini awakening. The word means life (prana) rising (uthan). It is the release of pranic forces. In 'Kundalini Tantra', Swami Satyananda Saraswati explains Pranotthana as follows:

'This preliminary awakening starts from Mooladhara and ascends the spinal cord via Pingala Nadi, only partially purifying the Chakras, until it reaches the brain where it is usually dispersed. However, it does prepare the aspirant for the eventual awakening of Kundalini, which is something altogether different and more powerful.' Or in common parlance, one can say it is a trailer of the unfolding of Kundalini.

Your author is still on this path. The experiences I have related do not fully illustrate the process of Kundalini awakening but portray what I have experienced in my journey so far.

Experiences are simply a by-product, not the main aim or purpose of the practice. Your inner world is not another screen for your entertainment. Experiences can be many and can vary depending on your individual seeking, personality, life experiences and many other permutations and combinations. Be careful not to psyche yourself up into having experiences.

Another pitfall to be strictly avoided is the desire for acquisition of powers through your Kundalini practice. We grow up on myths which tell us tall tales about various seekers who acquired powers such as that they could bring back the dead or walk on water. These distractions will derail you from the path and from reaching the final destination of Kundalini awakening. Ramkrishna Paramhansa said rather wryly, 'What is the point of doing years of hard practise only to be able to walk on water when you can easily take a boat?'

A refrain most frequently heard is that one must not practise Kundalini Yoga without a Guru. But it is equally true that the first and last Guru is within you. The external Gurus will come and go in many forms and often not just in human forms. Be clear and confident that awakening Kundalini is your goal. Then even if you start with just this book as your guide, the rest will unfold slowly and surely, just as a lotus opens up to the touch of the sun's rays.

I am mostly self-taught and have relied heavily on the vast number of writings and lectures given by enlightened people. Most people think that having a Guru is like having a doctor who will prescribe the medication to solve your problems. A Guru won't give you an easy solution for your Kundalini practice. With or without a Guru, you have to do all that it takes. I refrain from calling it hard work, because frankly, your practise is truly the most enjoyable and unique experience you can ever hope to have in this world.

Also, you must not get waylaid by the many quick-fix gurus floating around. How can you recognize a genuine yogi? This was Arjun's predicament too in the Mahabharat. In the Bhagwat Gita, in the second Chapter, from shloka 54 to 72, Lord Krishna, in reply to Arjun's query on how to recognize a true Yogi delineates, lists out some pointers. I have picked specifically those that apply to people who have not retired from the trials and tribulations of the world and yet are aspiring to explore their own ultimate potential and purpose in life.

Arjun asks in the 54th shloka, 'Krishna, what is the definition (mark) of a God-realized soul, stable of mind and established in *Samadhi* (perfect tranquillity of mind)? How does the man of stable mind speak, how does he sit, how does he walk?'

Lord Krishna in the 55th shloka says, 'Arjuna, when one thoroughly casts off all cravings of the mind, and is satisfied in the Self through the joy of the Self, he is then called stable of mind.' (Srimad Bhagavadgita)

He further states that the person will be stable, who will neither rejoice nor recoil when met with good or evil, will remain unperturbed in face of sorrow, who will be free of passion, fear or anger. He who is not led by his senses and has controlled his mind and is ever established in Me, is a true Yogi.'

While Lord Krishna sums it up in eighteen shlokas, I am reminded of Hermann Hesse's description of Gautama the Buddha in *Siddhartha*, which also answers Arjuna's question, 'His peaceful countenance was neither happy nor sad. He seemed to be smiling gently inwardly . . . he walked along peacefully, quietly. He wore his gown and walked along exactly like the other monks, but his face and his step, his peaceful downward glance, his peaceful downward hanging hand and every finger of his hand spoke of peace, spoke of completeness, sought nothing, imitated nothing, reflected a continual quiet, an unfading light, an invulnerable peace.' (Hermann Hesse, *Siddhartha*, The Timeless Books, 2012, page 31.)

Such a Guru is not easy to find for two reasons—they are a rarity and to recognize such a Guru, you must possess heightened awareness yourself.

In the End Notes section, there is a list of books, lectures and videos for your reference and learning. If you are a true seeker, you will be able to discover much for yourself.

To the youngsters, I would say, there are benefits in starting early. It can transform your mind and body into a healthier and more beautiful form. It will empower you, as nothing else will, to face the challenges of proving your potential in every sphere of life—professional, financial or personal. You have the advantage of taking your time for the practise to ripen, unlike people who turn to yoga late in life. These people start practicing after they are over with their tryst with the external world, are short of time and their physical state cannot withstand the rigours of the practice.

The Practise Begins section is so designed that everyone, from the adept to the uninitiated, will be able to practise and progress steadily. The Hatha Yoga system of cleansing your body precedes the Stage I so that you can start with cleansing your body and removing imbalances. Stage I of the practice is for beginners. It is designed to prepare your body and spine for the task ahead. Stage II tackles advanced practice with introduction to Dharana and mantra practice. Stage III will take you to primary Kundalini practices. Stage IV is the final Kundalini practice.

The practise section is prefaced with the dos and don'ts, dietary instructions and other necessary guidance to start you on this thrilling journey of Kundalini Yoga.

With humility and reverence to this universal power, Kundalini Shakti, I launch upon this effort to present to all aspirants a journey into exploring the primordial energy within us and crossing over from the limited existence to unlimited power, energy and bliss.

I humbly acknowledge the guidance I have received through the books and lectures of Swami Sivananda Saraswati and his protégé, Swami Satyananda Saraswati, who established the Bihar School of

Yoga and the Rikhiapeeth Ashram. The books and lectures provided by the Bihar School of Yoga have been the guiding light in my practise and understanding of a whole range of Yogic texts. The repeated visits to Munger and Rikhiapeeth to absorb the vibrations of both the ashrams and hear Swami Niranjananda Saraswati at Munger and Swami Satyasanghananda Saraswati at Rikhiapeeth have helped me immensely along the way.

I have also gained insights and inspiration from my readings of Ramkrishna Paramhansa, Paramhansa Yogananda Saraswati, Shri M and so many other beautiful texts, books and lectures.

Section I

THE WHY AND WHAT OF KUNDALINI YOGA FOR ALL

1

KUNDALINI FOR THE WORLDLY

Most people associate the achievement of higher states of consciousness as detached from worldly life. It is associated with renunciation, detachment from the world and giving up of life's pleasures. This thought process is antithetical to the fundamentals of yogic philosophy which is, in fact, all inclusive. If the purpose of yoga is to seek unity in all, then how can we divide the world into those who are engaged with the worldly matters and those who have renounced them? As a matter of fact, the people engaged in worldly life need help more than the others.

Renouncement of life's worldly pleasures is not crucial to this practice. What is crucial is that you adhere to the requirements of your practice wherever you are and in whatever state you are in.

We can put this matter to rest with advice from a realized soul, Swami Sivananda Saraswati of Divine Life Society, Rishikesh, 'When rightly apprehended and practised there is truth in the doctrine that man must make the best of both worlds. There is no incompatibility between the two provided action is taken in conformity with the universal law of manifestation. It is held to be wrong teaching that happiness hereafter can only be had by absence of enjoyment now, or in deliberately sought for suffering and mortification.'

Swami Sivananda exhorts, 'To neglect or deny the needs of the body, to think of it as something not divine, is to neglect and deny the greater life of which it is a part, and to falsify the great doctrine of the unity of all and the ultimate identity of matter and spirit.'

* * *

Sincerity of intent is of utmost importance. The story of two saints crossing a river illustrates the mere uselessness and external resolutions when the mind is still engaged in the opposite direction.

Two saints were crossing a river when they saw a lady standing on the bank of the river. The older saint offers to help her cross the river and picks her up in his arms and takes her across. The younger saint is aghast and angry that the older saint broke the dictates of sainthood by touching a lady. They walk in silence and ultimately the younger saint questions the older saint's action. The older saint smiles and says, 'I've left that lady long back, but you are still carrying her.'

Utmost sincerity and honesty of purpose are sufficient. Your yoga practice will help in every aspect, including transformation and finally transcending your own limited self. This in turn, will free you to embrace your true self and help you to work and focus on many tasks at once. You can take solace and encouragement from the fact that the author of this book wears several hats for the external world while quietly pursuing her yoga. If you have faith and continue to put in the work, you will experience and realize.

It is relevant here to mention the well-known story in yoga philosophy of Adi Shankaracharya's debate with Mandal Misra, a renowned authority on the Vedas, specifically the Mimosa philosophy.

Both debaters agreed that Bharathi, wife of Mandal Misra and a learned scholar, would be the judge for the debate. After months of back-and-forth debate, Mandal Misra accepted defeat in the face of the incisive, erudite arguments put forward by Shankaracharya, that were an engrossing treatise on Advaita philosophy.

However, Bharathi said that as the wife of Mandal Misra, Shankaracharya must defeat her too in the debate. Knowing he was a celibate, she put Shankaracharya in a spot by debating on the role of conjugal and marital relationships in spiritual life. He asked for time. Using his spiritual powers, he entered into the body of an old and dying king who had many wives. He experienced conjugal and marital state and returned to his body which was preserved by his followers. He came to face Bharathi's challenge and finally won the debate.

This story brings forth the importance of experiencing the world at all levels of manifestation of energy and consciousness. In every way, a householder or a worldly person is not exempt from the path to awakening their own potential.

* * *

This book will benefit youngsters starting off in life. As you take on life's challenges and establish yourself in the numerous spheres of life, stress takes a toll on your mental, physical and emotional state. Hence, many of you end up with typical health profiles—high blood pressure, diabetes, hyperthyroidism, heart problems or chronic digestive issues—by the time you reach your forties. But if you start the practice of Kundalini early in life, you will not only avoid common health issues but also achieve a state of immense energy, greater mental capacity and emotional stability with the possibility of achieving extraordinary levels of success as you discover your potential and the secrets of your own existence.

The only exclusions are people who suffer from chronic health problems like heart issues, high blood pressure, diabetes, ulcers and arthritis. They should get treatment for such bodily ailments before attempting to undertake the practice of Kundalini Yoga. However, those who cannot manage to fully treat their health problems can attempt to arouse their Kundalini or achieve a state of Bliss by following the paths of Bhakti Yoga, Gyan Yoga or any other yogic system. If you have the drive to achieve your goals, nothing can stop you. Defeat and despair have no place in the quest for spiritual realisation, whatever the hurdles may be.

2

WHY KUNDALINI?

The quest to play God is deep-seated in people. They have sought power unto themselves to control nature as well as other people. It is a crude manifestation of the quest to know God. Just as children love to imitate their parents, people try to know and imitate their own Creator, God. A person's quest to understand the meaning of life and creation has not only fostered scientific research but also driven the cause of spirituality. Scientists and spiritual who seekers are considered to be opposites by many, have come to recognize the fact that they must join hands to solve the puzzle.

Srinivasa Ramanujan, FRS, the genius mathematician, is a poignant example of science and divinity meeting within one mind. Ramanujan's uncanny brilliance challenged the frontiers of science itself—much to the consternation of his mentor, Prof. G. H. Hardy, who was an atheist. Astounded by the almost mystical ways in which Ramanujan accosted infinity through the equations, Prof. Hardy asked him about the source of the solutions for his unique derivations. Ramanujan told him that his village goddess, Namadari, sat on his tongue and spoke the derivations. Through the combined workings of science and spirituality, Ramanujan was able to arrive at mathematical calculations that were far ahead of his time.

Kundalini Yoga helps in the quest of discovering the mysteries of creation and the purpose behind it through a process which is both scientific and spiritual. You will find sound scientific and medical evidence to substantiate your understanding of Kundalini and the yogic principles which help unravel the experience of awakening of the Kundalini in the further chapters. Some of you may find wading through the anatomy of the nervous system to be a chore. You may skip it if you like in the first read, but you will find yourself coming back to it when you are ready to start your practise. It really helps in ascertaining the positions of the various Chakras, in feeling the connection of each Chakra with its associated organs and in understanding the impact of your practise on the nervous system.

* * *

Kundalini Yoga explains the logic behind those evolutionary processes which distinguish us from animals. Both animals and humans have Chakras. The Mooladhara, the root Chakra, resides in both humans and animals. The main difference being that in animals the Mooladhara Chakra is the highest Chakra while in humans it is the lowest one. Animals cannot go beyond the Mooladhara Chakra, which is responsible for their basic instincts of hunger, fear and procreation. This is how nature intended it to be. Humans, on the other hand, are sentient beings with the ability to rise above the basic animal state and evolve to their highest potential.

The world is poised at a stage where it has been able to attain material wealth, knowledge and scientific development, yet good health, contentment and peace are still elusive. Feelings of stress, anxiety and emptiness trouble the rich and successful too. Cancer, heart ailments, high blood pressure, diabetes and intractable viruses have risen in equal proportion to the advancements in medical science.

The reliance on the external world and neglect towards the phenomenal potential within all humans has left us weak. People resort to medicines, that are partly destructive, to treat the ailments caused by stress, tension and anxiety. Yoga not only holds the secret to managing everyday stress, tension and realising your greater potential but also allows you to be relaxed, happy and at peace.

In my many years spent as a Kundalini Yoga teacher, I have come across a number of hopeless cases of migraine, depression, cancer, heart ailments and much more. Yoga continues to surprise me with its phenomenal success in treating such ailments and in providing supportive and long-term corrective resolution for the entire body.

There was a journalist who, before taking up yoga lessons, was suffering from stomach disorders, fatigue and intermittent vomiting. When his doctors couldn't figure out how to help him, a suggestion from a friend brought him to the doors of yoga classes. Within a very short span of time, all of his maddening, intractable problems disappeared. The best feedback was that his mental capacities had increased; he was able to finish his tasks in less than half the time it used to take him before he had started practising yoga.

Another case that comes to my mind is of a German lady who was suffering from chronic depression. My Yoga Guru, Dr Rajesh Kumar, advised her to come to Mumbai and try out yoga, since she did not want to take psychiatric drugs and nothing else had worked for her. She came to Mumbai a day after the terrorist attack on the Taj and Oberoi Hotels. Against all advice not to travel to India and more so to Mumbai, she arrived; so desperate was her search for relief. Within a week of practising intensive yoga in the morning with a shorter session in the evening, she showed signs of improvement. She laughed a little while talking to her husband back home in Germany. He was in tears. It was the first time he had heard her laugh so openly in a while. She started expressing her desire to go out for a walk around the block (when in Germany, she would barely leave her room). She found her clothes drab and wondered why she had packed such a depressing wardrobe. Thus, cured, she was no more like a rag doll with limp hair and dull complexion. She flew back to Germany, a woman changed. Yoga had breathed new life into her.

Such real-life examples demonstrate the therapeutic effects of yoga. In Kundalini Yoga, these therapeutic rewards are the first rung of benefits or siddhis one acquires.

Even as one is writing this book, technology and medical science have been rendered futile against the COVID-19 virus that is only half alive. While the medical world did contain the virus with vaccines, even then the world has realized that only a person with a healthy body and a strong immune system will stand a chance against such a relentless disease.

3

KUNDALINI FOR ALL

Kundalini is the practise of knowing that our finite, mortal selves hold within themselves the power to know the infinite and become immortal.

Kundalini Yoga is for all because Kundalini Shakti resides in all. To live and not to have awakened the Kundalini within is to not know your full potential as a human being.

This book will take you through the theory and practise of this invaluable and ancient knowledge. There are no restrictions as to who can practise this yoga. In fact, this book has been specifically written for the worldly who wish to enhance their lives by awakening their latent Kundalini Shakti. You may be a corporate honcho, a sportsperson, a school teacher, a home maker or even a banker. The potential to awaken the latent powers of the brain and the body exists within everyone and Kundalini is the way to achieve it. Enlightenment is the final aim of Kundalini Yoga but along the way, you will expand your consciousness and energy, which will allow you to handle the usual stress, tensions and fears of everyday life with ease and equanimity.

In the past, Kundalini Yoga was shrouded in secrecy, its practise linked to madness and other baseless myths. For years, it has aroused fear and awe in people.

Kundalini Yoga was never the problem. As with most things in life the problem, if any, was within us and how we perceived things. Kundalini is the beautiful energy within you waiting to be awakened. Your purpose and the methods you apply for awakening this energy will determine if it benefits or harms you. In life, you find what you seek. Be forewarned; if you are tempted by the powers or experiences, you will attain through your Kundalini awakening, then be prepared for the attended risks of harm to yourself.

The world is now familiar with yoga and its efficacy. The time is ripe for Kundalini Yoga to come out from under the veil of secrecy because the collective consciousness of humankind warrants moving into higher states of evolution.

The saint of Rikhiapeeth, Swami Satyananda Saraswati, who established the Bihar School of Yoga in Munger, writes in his book *Kundalini Tantra* on the future of Kundalini—'Everybody must know something about Kundalini as it represents the coming consciousness of mankind.'

The 157th sutra of the Vijanana Bhairava Tantra states, 'O Goddess, this most excellent teaching, which is said to lead to the immortal state, should verily not be revealed to anybody.'

This stricture prohibits revealing the practice to simply anyone. However, Swami Satyasangananda Saraswati, in her commentary on the Sutra, says, 'Anything which is of great power and value should never be broadcast indiscriminately. There are two important reasons why secrecy is advised.'

'First of all, the practises and knowledge contained in the Vijanana Bhairava Tantra are of the highest order and will be useless to the ordinary person who is not prepared to comprehend the subtlety of these concepts. It would be a waste of time to discuss this text with people who are not able to understand or value such a high level of teaching and may even misuse or malign it.'

'The second reason for secrecy relates to the actual spiritual progress of the practitioner. Embarking on an inner journey is not a matter that should be discussed openly in society. It is a private affair, which concerns oneself and one's spiritual teacher alone.

Most importantly, she further writes, '[. . .]pride is also engendered, which fans the ego and will finally obstruct the attainment of the state necessary for higher practises.'

Thus, one can safely proceed with Kundalini Yoga without any sense of dread or inhibitions. Furthermore, the ancient texts on yoga—the Yoga Upanishads—do not contain any strictures on who can and who cannot practise Kundalini. Later writings warn against the practise of Kundalini Yoga out of the fear that novice practitioners will not be able to handle the awakening without the guidance of a Guru, without giving up worldly life or without becoming an ascetic. Fear not! Kundalini is not the problem. The shakti is very powerful, and if misused, it can lead to adverse situations. So, what you must fear is your own self.

4

WHAT IS KUNDALINI?

Let us start with the learning about the etymology of the word 'Kundalini'. 'Kundala' is the feminine form of the Sanskrit word coiled. It is also a conjunction of 'kund' and 'alini'. 'Kund' means a deep pit, 'alini' means coiled. Kundalini is the word used to describe the immense energy which is coiled like a snake at the base of the spine. There it rests for most of us, holding within itself the vast potential of dynamic energy. It is something like the atomic energy that is contained within every atom until brought forth via atomic fusion or fission. All matter is condensation of energy. Matter must undergo fission or fusion to be converted back into energy. Kundalini Yoga is something like the atomic release of energy when the brain and nervous system is subject to the Kundalini awakening.

The practice of Kundalini Yoga aims to awaken this latent energy from the base of the spine and make it travel upwards, along the spinal cord, awakening the various psychic points (Chakras) in the spine to culminate at the final psychic centre at the crown of the head, the Sahasrara Chakra.

As you scale each Chakra with unstinted daily practise of Hatha Yoga and Kundalini Kriya, your entire being gradually transforms into a transmitter-cum-receptor which starts resonating with different

levels of cosmic vibrations. As each Chakra is awakened, you connect
with the cosmic plane (or Loka) connected with that Chakra. When
all Chakras are awakened, you resonate with the universal cosmic
energy and consciousness.

Just as your TV, radio, mobiles and other electronic devices detect
frequencies and reproduce sound and images from afar instantly, you
too start detecting vibrations and see profound visions from beyond
this world. This encourages further development of your receptor,
the nervous system, and you get linked to the workings of nature
and the universe. The ultimate knowledge of mystery of the universe
unfolds before you. You may still go around following your daily
routine but a part of you is now in communion with the ultimate
source of energy and consciousness, call it what you like.

Location of the Chakras

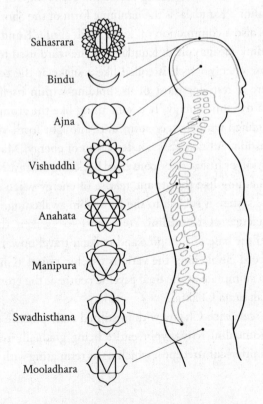

The Seven Lokas

Each Chakra belongs to a specific Loka or plane of existence. At this point, we must get acquainted with the fourteen Lokas, planes of existence other than the one we live in. After all, there is the imminent possibility of you experiencing or getting a glimpse of these Lokas during your practise.

There are seven planes below and seven above our plane of existence. The seven planes below are the under-worlds—Atala, Vitala, Sutala, Talatala, Rasatala, Mahatala and Patala. The seven planes above are—Bhu, Bhuvah, Swaha, Maha, Jana, Tapa and Satyam.

The seven underworlds are the regions denser and deeper than Earth and are inhabited by creatures like ghosts, goblins, snakes, demons and such. We will not go into a detailed description of each of these as we are concerned with scaling the higher realms and consciousness.

Here is a brief description of the seven upper Lokas:

1. Satya Loka: This is the realm of Brahma which is eternal. The atma becomes free of the cycle of birth and death.
2. Tapa Loka: Abode of deities.
3. Jana Loka: Abode of the sons of Brahma.
4. Maha Loka: Abode of great sages and enlightened beings known as Rishis.
5. Swaha Loka: The region between the Sun and the polar star, the abode of the God Indra.
6. Bhuva Loka (Pitr Loka): This is the realm above the earth. The Sun, the planets, stars and space between the Sun and the Earth, inhabited by semi-divine beings. It has an atmosphere and life force.
7. Bhu Loka: This is the earth along with all the inhabitants of this planet.

With the opening up of each Chakra, your astral body gets connected with the Loka associated with that Chakra. The Yogic assertion is that after death, depending on which of the Chakra was awakened, your astral body moves up to the Loka associated with that Chakra. If no Chakra was open, then the astral body remains trapped in the Earth's atmosphere and depending on the karmic load of that person, it is reborn. However, if the Anahata Chakra was open at the time of death, then the astral body of the person will go to the Maha Loka, where sages and enlightened beings exist. There is no return to the human body from this plane of existence.

Let us now dive into each Chakra as we seek to awaken them:

Mooladhara: As seen in the image, there are eight Chakras in the body. The lowest Chakra, Mooladhara, situated below the base of the spine, is the first one which is awakened with the practice of Kundalini Yoga. With the awakening of the Mooladhara Chakra, you connect to the Bhu Loka, the lowest of the seven higher planes associated with the Earth. It is the physical realm associated with food. In physiological terms: you connect with the energy managing your excretory systems and reproductive and sexual organs.

The awakening of this most basic Chakra cleanses and energizes the organs connected with this Chakra. On a physical level, your sense of smell intensifies along with your intuitive facility. At the psychic level, it is associated with the baser instincts of hunger and sex. This Chakra frees you from the feelings of guilt and the conflicts and complexes associated with sex.

Swadhisthana: As Kundalini moves from the Mooladhara to the Swadhisthana Chakra at the tailbone, you connect with the Bhuva Loka, the next plane which is contained within the earth's orbit and the pull of gravity and all worldly things. It is the world between the Earth and the Sun. This Chakra manages the workings of your kidneys, prostrate and utero-vaginal organs. It is another step towards freeing you from the attachments of this world.

Manipura: With the awakening of the Manipura Chakra at the navel centre, you resonate with the Swara Loka, the heavenly plane beyond the sphere of the earth and its pull. It is the realm of solar light—the heat, the brilliance and energy of the Sun. This is a centre for dynamism and strong will-power. It is associated with all the digestive organs at the solar plexus. Its element being fire, the sheer radiance from the awakening of the Kundalini at the Manipura Chakra energizes your whole body. At the Manipura Chakra, higher intelligence guided by noble ideas, creativity and foresight become your disposition. These bestow the psychic power of freedom from disease and the power to create wealth, as Manipura stands for the 'City of Gems'.

Kundalini may still slip back if you are lax in your practise. Once it crosses the Manipura and Kundalini opens up Anahata Chakra then and only then the Kundalini does not return.

Anahata: With the awakening of the Anahata Chakra at the heart centre, you resonate with the Maha Loka, the abode of the Rishis and Enlightened Souls. It is the realm of cosmic illumination and knowledge. The Anahata Chakra is the centre for understanding love beyond the limits of ego. At this Chakra, you break free from the limited self to experience expansiveness in every dimension. Such a person wins the love and admiration of others and attains the powers of healing. The Kalpa Vriksha, the wish fulfilling tree, is supposed to reside here. The practicioner finds that all of their wishes are fulfilled. But because of their awakened state and heightened intelligence, they also know not to abuse their powers and the pitfalls therein.

From here on, Kundalini does not return.

Vishuddhi: With the awakening of the Vishuddhi Chakra at the throat pit, you ascend to Jana Lok, which is the seed of creation. According to mythology, it is the abode of the sons of Brahma. Here we accost the subtlest of all elements—ether. As its name suggests, this Chakra purifies. All opposites dissolve as you scale higher. It is at this Chakra that the nectar that flows from the Bindu Chakra is split into *amrita* and poison and duality ensues as Kundalini descends to lower Chakras. As these dualities dissolve, you move closer to the centre of unification. It bestows telepathic and telekinetic powers.

Ajna: With the opening of the Ajna Chakra at the centre of your eyebrows, you scale up to the Tapa Loka, the abode of Gods and deities. Ajna is the confluence of the three Nadis: Ida, Pingala and Sushumna. It is known as the command centre because it controls two crucial glands—the pituitary and the pineal glands. At this stage of awakening, you can finally understand the laws of cause and effect as well as the laws that govern karma. By possessing the knowledge and understanding of the underlying laws of the universe, you become peerless.

Bindu: The journey from the Ajna to the Sahasrara Chakra at the crown of the head is a short one, with the Bindu Chakra placed between them. The Bindu Chakra resides in the soft spot on the head. It is represented by a full moon and is the source of nectar— ambrosia, which flows from the moon through the Bindu Visarga and into the Ajna Chakra. As mentioned earlier, this nectar splits into *amrita* and poison when it reaches the Vishuddhi Chakra.

Sahasrara: The Sahasrara Chakra is the Satya Loka, the abode of Truth. Here the individual Atma merges with the Supreme and is freed from the cycle of birth and death. It is the culmination of the purpose of life. In a nutshell, this is the journey that one undertakes in Kundalini Yoga practice.

Origins of Kundalini Yoga

The origin of Kundalini Yoga is buried in the annals of time. Although there is an absence of a clear source for the history or origins of the yoga, the mentions of Kundalini Yoga can be traced in the origins of Tantra, Samkhya and Hatha Yoga. Sir John Woodroffe, the Chief Justice of Calcutta High Court, who became a Tantrik and translated many Tantrik texts into English, writes, 'Thus the Tantra is that presentiment of *sruti* which is modelled as regards its ritual to meet the characteristics and infirmities of the Kali Yoga.'

One of the earliest references to Kundalini is in the Yoga Upanishads. Out of twenty volumes, twelve refer to Kundalini Yoga. Of the thirty-five sutra, the very first sutra of the Yogakundaliniupanishad makes a rather cryptic yet scientific and emphatic statement; it says, 'The two causes that operate on the mind and bear on its activity or inactivity are the forces of revived memories and the vital air breathed in and breathed out, without proper regulation and control. When either of the two ceases to operate, both of them alike become inoperative. Of the two, a man must first conquer forever, the vital air. The means to be employed for attaining this are temperance in food, assuming the proper Asana or posture and the rousing of the power as the third step.'

Right at the beginning, this Upanishad emphasizes the importance of breath, not just for Kundalini Yoga but life itself. Also, how when there is no proper regulation or control of the breath it impacts the functioning of the brain in storing and retrieving memory, which can mean information also.

It is interesting to note that the practises for Kundalini Yoga mentioned in the Yoga Upanishads are still a major part of Kundalini practice with some temporal changes that have crept-in in consonance with changing life patterns and that the sutras also stated the various therapeutic benefits.

For example, in the description of Sitali Pranayama, sutra 30, 31 of the Yogakundaliniupanishad, page 407 states, 'The man of clear intellect should, after performing Kumbhaka as before, draw in the air through the tongue and should slowly expel it through the two nostrils. Gulma (abdominal affection), diseases of the spleen and the like disorders, consumption, biliary; disorders, fever, thirst and poisons, are destroyed by this Kumbhaka known as Sitali.'

I was earlier under the impression that it was only recently that the medical world had established the physiological and therapeutic effects of yoga on the body.

Swami Sivananda Saraswati of Divine Life Society, Rishikesh, clearly says, 'One cannot alienate Kundalini from any form of yoga, be it Hatha Yoga, Tantra Yoga, Raja Yoga or even Gyan or Bhakti Yoga. Whatever the path or system of practise, awakening of Kundalini is its result.'

Kundalini Yoga marks its presence in all ancient Indian texts— from the Upanishads to the Puranas, to texts on Tantra and Hatha Yoga. Before the rise of Buddhism, ritualistic practises fell out of popularity as they were too complex and mis-represented. As a result, Buddhism brought much needed relief to the people with its simple moral and ethical codes and the practise of meditation as the way to salvation and freedom from suffering.

The world, however, lost invaluable systems and techniques for preparatory practises that were used to achieve meditation. It was much later that the school of Yogis called the Nath Sampradaya, starting with Matsyendranath and Gorakhnath and later, Swami Swatmarama, culled valuable practises from Hatha and Tantra Yoga and made it simple enough for people without the burden of complex ritualistic practises. The Hatha Yogis said that practising a combination of Hatha Yoga and Raja Yoga would allow people to achieve the highest level of spirituality. Kundalini Yoga makes up an intrinsic part of it all. Swami Sivananda advocates for Hatha and Kundalini Yoga practice as opposed to those practices that aim at deathlessness.

Swami Sivananda writes in *Kundalini Yoga*, 'The Hatha Yogin who works for Liberation does so through Layla Yoga Sadhana or Kundalini Yoga which gives both enjoyment and Liberation. At every Centre to which he rouses Kundalini he experiences special form of Bliss and gains special powers.'

The third chapter of *Hatha Yoga Pradipika* by Swami Swatmarama is devoted to practises for Chakras and Kundalini awakening. Most of the practises detailed in this book are derived from the *Hatha Yoga Pradipika*, *Gheranda Samhita*, *Shiva Samhita* and *Kundalini Tantra* by Swami Satyananda Saraswati and *Kundalini Yoga* by Swami Sivananda Saraswati.

* * *

Kundalini practice impacts not just the body but also the brain. It is contended that out of the ten parts of our brain, we manage to use just one. Kundalini practice is the effort to activate the remaining dormant parts of our brain which hold the key to unlocking latent, supernatural powers. Later in the section on the brain, this topic has been discussed through scientific enquiry and yogic rationale.

The understanding of Kundalini will remain incomplete unless the theory of creation and the role of Maya is understood.

According to Yoga philosophy, Cosmic Consciousness and Energy exist in unison and Creation itself happens when these two divide into many. Everything animate and inanimate is pervaded by both consciousness and energy. An amoeba, electrons, a speck of sand to the most complex organism is but a manifestation of energy and consciousness. Before you launch into the step-by-step understanding of the creation of the universe, let's first try to understand the building blocks, that is, Consciousness and Energy. All doubts and misconceptions must be cleared because the success of your voyage will depend on how well you know the waters you are cruising in.

Section II

STEPS TO OUR CREATION, ANTAHKARNA AND PRATYAHARA

1

CREATION

Consciousnesses: the meanings of consciousness range from, 'the state of understanding and realizing something' (Cambridge) to 'the state of being aware of and responsive to one's surroundings' (Oxford). All dictionaries give sumptuous meanings to chew on, but these do not suffice for the purposes of understanding yoga.

For our purpose, I have broken it down into two kinds of consciousness. When you drive a car, you are conscious of the fact that you are driving the car. What you don't think of is how the car is running or how the fuel propels so many functions of the car so that it follows your command. On the other hand, the engineers who have made the car are conscious of such mechanisms. There is a limited consciousness of the driver and a broader consciousness of the engineers who have designed the car.

Hiroshi Motoyama puts it in yet another way, the esoteric and the exoteric, the yin and the yang.

As I understand his writing, he said that all things have an exoteric aspect, that is, exposed to light, and an esoteric aspect, which is hidden. A tree has an exposed portion like the trunk, the branches, the leaves, flowers and the fruit. You can also see it change with the changing seasons. In Autumn, the leaves fall off, then in Spring, they come back to life. You cannot see nor are you generally aware of the esoteric aspect of the tree, that is, the roots, hidden under the surface, without which the tree wouldn't survive.

Similarly, with the consciousness and energy. Both have exoteric and esoteric aspects. This can be easily seen in our body too.

You see with your eyes. This is your individual consciousness. That which engineers you, enables you, powers you to see is the Cosmic Consciousness. The individual consciousness is distinct and unique to each person, depending on complex factors like physical abilities, nature, nurture, experiences, etc. It is powered by our sense organs and by the brain.

In contrast Cosmic Consciousness is universal, all pervading and is present in everything animate and inanimate. This pure, all-pervading consciousness is referred to as Chaitanya or Chitta in the Vedas, Shiva in the Tantra and Purusha in the Samkhya.

The goal of yoga is to expand our limited individual consciousness to experience and become one with the universal super-consciousness. You come to know the secrets of creation itself. This is the consciousness that you try to achieve through your Kundalini Yoga.

Energy: The energy which powers us and our world is distinct from the vital life force, the cosmic energy, which is also called the pranic energy. For example, breathing is a process of inhalation of oxygen and exhalation of carbon dioxide. It is our lifeline. But what powers the process of breathing? The answer is the energy, which in Yogic parlance is called Prana, the vital life force. In Vedas, it is Chitta Shakti, in Tantra philosophy, it is called Shakti. In Samkhya philosophy, it is called Prakruti.

Manifestation of Consciousness and Energy

If you look around, all things are a manifestation of consciousness and energy in millions of forms.

Every philosophy, religion and scientific exploration has put out theories about the beginning of creation.

For the purposes of Kundalini practice, it is crucial to understand the creation of the world as postulated by Samkhya and Tantra. It forms the crux of your Kundalini practise. It is a beautiful, scientific-cum-theological, engrossing rationale on creation, your position in it, and the purpose of your life, which is linked with wherefrom you came and wherefore you have to return.

Those who want to know more about the chronological creation can read *Tattwa Shuddhi: The Tantric Practise of Inner Purification* by Swami Satyasangananda.

Unlike scientific enquiry, which tries to hypothesize on the beginning of this universe through theories such as 'the Big Bang' or 'God Particle', Samkhya and Tantra theorize that there is no beginning or end. Energy and Consciousness, Shiva and Shakti, Prakruti and Purusha, the building blocks of the universe have always existed and will continue to exist in a state of eternal union in a timeless frame.

Shiva is pure cosmic consciousness and Shakti is pure cosmic energy. They are immanent, eternal and pervade the whole universe, from the beginning of time to infinity. Shiva is at eternal rest and Shakti has enormous potential energy. We will be using both the traditional yogic terms and the scientific terms, Shiva-Shakti and Cosmic Consciousnesses and Cosmic Energy or just Consciousness and Energy

So how was this universe created? According to Yoga philosophy and Tattwa Shuddhi, Shiva and Shakti or Cosmic Energy and Cosmic Consciousness, which exist in unison, began the process of creation by separating from each other to create many. Shiva remains the inactive principle and manifests as consciousness in all creation. Shakti is active and diversifies into form and matter and manifests as energy in all matter. In every speck of creation, both are ever present.

In people, cosmic consciousness and cosmic energy enter through the crown of the growing foetus in a state of union. Consciousness or Shiva remains at the crown of the head at the Sahasrara Chakra while Shakti, cosmic energy, travels along the spinal cord, and settles down at the Mooladhara Chakra at the base of the spine as Kundalini Shakti. There it remains with an inherent urge to unify again with Shiva at the crown of the head.

Kundalini practise is the effort to arouse Kundalini from its latent state at the base of the spine and make it travel up the spinal cord, arousing the six Chakras along the way, to finally unify with Shiva, the super consciousness at the top of the head. Thus, the cycle of unity to diversity and back to unity can be seen as the purpose of creation of mankind. Until this is achieved, the cycle of birth and death continues. The individual continues to exist in the world of duality of pain and pleasure, light and darkness, birth and death and so on.

When Consciousness and Energy separate, the duality, which is the inherent nature of this universe, starts to manifest. This state of duality is called 'Maya'. Maya means illusion. It is distinct from the unified state it arose from. It has a beginning and an end, like birth and death, it is the veil obscuring the Truth, the Source of all creation. Maya is the limiting power which binds us to our ego; it blinds us to our true self, which possesses unlimited powers. The practise of all yoga and other spiritual systems is to break through the veil of Maya so that an individual, a jiva, can know and experience that which exists on the other plane beyond this dimension.

In the fables for children, a prince rescues a princess. The prince is warned that the journey to find her will be arduous. He will have to cross wild rivers, travel through dark forests and scale frozen peaks but after every challenge there will be a clue that will take him one step closer to his goal and he has to keep moving forward. The prince is the Yogi, and the princess is the Kundalini. His task is to awaken her from her deep slumber. Maya, as the villain in the fables, creates the obstacles. The eight Chakras hold the clue for the prince to move forward.

2

STEPS TO OUR CREATION

Let us set upon knowing about the steps to the creation of the world and the people. If you follow the Tattwa Shuddhi and Sankhya for 'Theory of Creation', it becomes easy to connect it with your daily yoga practise. It allows us to experience how our yoga practise takes us from the gross state to the subtle state—the final reality beyond our present realm of existence.

In the first step towards creation, Shiva and Shakti divide into the following:

1. Vibration (Nada)
2. Particle (Bindu)
3. Wave (Kaala)

This is similar to what science has laboriously discovered over the years; the truth is that light is both wave and particle vibrating at various frequencies.

At this stage, everything is still unmanifest (avyakta). These three attributes—nada, bindu and kaala—interact with each other and multiply into thirty-six elements and fifteen supplementary elements.

Out of the fifteen supplementary elements, we get the first stage of the building blocks that make up the foundation of our body. They are the seven humours, also known as Sapta Dhatu (seven elements).

Sapta Dhatu are as follows:

1. Bone
2. Plasma
3. Blood
4. Bone marrow
5. Muscle
6. Fat
7. Nerve

The other two unmanifest creations are the five vital airs (Panch Vayu) and the three vital qualities (Triguna) which function in a human being throughout their life.

Panch Vayu

Panch Vayu stands for 'five winds' or 'five airs'. It refers to the various energy systems which move around in our body, much like wind, which remains unseen but can still be felt.

The Panch Vayu are five energy systems in your body, which aid in the functioning of different organ systems. They are responsible for various functions of the human body such as excretion, procreation, digestion, respiration, mental activity and so on. Kundalini Yoga practise aims to manipulate these vital airs to enable the nervous system to make a pathway for Kundalini to move from the base of the spine to the top of the head.

The Panch Vayu are:

1. Apana (Operates between the genital area and the navel)
2. Samana (Operates between the navel and heart)

3. Prana (Operates between the heart and throat)
4. Vyana (Operates between the throat and the head)
5. Udana (Operates in the entire body)

It is essential for you to understand the role each of the Vayu play in the efficient functioning of the human body.

Apana Vayu

Apana Vayu circulates between the navel and genital area. It is responsible for the excretory, reproductive and sexual organs as well as the kidneys and both of the intestines.

Apana Vayu moves downward. Ejaculation in men, menstruation in women and pushing a foetus out during labour are all directed by the Apana Vayu. Malfunctioning of the Apana Vayu can result in constipation, diarrhoea, piles and other ailments associated with the organs under the Apana Vayu's control. Most of the mudra and bandha practise aim to prevent the downward movement of Apana and make it move upwards (see section VII). This also assists in freeing the Mooladhara Chakra from its animal state.

Samana Vayu

The Samana Vayu operates between the navel and the heart. It is responsible for most of the digestive system and the organs associated with it—the stomach, the liver, the pancreas, the spleen, the small and the large intestine. It is a Vayu associated with the Manipura Chakra.

The Samana Vayu moves sideways and controls the bodily functions of digestion, assimilation of nutrients as well as other miscellaneous functions associated with the digestive organs. Malfunctioning of this Vayu results in indigestion, gas, constipation and other gastric ailments. In our practise, we try to unite the Apana Vayu with the Samana Vayu and make them both move upwards with the Prana Vayu. This is further explained in the practise session of Bandhas.

Prana Vayu

The Prana Vayu plays an important role as it functions between the heart and the throat. The organs of the thorax, that is, the lungs and the heart are controlled by the Prana Vayu. It can be visualized as moving upwards. Any disturbance in its functioning will affect the heart and the lungs, both of which play a central role in our survival. It is associated with the Anahata Chakra.

Udana Vayu

The Udana Vayu, which can be visualized as moving upwards, plays an important role as it is responsible for the functioning of the brain. It moves from the throat to the brain. In addition to the brain, it controls the organs of speech in the throat, as well as the movement of hands and legs. It is associated with the Vishuddhi Chakra.

Vyana Vayu

The Vyana Vayu pervades the entire body and carries energy from the nutrients obtained from the digestion of food substances to all the parts of the body through the circulatory system. It provides energy to the cells of any part of the body as and when they need it. It acts like a storehouse of energy for the body. It is also responsible for controlling muscular movements and carrying sensory and motor impulses to different parts of the body. Moreover, it controls perspiration and other bodily phenomena such as 'goosebumps.'

Understanding the Panch Vayu is crucial to the practise of yoga. It helps fix the malfunctioning of these vital forces within your body. The Nadis, subtler channels of energy, will not be able to function optimally if Panch Vayu don't work properly in a body. This will tamper with the distribution of pranic energy from the Chakras when they are awakened.

Triguna

The Triguna are the three basic attributes that control the whole gamut of creation.

Through your yoga practise you achieve and stay mostly in the Sattwic or pure state.

The Triguna are as follows:

1. Sattwa (pure)
2. Rajas (dynamic)
3. Tamas (dull)

As the word itself suggests, Triguna stands for 'three qualities'. In our everyday lives, we get to meet a vast range of personality types—the hyper-active, the indolent, the angry, the calm, the eccentric and so on. Samkhya and Tantra claim that all human behaviours and attitudes can be classified under three broad categories Sattwa, Rajas and Tamas.

Western psychology does not account for Eastern traditions, cultures and religious practises in understanding personality types or psychological disorders. Acclaimed psychologist Carl Gustav Jung dived into Eastern and specifically Indian philosophy after some mystical experiences he himself had to which he could not accord any explanation.

Jung's seminar on Kundalini Yoga, presented to the Psychological Club in Zurich in 1932, is regarded as path-breaking in understanding Eastern thought and symbolism connected with inner experiences.

'Kundalini yoga presented Jung with a model for the developmental phases of higher consciousness, and he interpreted its symbols in terms of the process of individuation.'

After Jung's seminar, much of yoga, Tantra and the Vedas served as the foundation for Jung's understanding of psychological phenomena through the lens of Indian, Buddhist and Zen philosophy, symbolism and psychic representations.

The Triguna established itself as an occidental system for the classification of personality types. Tantra and Samkhya state that in the process of creation, Chitta Shakti breaks up into three Gunas or qualities, namely, Sattwa, Rajas and Tamas. Shakti propels each of these qualities as follows:

1. Tamas Guna represents inertia, denseness and dullness. Its propellor is Ichcha (Desire) Shakti.
2. Rajas Guna represents dynamism, dissipated energy and ambition. It is propelled by Kriya (Action) Shakti.
3. Sattwa Guna represents knowledge, radiance and bliss. It is activated by Gyan (Knowledge) Shakti.

These three characteristics dominate your life from birth to death. They coexist simultaneously but the one that is more dominant than the other two determines your personality type. The dominant characteristic keeps changing throughout life.

The aim of yoga is to be in the Sattwa Guna. For most people, especially those living in urban areas, the Rajas Guna dominates. It is definitely better than having a personality dominated by the Tamas Guna. You may be born with a dominant Guna or with all three in a state of balance. If either Rajas or Tamas is dominant, the Hatha Yoga practises of body cleansing along with a combination of asana and pranayama keep the negative attributes of Rajas and Tamas in check, ensuring that you gradually move towards the Sattwic state.

* * *

Next, we must dive deep into the various stages of evolution. The most significant point of these stages comes when we, along with this whole universe of creation, cross over from being unseen to being seen. In spiritual parlance, this is termed as crossing over from the unmanifest to the manifest. Maya serves as the dividing line between these two planes of existence. From this point onwards, Shakti, with her inherent powers, creates this temporary universe which is broken into dualities and has a beginning and an end.

The above inherent elements multiply into three major Tattwa. Tattwa is a Sanskrit word which can be translated into English as thatness, principle, reality or truth. These Tattwa, in turn, create the thirty-six elements. The three major Tattwa are—Shiva Tattwa, Vidya Tattwa and Atma Tattwa.

Shiva Tattwa

The Shiva element, at this point of creation, is composed of five elements but they exist in a unified and unmanifest state. These are:

1. Shiva as pure consciousness
2. Shakti as pure energy
3. Vidya Tattwa
4. Kanchukas
5. Atma Tattwa

Inherent in Shakti are three creative aspects that hold the seeds of creation, namely, desire, action and knowledge. Desire is the seed which propels action to fulfil it, which ultimately results in knowledge.

These aspects remain dormant until the point of creation. Until the exact moment of creation, these five elements that comprise the Shiva Tattwa, remain unified as one. There is no division or diversity. The first indication of division in this unity leads to the development of the Vidya Tattwa, which is a part of the micro-cosmic consciousness.

Vidya Tattwa

We must approach an important distinction, something that you must hold within yourself as a significant event to contemplate upon during your Kundalini practise. It is this point at which

Maya, the illusory world of our existence, begins to take shape. An important distinction you must be aware of is that the Absolute Consciousness and Absolute Energy exist in their unlimited, unconditioned, unified state, but now appear differentiated because of the conditional, limiting and divisive nature of Maya.

Even in the micro-cosmic state, Shiva and Shakti continue to exist in unison in all creation. But because of Maya, they appear to be separate from your individual consciousness. Thus, begins the process of duality, which separates you from the Cosmic Consciousness and Energy which resides in every creation. This creates the world of subject and object; of Jiva, your individual soul, which appears to be separate from the Paramatma, the universal soul.

We progress towards other elements of the Vidya Tattwa, which are instrumental in giving power and expression to an individual's will, desires, actions and discriminatory faculties.

It is through the development of the Vidya Tattwa that the power of Maya, inherent in Chitta Shakti, begins to manifest. From here on, Shiva or Pure Consciousness is hidden behind the veil of Maya. Maya operates through her five kanchukas or sheaths to create a shell that envelopes Shiva.

The five Kanchukas/Sheaths

The Vidya Tattwa breaks up into five attributes. These attributes prevent us from breaking free from the bonds of Maya. The permanent and limitless aspects of Shiva-Shakti become riddled with limitations and impermanence. These are:

1. Kalaa: that which limits the power to do all.
2. Avidya Vidya: that which limits the power to know all.
3. Raag: that which limits by creating attachment and desire which gives rise to discontent.
4. Kaala: that which limits perpetuity by creating time, thus giving rise to birth, growth and death.

5. Niyati: that which limits free will by creating the notions of fate and destiny, thus binding it to birth and death.

Atma Tattwa

The final stage of our evolution brings us to the Atma Tattwa. It has twenty-five components. The instruments and tools of action and the five elements of which this universe is made are explained concisely below.

Four Antahkarna

1. Buddhi: Intelligence
2. Manas: Thought and counter-thought faculty
3. Chitta: Storehouse of memories from present and past lives
4. Ahankaar: Ego

Five Tanmatras

1. Shabda: Sense of sound associated with the Vishuddhi Chakra and Akash (sky) Tattwa
2. Sparsha: Sense of touch associated with the Anahata Chakra and Vayu (air) Tattwa
3. Roopa: Sense of form associated with the Manipura Chakra and Agni (fire) Tattwa
4. Rasa: Sense of taste associated with the Swadhisthana Chakra and Apas (water) Tattwa
5. Gandha: Sense of smell associated with the Mooladhara Chakra and Prithvi (earth) Tattwa.

Five Tattwas (the five elements)

1. Akash: Ether, void
2. Vayu: Air, motion
3. Agni: Fire, heat

4. Apas: Water, flow
5. Prithvi: Earth, gravity.

Five Gyanendriyas (the instruments of knowledge, the sense organs)

1. Srotra: Ears, auditory
2. Twacha: Skin, touch
3. Chakshu: Eyes, sight
4. Jihva: Tongue, taste
5. Gharana: Nose, smell.

Five Karmendriyas (the instruments of action)

1. Vak: Speech
2. Pani: Hand, touch, grip
3. Pada: Feet, locomotion
4. Upastha: Reproductive organs
5. Payu: Organ of excretion

Maya

This is the twenty-fifth component of the Atma Tattwa. (See Section I, Chapter One)

3

THE ANTAHKARNA

The mind has been a subject of endless study and scientific inquiry. We will limit ourselves to understanding it from the standpoint of the Samkhya philosophy which is a part of the Theory of Creation. According to Samkhya, the mind is made up of four basic tools—Buddhi, Manas, Chitta, Ahankara—which are known as the Antahkarna ('Antah' means inner and 'karna' means tools). Thus, Antahkarna refers to our Inner Tools. The following are the four tools that play a role in the functioning of our mind. Each of these is influenced by the three gunas—Sattwic, Rajas and Tamas.

Chitta

We often wonder why an individual is born with specific traits and quirks. Sometimes siblings possess such opposite personalities and attitudes that it becomes hard to imagine that they were conceived and raised by the same set of parents. This is because of Chitta, which is the link between your past lives and the present one. It is the most basic instrument of your brain and mind. It is connected with all levels of Consciousness—the conscious, the unconscious and the subconscious. It is connected to your memories of not only this life but also your past lives. It serves as the storehouse of your *samskaras* (the accumulation of your karma, whether good or bad, from all the lives you have lived, including the present one). It is the foundation upon which our personality is formed at birth.

The purpose of yoga and its practises is to free our Chitta and discover its hidden memories and samskaras. These form a part of our subconscious and unconscious mind. If they remain unresolved, they tend to manifest in the form of irrational fears, dreams, questionable likes and dislikes and more. As we progress in our practise, a healthy body and a well-functioning brain help us process information better. The meditation and mantras help us cleanse our subconscious and unconscious mind.

I will share my own experience on how mantras can affect us in unfathomable ways. Since childhood, I had an irrational, debilitating fear of ghosts, which I was unable to shake off even in adulthood. It was debilitating because it made sleeping alone or in the dark a major challenge for me. I almost always left one light on. My Yoga Guru, Dr Rajesh Kumar, advised me to recite the 'Das Mahavidya' every day. These are *stotra* of Ten Goddesses and fills one with fearlessness and courage. It took me forty-five minutes to recite these every day and I practised this for three years.

After completing two years of doing those daily recitations, there was an occasion when my son was traveling, and I knew I would have to be alone. Earlier, I would have been completely psyched out and would have slept with the lights on. Strangely enough, I managed to sleep with the lights off and didn't even think about ghosts. At some point that night, I woke up and saw a white apparition standing near my bed. The apparition had a face, though the features weren't distinct. I got the feeling that it was looking at me with its lifeless eyes. I felt no fear. On the contrary, I tried to get a better look at it. It slowly moved away from my bed and settled near the wardrobe. I couldn't stop looking at it. I don't know how long I kept this up. Eventually, I managed to drift back to sleep. The next morning, I was surprised that I could still vividly remember the dream or whatever it was. Thinking about it, I was glad to realize that what would have once driven me crazy with irrational fear, I dismissed as an insignificant dream.

There are many ways to cleanse your Chitta. The vibrations produced by these Sanskrit shlokas connect with your deeper self and work on building your inner strength by removing mental or emotional blockages. Similarly, the Gayatri Mantra helps stimulate your intellect; the Mahamrutyunjaya Mantra helps build immunity and strength and improves your overall health.

Buddhi

This inner tool provides the faculty of thought and counter-thought. It engages in internal debates, fluctuations of mind and considers available options to help Buddhi make all sorts of decisions. This is the faculty which distinguishes people from animals, because of the faculty to discriminate and rationale to choose.

It is clear that none of these tools work independently. They are always interacting and the outcome of their interaction depends on the level of refinement of each of these tools. This will also depend on which of the Gunas is dominant in a person at any given time. For example, if Rajas is dominant, then Manas will be dynamic, over-active and will result in dissipation of energy and a fragmented life. If a person is dominated by Tamas, then their mental faculty, Manas, will be dull, inactive and not energetic enough to pursue anything and make the right decisions. The Sattwic state is the most balanced state. There is clear perception of their surroundings and experiences, which is guided by neither a dissipated nor a dull mind. A cleansed Chitta and a balanced Manas helps Buddhi or intelligence to make use of knowledge in the right manner, followed by the right actions and resulting in peace, calm and bliss.

Manas

It is the tool with the discriminating faculty, and which navigates between the instinctual, primitive pulls of Chitta, the vacillation of Manas and arrives at an understanding depending on its own level of sharpness. Here again, the three Gunas hold sway, and the intelligence, Buddhi, is at its best when the Sattwic Guna is dominant in the person. The purpose of our Kundalini awakening is to enlighten our intellect so that it can guide our Ego to the goal of self-realization.

Ahankara

Ego is that tool that gives you a sense of self. Ego is one of Maya's strongest instruments which makes it one of the most difficult to subdue. The ego, however, is not your enemy. The ego serves as the driving force that makes the other tools of the Antahkarna function.

All the four tools of the Antahkarna work according to the Ego's wishes. It is through this tool that Maya keeps the individual attached to the world. Yet, it is the same Ego, when coupled with a refined Buddhi, Manas and Chitta, that has the potential to reach the highest level of self-realization by breaking free of Maya's control and merging with the transcendental, greater Self.

The three Gunas influence the working of Ego in the same way they impact the other tools. In a Rajasic person, the Ego is dominant and pushes them to achieve and prove themselves in worldly sense. Their life is influenced and guided by the workings of Maya which compels them to pursue success, recognition, and materialistic attachments. In a person where Tamas is dominant, the Ego manifests as a negative force, guided by doubts, fears and avoidant tendencies resulting in procrastination and indecision.

In a Sattwic state, the Ego is guided towards self-realization. However, as Patanjali states in his chapter on Samadhi, remnants of the Ego and the three Gunas can be found even in the highest states of Samadhi. It is only when man becomes free of the Ego and the Gunas, that he becomes one with the Universal Consciousness.

Each inner tool exists within us in the gross state. The purpose of Kundalini practise is to refine each of these so that they become pure and subtle and expand to overcome the limitations imposed upon them by Maya, which keeps us attached to the pull of the gross, the senses, the gravity and the world of duality. In Yoga and Tantra, that which pulls you down is used to help you overcome it. To shun or negate any of these is to create a conflict within ourselves, thus becoming a problem in itself. For example, sex generally is dissociated with higher attributes and spiritual practices. Tantra does not exclude or shun it but brings it into the light of awareness and thus helps the practitioner, the *sadhak*, to overcome its lower associations to proceed to transform it into higher energy.

The journey of yoga allows you to trace back the steps of creation and return to the primary source. The first stage is to get our instrument of awakening, our body, into a healthy and energetic state through the practise of Hatha Yoga which involves body cleansing, asanas and pranayama. This assists in the removal of the bodily distractions of pain and suffering which can hold you back from finding awareness beyond the body. The first rung of obstacles we face are our own sense organs and our tools of action, the limbs. For this reason, Pratyahara practice is of vital importance.

4

PRATYAHARA—WITHDRAWAL OF SENSES

The bedrock of Yogic philosophy rests on achieving a quiet, relaxed and peaceful mind. This may seem like a tall order but it is not. The Rishis and the Yogis focus on the simple connection of the senses to the mind. The senses are what keep the mind occupied, stimulated and distracted. The practise of disassociation of your mind from the sense organs and their incessant feedback is the key to achieving a quiet and relaxed state of mind.

The senses stimulate and serve the mind as well as the body that obey the mind's commands. But as you progress in your practise of yoga, which includes asanas, pranayama, mudra and bandha, your mind will begin to internalize and withdraw from external stimuli. It is a natural progression from the practise of asanas which is mostly performed with open eyes, to the yoga practises which are performed with closed eyes. With this starts the internalisation of the mind. The eyes turn inward. Gradually, the other sense organs follow suit. This automatically results in the senses and the sense organs becoming quiescent, which automatically makes the mind quieter.

Behind all your sense organs are other higher sense organs. Behind the eyes is the Third Eye. Similarly, behind the ears, nose, tongue and skin are other higher sense organs. As a result of your Pratyahara practise, these awaken as you withdraw from your worldly sense. After all, in your journey to tracing your footsteps back to the source of creation, when you pierce the veil that divides this world from the world beyond Maya, your unawakened sense organs will fail to see, hear, smell, taste or touch the higher reality in another dimensional plane. You have to awaken your higher sense organs in order to experience the indestructible, eternal reality of the other world. The shutting down of the limited senses shuts the limited mind, just as the awakening of the higher senses awakens the higher mind. Thus, you encounter through your Third eye, which is located between your eyebrows, the Chidakasha, the sky beyond our sky. At the heart's centre, you experience the Hridyakasha, the cosmic heart of the universe and hear its slow, rhythmic beat.

Each of your Chakras is associated with one of your sense organs. When the Manipura awakens, the Third Eye begins to awaken. Similarly, with the awakening of the other Chakras, the higher sense organs linked with them begin to awaken. This entire process is like a well-conducted, synchronous orchestra.

At this point, the emphatic assertion of Kundalini Upanishad becomes an experience. To recall the opening sutra of this Upanishad which states that—two causes which affect the mind's activity and inactivity are the past memories and the vital air breathed in and out without proper control. Therefore, it asserts that man should master the vital air, that is, the pranayama practise. When breath is irregular, the mind wanders. When breath is controlled, the mind stays focused. Thus starts your journey of understanding the nature of the mind and its vagaries by learning how to control your breath through pranayama practise.

If you follow the flow-chart of creation backwards, you will see that after controlling the mind, you begin to encounter the Tattwas, the Triguna and the Antahkarna. You begin to break free of the

Kanchukas, the limiting powers of Maya. Thus, you retrace your steps back to unite with your origin, Shiva-Shakti.

This is why it is essential that you know how you were created and how you can trace your steps back to the origin—Cosmic Consciousness and Energy.

Section III

SYMBOLISM AND THE GROSS AND SUBTLE STATES

1

SYMBOLISM IN KUNDALINI YOGA

Symbolism is an inextricable part of Kundalini Yoga. It acts as a connection between the abstract mysticism of the practice and the imagination of the practitioner. Symbolism is not a random visualization of images.

The Serpent as Kundalini Shakti

Fear and reverence are a part of the worship of God. In the same way, the snake, as a symbol, evokes the same feelings of fear and reverence. Therefore, across cultures around the world, the snake is seen as a symbol of the unknown.

The world of science also uses the snake as its official symbol. The World Health Organization's logo depicts the staff of Asclepius from Greek mythology with a snake coiled around it. The medical world also uses the same staff of Asclepius with two snakes intertwined around it, overlapping each other at several points, just like Ida and Pingala meet at various Chakras in our spine in Kundalini.

In humans, the serpent symbolizes the unconscious. Since the beginning of civilization, the snake has been a constant feature in mythology and religious symbolism across the world. In Bible's

Genesis, Adam and Eve were tempted by Satan, who had presented himself in the form of a snake, to take a bite of the forbidden fruit, which resulted in their eviction from the Garden of Eden, the paradise created for them by God.

The snake is also one of those creatures which represent the multi-dimensional planes of existence. It lives on land, water and can even fly! In Indian mythology, the power of snakes can be observed in many myths. The gods and the demons used the snake Vasuki to churn the ocean to get the nectar of immortality. It is Sheshnath, the thousand-headed cobra, that holds the earth on its head. Vishnu rests on several coiled layers of snake known as the Kalaswarup Sheshnag. It was Kalia, the many-hooded cobra that shielded Baby Krishna from rain and storm as Krishna's father, Vasudeva, carried him in a basket across the river Yamuna. Shiva is often portrayed with a cobra coiled around his neck and arms. The Shiva Lingam is depicted with a snake coiled around it with its head hovering over the shrine. In Tantra, the snake is known as Mahakala, which stands for great or endless time.

The snake is symbolic of passions, desires, fears as well as the poison of evil that exists in us and that is capable of consuming all these emotions. As a symbol of Kundalini energy, the snake represents the base energy within us and the pure energy that is released to move up to the higher planes of existence.

The Lotus as Chakra

The Chakras are depicted as lotuses in Kundalini Yoga and Tantra. The lotus symbolizes the three stages of spiritual purification. The lotus grows in turbid waters, which represents the world of Maya which is rife with pain, duality and suffering; the stem of the lotus which rises above the mud represents our efforts to rise above the illusion of Maya; the blossoming of the lotus flower represents the enlightened state we achieve after overcoming Maya's illusions.

Animal and Divinity as symbols of Chakras

There is an animal, a god or a goddess associated with each Chakra. The animal represents the various stages of evolution humans must undergo at the lower levels. The deities represent the higher levels that humans aspire for and can ascend to.

2

THE SUBTLE (SUKSHMA)
AND THE GROSS (STHULA)

Understanding the gross and the subtle forms the basis of all Yogic philosophy. The gross is destructible and finite. The subtle is the basis of all existence; it is indestructible and limitless. The astral is the non-physical realm of existence to which various psychic and paranormal phenomena are ascribed to and in which the physical human body is said to have a counterpart. This astral body does not get destroyed in death. It lives on forever.

The Kenopanishad succinctly explains the power of the subtle in every creation. The sutras 4–8 of Part One beautifully explain that which we worship is not the Brahman; it is verily the power which powers all. It is that which cannot be seen with the eyes, but by which the eyes are enabled to see; that which is not uttered by speech, but powers speech; that which mind cannot comprehend, but powers the mind to think.

Another example of the subtle is the state between sleep and wakefulness. Wakefulness is the gross state of consciousness. In this state, both breath and thoughts are active. Sleep is the gross state of unconsciousness when there is breath, but no thoughts. The subtle is an in-between state when you are awake and conscious, but there are no thoughts and the breath is quiescent. This is the meditative state. It is the doorway to the knowledge of the subtle and its powers.

As a Kundalini Yoga practitioner, you cannot progress in this path, regardless of the practise of asanas and pranayama, unless you acknowledge and understand the subtle. Kundalini Shakti, the serpentine power, the Chakras, the Nadis and the pranic energy, all have no gross presence. You have to use your power of imagination to graduate from the gross to the subtle in order to tap into the phenomenal storehouse of energy that is the Kundalini Shakti.

In the following pages, you will weave your way through the gross (anatomical) and subtle (yogic physiology) aspects of your body as you attempt to understand how the gross and the subtle work together as we awaken the Kundalini energy from its dormant, resting state.

* * *

Words like Samadhi, Nirvana, Moksha and Super-Consciousness seem to belong to some state that is not associated with our body. This is fallacious. The beginning has to be made within the body at every level. The whole process of yoga attempts to merge our individual physiology with that of the universe. If you look at it dispassionately, without any religious or philosophical appendages, you will be able to realize that it is a completely physiological phenomenon. Thus, it is necessary to understand the physiology of our body so that as we do our practise, we experience the phenomenal changes which will take place at the gross and subtle levels of our entire being.

Before you proceed into understanding the anatomy of our physical or gross body, it is important to know the subtle body—the astral body.

The Five Koshas

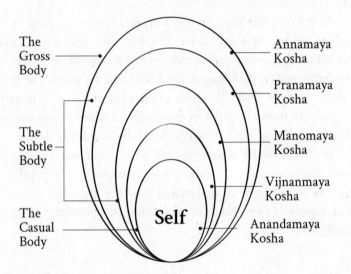

Pancha Kosha Tattwa

The
Gross — Body

The
Subtle — Body

The
Casual — Body

Self

Annamaya
Kosha

Pranamaya
Kosha

Manomaya
Kosha

Vijnanmaya
Kosha

Anandamaya
Kosha

The simplest way to understand the koshas is to think of them as the aura that surrounds your body. They are subtle and invisible to the eye but can be sensed when your faculties of awareness are sharpened through daily practise.

And each of these auras or koshas are arranged as Russian dolls encased one inside the other. Let us start with the outermost kosha, the food body or Annamaya Kosha and then move outwards to the last kosha, the Anandamaya Kosha. (Starting with the gross aura furthermost to your body, the food body or the Annamaya Kosha, you will progress to the other koshas as you move inwards.)

1. Annamaya Kosha: It is related to the gross body, our food body associated with eating, digestion and maintenance.
2. Pranamaya Kosha: It is related to the energy body, the vital force which powers the working of our body.

3. Manomaya Kosha: It is related to the mental body, which powers the functioning of your brain.
4. Vijnanmaya Kosha: It is related to the discriminative mental capacity; it powers your mind.
5. Anandamaya Kosha: It is related to the bliss body.

Annamaya Kosha: Most people are never in communion with their gross body. Unless they experience discomfort, injury or pain, people may never even notice the existence of the various body parts and organs. The body is always giving feedback on how our activities affect it.

The goal of Annamaya Kosha awareness practice is to correct this gross injustice. We must acknowledge the fact that our body is made up of individual parts which make up our basic body. Annamaya Kosha can be described as our food body (*Anna + Kosha* = Food + Sheath). While doing your asana and pranayama practice, you can attempt to develop an awareness of your body by turning your gaze inward, sensing how every posture affects the different parts of the body. Studying about the basic physical anatomy will also help in your practise. This will ultimately help you understand the nature of your true self.

For example, the liver is a dark-reddish brown organ and usually weighs 1.36 kilograms for an adult person. It holds approximately thirteen per cent of the body's blood supply at any given moment. It consists of two main lobes that are divided into eight segments that consist of 1000 smaller lobes. The liver performs more than 500 important bodily functions—the production of bile, which helps break down the food we eat; regulates the levels of toxins and chemicals present in our blood, and so on. Leading a poor lifestyle can harm our liver and result in the obstruction of all those functions that it performs to keep our body healthy.

Similarly, when you familiarize yourself with the workings of the body's most indomitable organ, the heart, you will start appreciating all the work it does. Most of the asana practise is done keeping in mind which organs of your body are being impacted and in what manner. This, along with the theoretical knowledge of your body parts and their functions, makes you gradually aware of your innermost sheath. The theoretical awareness of the Annamaya Kosha will help you stay grounded when you go about performing your daily activities.

Pranamaya Kosha: This is the energy body. From here on, you enter the subtler aspects of your being. We are normally unaware of the existence of our energy body when the truth is that without it our gross body cannot exist. Just think what powers the continuous beating of your heart from birth to death, and you have hit upon that energy known as Prana. Since this is a part of our autonomic system, we take it for granted and fail to acknowledge or understand its presence. Yet, as you become better at pranayama practise, you will slowly but surely start to feel the presence of this energy sheath.

It is crucial that this energy flows unimpeded, or else disease and health problems will surely manifest. Like the electric current, this energy also has negative and positive flows. Ida is the negative flow and Pingala is the positive flow. When these flows are imbalanced, your body doesn't function at its optimal capacity. With the regular practise of pranayama and a healthy lifestyle, you balance these two forces, which allows the third energy force, the central channel to open up, which is called Sushumna Nadi. There will be more about the Sushumna Nadi in the chapter on Nadi.

Starting out with just observing the flow of breath to practising pranayama along with a mantra like SoHum awakens your awareness of your astral body. Awareness of these Koshas brings you closer to the third sheath, the Manomaya Kosha.

Manomaya Kosha: This is your mental body. The Pranamaya sheath is unmanifest. But the Manomaya sheath is a mix of the manifest and the unmanifest. The brain is considered to be the seat of mental activities but the forces which power it are unmanifest. You can think but don't know how you do it. You have thoughts but don't know what thoughts really are. Can you know your mind through your mind? No. When you practise mantra, Ajapa japa, you begin to understand your mental sheath. Once you have understood it, you are ready to know your wisdom sheath, the Vijnanmaya Kosha.

Vijnanmaya Kosha: This is your wisdom body. As you encounter each of these sheaths, it is but natural that you will end up experiencing the wisdom sheath. When you have experienced your food body, the vital energy body and the mental body, your operating systems start working at a higher level. Your thoughts and actions have changed profoundly; they are now coming from the Vijnanmaya Kosha. Every moment of your life is impacted and you are on the verge of experiencing your final sheath, the Anandmaya Kosha.

Anandmaya Kosha: This is your bliss body. To experience and realize it is the culmination of your Kundalini practice. This sheath is the home of unadulterated bliss.

Now you must confront your gross body. The two main anatomies to be understood completely for the purposes of our Kundalini Yoga practice are the spine and the brain.

3

THE GROSS BODY

Anatomy of the Spine

Your spine is the kshetra (the field) of Kundalini Yoga. In today's parlance, this is where all the action takes place. Therefore, you must familiarize yourself with your spine. The spine allegorically signifies a person's strength. If you wish to be someone with courage, then understanding it is the first step in that direction.

An insight into the form and function of your spine will help in visualising the location and working of the Chakras, within the spine as well as the Nadis, the carriers of this subtle energy in your whole body.

Anatomically, the spine is made up of the spinal column, the bone structure of vertebrae, which supports the head, thoracic area and whole torso. The spinal cord is a bunch of nerves which run inside the hollow of the spinal column. These nerves connect the brain to the body and act as a communication system between the two. As you progress, there will be frequent references to the Nadis and Chakras, both of which reside in the spine. The central canal of the spine contains the cerebrospinal fluid (CSF). This acts as a cushion which provides mechanical and immunological protection to your spinal cord. The central nervous system is made up of the brain and the spinal cord.

Yoga philosophy from Bhagwat Puran ascertains that man is a microcosm of the universe. Everything that the universe is made of is seen in the human body too. The spine is called the Meru Danda which is the counterpart of Mount Meru, which in the Bhagwat Puran and other texts, is the axis of our universe, just as the spine is the axis of the human body.

The spine begins from the medulla oblongata in the brain and ends near the genitals, thus covering almost the whole body, from the head to the pelvis. The medulla oblongata is a cone-shaped neural mass responsible for autonomic (involuntary) functions. It is responsible for controlling the cardiac, respiratory, vomiting and vasomotor functions and therefore controls breathing, heart rate, blood pressure as well as the sleep cycle.

The spinal cord is made of thirty-three bones called vertebrae which are divided into five regions:

1. The Cervical region in the neck with seven vertebrae
2. The Dorsal region in the mid-back with twelve vertebrae
3. The Lumbar region in the waist area with five vertebrae
4. The Sacral region in the buttocks area with five vertebrae
5. The Coccygeal region in the coccyx area with four vertebrae.

The vertebrae are stacked on top of each other and form a pillar of support for your torso. Each of your vertebrae has arches that create a hollow cylinder which serves as a passage for the spinal cord. Through this passage flows your Sushumna Nadi after it has been activated through regular practise. The size of the vertebrae varies for each region. The cervical vertebrae are smaller than others, but their arch is bigger. The dorsal vertebrae are bigger, but their arch is smaller. The lumbar vertebrae are the largest. The spine is not stiff but has a curvature that gives it the spring action.

The spinal cord ends at the second vertebrae of the coccygeal region where it tapers off into fine threads known as Filum Terminals.

The spinal cord is further divided into two symmetrical halves, the anterior and the posterior fissure. In its centre is a minute canal called the Canalis Centralis.

Moreover, between each pair of vertebrae, there are apertures through which the spinal nerves extend from the spinal cord to other parts of the body. These spinal nerves are numbered according to the spinal vertebrae above which they exit the spinal column.

- The eight cervical spinal nerves are C1 to C8.
- The twelve thoracic spinal nerves are T1 to T12.
- The five lumbar nerves are L1 to L5.
- The five sacral spinal nerves are through S1 to S5.
- There is one coccygeal nerve.

These five centres in your spine correspond to the five Chakras—Vishuddhi, Anahata, Manipura, Swadhisthana and Mooladhara.

This takes us to the central nervous system wherein the five Chakras and the Nadis which extend from each of these Chakras are located, including the three most important Nadis—the Ida, the Pingala and the Sushumna.

The Central Nervous System (CNS)

The central nervous system (CNS) controls all the functions of the body and the mind. It consists of two parts—the brain and the spinal cord.

The spine which is a part of the central nervous system is precious for two reasons—it is the bridge between the brain and the body and unlike other organs, the CNS cannot be replaced nor does it divide and create new cells. Neither a doctor nor your own body can help resurrect any part of the CNS if it is damaged. Any injury to the spinal cord disrupts the exchange of information between the brain and other parts of the body.

The brain is the centre of our thoughts, the interpreter of our external environment and exercises control over the body's movements. Like a central super-computer, it interprets information from our eyes (sight), ears (sound), nose (smell), tongue (taste), and skin (touch), as well as from the internal organs.

The brain is responsible for integrating sensory information and coordinating body function, both consciously and unconsciously. Complex functions such as thinking and feeling as well as regulation of homeostasis are performed by different parts of the brain.

There are two types of tissue that can be found in the CNS:

1. Grey matter consists of nerve cell bodies, dendrites and axons. Neurons in grey matter organize either in layers, as in the cerebral cortex, or as clusters called nuclei.
2. White matter consists mostly of axons, whose myelin sheaths give it its white appearance.

In the early stages of embryonic development, the CNS is formed as a relatively uniform tube. The major regions of the brain develop as enlargements at the top of this tube and not as a separate organ.

Within the central nervous system is the autonomic nervous system, which controls involuntary processes like blood circulation, digestion, breathing, excretion and more. It is called autonomic because it works without conscious effort. The basic function of the autonomic system is to maintain homeostasis.

The autonomic nervous system can be divided into:

1. The sympathetic nervous system
2. The parasympathetic nervous system.

The basic function of the sympathetic nervous system is to manage the body's response in a fight-or-flight situation. It is located close to the thoracic and lumbar regions in the spinal cord.

The parasympathetic system maintains the bodily functions when the body is at rest. It regulates the body's 'rest and digest' and 'feed and breed' responses. It is located between the spinal cord and the medulla.

At the subtle yogic level, the sympathetic system is the Pingala Nadi and the parasympathetic system is the Ida Nadi. The central cord is the Sushumna Nadi.

The Ida Nadi extends from the left side of the Sushumna Nadi and the Pingala from the right. They both travel up along the Sushumna, criss-crossing at the various Chakras along the spine to finally culminate at the Ajna Chakra, between the eyebrow centre.

4

THE SUBTLE

What are Nadis?

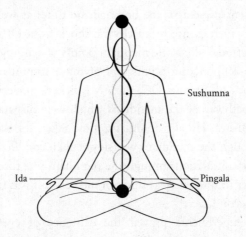

Ida — Sushumna — Pingala

The word 'Nadi' means flow. One can say they are the yogic system of energy flow in your body. Understanding Nadis is crucial as they are responsible for transmission of energy from the Chakras to all parts of the body. They are distinct from the nerves and the nervous system. The western world has been sceptical about their existence as they do not have a physical presence in the body. However, experiments conducted with specially designed equipments to measure electric currents in the body have proved the existence of such energy flows in the body distinct from the nervous system. Japanese, Russian and Korean scientists have studied the meridians of acupuncture and the Nadis through biophysical and bioelectric systems and have confirmed their existence and nature.

For the rationalists, it will be interesting to have a glimpse at what the scientists discovered through their experiments to locate and prove the existence of Nadis and the three meridians of acupuncture.

The most extensive research on this was done by Dr Hiroshi Motoyama, a Japanese para-psychologist, scientist and author. In his quest to research into Nadis and the meridians, he developed an instrument called AMI which was designed to measure the flow of electric currents in the body. Dr Motoyama used it to measure the steady current present in the body all the times as well as current in the body in response to an electric shock from DC voltage. By placing electrodes along the meridian points of acupuncture as well as the non-acupuncture points and giving a stimulus through an electric shock of 20 volts DC, the AMI picked up electric currents along the pathway of the meridians which were disparate from the neural pathways. He also found the time taken for the sensations to pass through the meridians was slower than conduction through nerves. The conduction through the meridians was fifteen to forty-eight cm per second whereas through the nerves it was five to eighty meter per second.

These experiments proved the existence of energy systems within the body that were distinct from the nervous system. Later he used this instrument to predict the onset of malfunction within the body by studying the state of Nadis. This again established the Yogic theory that disease is a manifestation of energy blockages and malfunctioning of the energy flows in the body. The Nadis are connected to the lungs, the nervous system and the Chakras. They are instrumental in maintaining a healthy body and mind.

According to ancient texts, there are 72,000 Nadis in the human body, but as per the Shiva Samhita that figure is closer to 3.5 lakhs. Regardless, we are more concerned with three main Nadis—the Ida, the Pingala and the Sushumna.

The Ida, Pingala and Sushumna Nadis

Our universe is a dance of opposites that interact with each other resulting in a whole lot of creation. Birth and death create life, light and dark make a day, positive and negative charge make electricity, left and right hemispheres of our brain work together to create cognition and so on. Most of life is an attempt to find a balance between opposites.

Similarly, in the Nadis we have the opposites in Ida and Pingala, which when harmonized awaken the third force, the Sushumna Nadi.

It is fascinating to understand how these Nadis function within the body. This will allow you to not only understand your personality type but also change it by inter-changing the function and character of the Nadis. Let us embark on this adventure.

Ida Nadi originates from the base of the spine from the left side of the Sushumna Nadi. As it travels up, it criss-crosses at the various Chakras on the spine and ends on the left side of the Ajna Chakra. Ida Nadi is connected to your left nostril. Your left nostril in turn is connected to your right hemisphere of the brain. The right hemisphere controls the left-side of your body. In short, the Ida Nadi controls the functions of the left-side of your body. The Ida Nadi has certain characteristics. When the Ida Nadi dominates in you, certain characteristics manifest in you and determine your personality type.

Ida Nadi can be described as feminine, lunar, intuitive, emotional, negative (as a charge, not as a quality), passive, inert force and yin energy. It is the parasympathetic nervous system and inwardly directed. It controls our sense organs, the gyanendriyas, to understand the world we live in. It is mind over the body. In Yogic parlance, it is the Chitta, the consciousness; it is the mental force. If your Ida Nadi is more dominant, then you will tend to be emotional and intuitive rather than rational and logical. Therefore, most artistic people are left-handed.

Similarly, Pingala Nadi originates from the right side of the Sushumna Nadi, travels up the body, criss-crossing at the various Chakras along the spine to terminate on the right side of the Ajna Chakra. It is connected to the right nostril, which is connected with the left hemisphere of your brain. The left hemisphere controls the right side of your body.

Pingala Nadi can be described as masculine, solar, physical, positive, dynamic, logical, active and yang energy. It is the sympathetic nervous system and is outwardly directed. It controls the organs of action, the karmendriyas. It is prana shakti, the vital life force. If your Pingala Nadi is dominant, then you will be dynamic, logical, extroverted, rational, ambitious and a go-getter. Most people into today's materialistic world are Pingala dominated.

The Brain and the Nadis

Scientific research has established that the left hemisphere of the brain connected to the Pingala Nadi is what controls speech, logical and analytical abilities and temporal and linear functions. The right hemisphere of the brain connected to the Ida Nadi is silent, dark, lunar, intuitive, emotional, spatial and holistic in function.

Thomas Hoover, a researcher who studied the comparison between Zen and neurological discoveries pithily sums up when he states, 'The hemisphere that speaks, does not know; the hemisphere that knows, does not speak.'

This demonstrates the wisdom of the Creator; had the whole brain been performing all of its functions as a whole, then injury to any part would affect the whole brain and render the person dysfunctional. Also, at another level, these seemingly disparate halves complement each other.

The following list states the distinct functions performed by each side of the brain:

The Left brain (Pingala Nadi)	The Right brain (Ida Nadi)
Active	Passive
Analytical	Understanding
Temporal	Here and now
Partial	Holistic
Explicit	Implicit
Argument	Experience
Intellect	Intuitive
Logic	Emotion
Thinking	Feeling
Verbal	Spatial
Extrovert	Introvert

These opposite energy forces work together to run our entire body system by controlling the faculties of knowledge, cognition and action.

Swara Yoga states that on the day of a full moon, during the wee hours, the left nostril is more active than the right nostril. After ninety minutes, the right nostril takes over and the left nostril is subdued. This cycle goes on for the rest of the twenty-four hours.

The opposite happens on moonless nights, that is, the cycle begins with the right nostril being more active during the wee hours. Thus, in the present-day work culture, people who have desk jobs end up with numerous health problems. This happens because your natural bio-rhythm changes every ninety minutes or so. When the right nostril is dominant, the dynamic, extroverted part of the brain is active. During this time, your natural urge is to get up and engage in physical activities. But if you continue to sit at your desk and do mental work, you go against your natural cycle and urges. Realising this, corporates have made exercise a part of their work culture for the benefit of their employees.

The fluctuation between dominance of one or the other Nadi is constant throughout the day. Studying the pattern of your breath in the nostrils is an easy way of knowing which Nadi is dominating at any given point of time. Keeping a log of the fluctuations of flow of your nostrils to understand their pattern will ultimately help your yoga practise. Yogic practise attempts to bring about balance between these opposites. When this happens, it results in the awakening of a third force, the Sushumna Nadi. This is an important event in your journey of Kundalini awakening. Kundalini energy moves along the Sushumna Nadi and therefore the first step is to ensure that your Sushumna is awakened.

Sushumna Nadi

Let us go back to the brain and the spinal cord to understand the interplay of the gross and subtle as manifested in the interplay between your nerves and the Nadis. Your spinal cord extends into the brain. All the cranial and spinal nerves are connected to this cord. Thereby every nerve and function of the body is controlled by the spinal cord. The spinal cord enters in to the fourth ventricle of the brain in the medulla oblongata. From there on it runs along the third and finally the fifth ventricle and reaches the crown of the head.

Parallel to the spinal cord in the gross body is the subtle Nadi, the Sushumna Nadi which starts at the base of the spine and ends at the crown of the head. It runs inside the spinal cord. The Sushumna Nadi plays a critical role in Kundalini practise. It is the channel through which the awakened Kundalini will travel upwards from the base of the spine. Therefore, before awakening the Chakras, it is important to awaken the Sushumna Nadi.

Within the Sushumna Nadi is yet another Nadi, called the Vajra Nadi. While the Sushumna Nadi is red like fire, the Vajra Nadi is lustrous like the Sun. Understandably, its character is Rajasic, which means dynamic. Within the Vajra Nadi is another Nadi, the Chitra Nadi. It is pale in colour and has Sattwic, unstinted attributes. It is pure and reflects the moon. Within the Chitra Nadi is a minute, fine Nadi, the Brahma Nadi. It corresponds to the Canalis Centralis in the gross body. It is through this Brahma Nadi that the Kundalini travels from the Mooladhara to Sahasrara Chakra. In this Nadi exist all the six Chakras: Mooladhara, Swadhisthans, Manipura, Anahata, Vishuddhi and Ajna.

5

THE BRAIN

Your brain is like a coiled mass of snakes. It is a mass of nervous tissues made up of grey and white matter. How well do you know this coiled mass situated inside your head? The brain is the most crucial organ of the body. Yet, despite the essential role it plays, it is the most misused and the least understood organ.

Yogis claim that your cognition and action comes from one part of your brain. The other nine parts make up the inactive or the sleeping brain.

'Why are these compartments inactive?' Swami Satyananda Saraswati says, 'Because there is no energy. The active portion of the brain is powered by the energies of Ida and Pingala, but the other nine-tenths have only Pingala. Pingala is life and Ida is consciousness. If a man is alive but unable to think, in yoga it is said that he has prana shakti but not manas shakti.

Up until the 1990s, scientists debunked this theory and claimed that humans use most parts of their brain throughout life unless they have sustained brain damage. However, in the 1990s and later, studies found that the truth lies somewhere between the two clashing assertions.

Scientists have discovered that a small number of neurons fire hundreds and thousands of times more than the others in the brain.

They found that there was a kind of reserve pool of dormant neurons in the brain. Why were these neurons dormant? Neuroscientists studied neuron activity in rats before and after trimming off one of their whiskers. They found that the less active, quiet neurons became more sensitive and active in relation to the spared whiskers.

In an article published in the Nautilus, a science magazine, Dr Kelly Clancy, a neuroscientist, concludes that, 'we really do have latent mental capabilities, as suggested by the ten per cent myth.'

Having settled this, we can now get started on how we can activate the latent parts of our brain in ways that don't involve losing a body part. When spirituality and science come together, the many mysteries of life unravel and make the impossible happen.

Dr N.K. Venkataraman, a neurosurgeon and Sri M, a contemporary spiritual master, in an interesting conversation on 'The Unknown Dimensions of the Brain', bridge the gaps between science and spirituality. Dr Venkataraman acknowledges the claims of yoga and, specifically, Kundalini Yoga's potential to change the capacity and character of the brain through pranayama, meditation, Chakra awakening and attitudinal and lifestyle changes.

Dr Venkataraman says that science has empirical evidence of what the spiritual world claims is the path to Bliss. He says, 'Love and empathy change the functioning of the brain. When you have love and empathy, the dendrites which receive sensory messages, the synapses which link up the cells, the neurotransmitters which make the chemicals to transmit messages across the synapses, undergo a change. The brain produces dopamine and oxytocin which transport the person to a blissful state.' Dr Venkataraman likens this state to the Anandmaya Kosha.

He says, 'Modern science knows that you have the ability to completely handle your brain. The way you think can change your brain; through it, you can modify your brain structure, the nerve structure and the neuro transmitters.' Rene Descartes said, '*Cogito, ergo sum*', meaning 'I think, therefore I am.' But we can now safely say, 'I am what I think.'

The secret to utilizing your brain to its full potential lies in your breath. Over the years, several experiments have established the effects of sustained practise of pranayama on the brain, especially the reticular activating system (RAS) which, along with the vagus nerve, impacts the brain.

You may be wondering about the connection between the mind and the brain. Earlier, it was thought that the mind is a product of the brain. But according to modern science, the mind does not exist in just the brain but also in other parts of the body and even outside the body (quantum theory). Every cell in the body possesses its own intelligence. The gut, the heart, the lungs and all the other organs have neurons similar to the brain and thus, there are lesser brains in the body. Moreover, this explains how a powerful mind can so to say 'jump out of the body' and control and influence a weaker or lesser mind. The mind is not simply brain matter but waves of energy which can reach out of your body too. Dr N.K. Venkatraman says a stronger mind can permanently change the structure of the brain of the weaker mind.

What is RAS?

The reticular activating system (RAS) is a bunch of neural circuits between the brainstem and the cortex. These circuits let the brain modulate between slow and fast sleep rhythms, as seen on an EEG. The nuclei of the RAS coordinate both the sleep-wake cycle and wakefulness. The groupings of neurons that together make up the RAS are ultimately responsible for attention, arousal, modulation of muscle tone, and the ability to focus.

All of this affects the circulatory, digestive and excretory systems. God, in all his wisdom, has given us the power over this autonomous structure. He gave us the reins to our involuntary system through our breath. It is the only conscious activity which is connected to the RAS. Thus, by regulating your breath you can regulate the whole gamut of your being.

While the RAS resides in the brain and activates it, the vagus nerve originates in the brain and moves around your whole body. It is this characteristic of this nerve that it takes its name from the word vagabond. This nomadic nerve connects the brain and the body for the voluntary, autonomous working of our respiratory, circulatory, digestive, sexual and excretory activities. The vagus nerve is also affected by our breathing.

Inside the Brain

The core of your brain is made up of 100 billion nerve cells. It was earlier believed that we are born with a fixed number of neurons; during old age, the number of neurons decreases and the lost neurons are not replaced. However, research has proven that even in adulthood the number of neurons can increase. What is more, the research links up with what the spiritual world also claims is a way of increasing brain power and even defying age-related decay. In the following section, we will take a ride through the two systems of empirical and experimental knowledge to explore possibilities of defying age and decay.

The Pineal and Pituitary Glands

You must understand the function of two important glands in your brain—the pituitary and the pineal gland. These glands are directly connected with the Ajna Chakra.

The pineal gland situated in the brain is another example of something that the spiritual seekers intuitively knew about before it was discovered by the scientific world. This mysterious gland was referred to as the Third Eye. It is the place of Ajna Chakra. Yogis believe it to be a powerful centre and it is used in Kundalini Yoga and many other advanced yogic practises. It was not until recently that the scientific world verified the assertions of the yogis. It was considered a vestigial gland.

In 1886, H.W. De Graf and E. Baldwin Spencer independently discovered that the pineal gland was a kind of eye, possessing all the features of the external eye with pigmentation and retina cells surrounding an inner chamber filled with a globular lens like mass. Subsequent research has established that this inner eye responds to light, both direct and through the nervous pathway from the eyes.

The pineal gland is located behind the centre of the eyebrows, at the central intersection of the two hemispheres of the brain. It is barely ¼ of an inch and weighs less than 100 milligrams in an adult.

In 1958, Aaron B. Lerner, a dermatologist working at the Yale Medical School, isolated the hormone melatonin from the pineal gland. It is a hormone that regulates the sleep-wake cycle. It also affects the onset of puberty in a negative way (it inhibits the function of the pituitary gland, which is primarily responsible for the onset of puberty). When children reach adolescence, the size and the function of the pineal gland diminishes prompting the pituitary gland to take over. Pituitary glands become active and releases hormones necessary for facilitating the onset of puberty and development of the reproductive organs in men and women. However, despite its diminished function in our physical body, the pineal gland is directly connected with our Kundalini practice.

Later, another hormone known as serotonin was also found to be released by the pineal gland. This hormone is a mood stabilizer and induces feeling of well-being and happiness. It also helps with sleeping, eating and digestion. The lack of serotonin can cause depression and anxiety.

In the Yoga Magazine of March 1979, Swami Karmananda Saraswati, MBBS, Sydney, put together some amazing facts about the discovery and the role of serotonin in human consciousness, which is of utmost importance to the practise of yoga.

It is also worth acknowledging that children display a combination of innocence and intuitive intelligence, which is attributed partially to the pineal gland and its release of the two hormones—serotonin and melatonin. They sense unspoken tension between parents, they hold the ability to create alternate universes, of turning ostensible objects into make-believe worlds of their own creation, by imagining a chair as the driving seat of a car and with an imaginary wheel at their hands as they speed away.

It is for this reason that so many practices of yoga target awakening the pineal gland through practises like the Shambhavi mudra, Trataka and more. When the pineal and the pituitary glands are active, an individual can manage their worldly affairs with the help of hormones released by the pituitary gland and gain access to intuitive powers through the pineal gland.

Section IV

WORLD OF CHAKRAS, LOCATION, FUNCTION, SYMBOLISM

1

THE WORLD OF CHAKRAS

The word Chakra means a wheel. For the purposes of Kundalini Yoga, it is a vortex of subtle cosmic energy. Kundalini Yoga practise rests on the complete understanding of these Chakras in all their dimensions, that is, their location in the spine, their functions, imagery, symbolism, their animal association and their divine representation.

The location of the Chakras

In the spinal column, there is interlacing of several nerves, arteries and veins. These are known as plexuses. The plexuses of the spinal column, from top to bottom, are listed below:

1. Cervical: connected with the head, neck and shoulders
2. Brachial: connected with the chest, shoulders, arms and hands
3. Lumbar: connected with the back, abdomen, groin, thighs, knees and calves
4. Sacral: connected with the pelvis, buttocks, genitals, thighs and feet

5. Sacrococcygeal: connected with the movement of the lower
    limbs and the sexual organs

Except for Ajna Chakra, which is associated with the pituitary
and pineal glands, the rest of the five Chakras from Vishuddhi to
Mooladhara are associated with the above five plexuses.

The Ajna Chakra at the cerebellum is connected to the pineal
and pituitary glands and controls the muscles and the onset of
sexual activity. These two are the command centre for the whole
body.

The other Chakras and their functions are as follows:

1. The Vishuddhi Chakra at the laryngeal region controls the
    thyroid gland, the speech centres, the upper palate, the epiglottis
    and corresponds to the cervical plexus.
2. The Anahata Chakra is at the cardiac plexus. It manages the
    functions of the heart, the lungs, the diaphragm and other organs
    in this area of the body and corresponds to the Brachial plexus.
3. The Manipura Chakra is at the solar plexus. It controls
    digestion, assimilation and temperature fluctuations in the body
    corresponds to the Lumbar plexus.
4. The Swadhisthana Chakra is at the sacral plexus. It is connected
    with the lower abdomen and the organs associated with it.
5. The Mooladhara Chakra is at the sacrococcygeal plexus. It
    controls the excretory and sexual functions.

There are two higher Chakras that are connected to the Cosmic
Consciousness and therefore have no association with any specific
bodily system. They are:

6. Bindu Visarga is at the soft spot on the head. It is connected with
    the Sahasrara Chakra.
7. The Sahasrara Chakra is at the crown of the head, the ultimate
    destination of the Kundalini Shakti. At this Chakra resides

Cosmic Consciousness, also known as Purusha in Samkhya and Shiva in Tantra.

These are the eight fundamental Chakras. Hatha Yoga texts and other texts mention other Chakras, numbering from fifty-two to 144, present in various parts of the body. However, we are mainly concerned with the eight Chakras mentioned above.

Swami Satyananda writes in the Kundalini Tantra—'If you cut open the spine transversely, the grey matter appears like the petals of a lotus flower and the nerves that extend from the junctions appear like the Nadis.'

Functions of the Chakras

Chakras are subtle and don't have a physical presence in the body. Each Chakra serves as a switch or centre of cosmic energy.

The awakening of each Chakra invokes certain experiences, especially at the experiential level. This depends on the practitioner's personality and focus of practise.

Every Chakra is directly connected with the brain and exists independent of the other Chakras. Once a Chakra is awakened, you move on to the next and the previous Chakra becomes quiescent. This will affect not just the present life but all of the next lives. The astral body does not disintegrate upon death. The state of awakening of the Chakras remains in your astral body even after the destruction of the physical body. Hence, the state of awakening of your Chakras in this life will be instrumental in their awakening in your next life.

There are a number of practical techniques that can help one concentrate on and develop an awareness of each Chakra. You may find it difficult to fix your mind on its location or its symbolic representation. One of the easiest ways to accomplish this involves starting with visualising the anterior side of the body which is the field or kshetra of the Chakras. For example, the Manipura Chakra is located behind the navel centre in the spine. If locating the Chakra inside the spine is difficult, you can focus on the navel centre in the anterior side of the body. Every Chakra except the Mooladhara has a corresponding focus point on the anterior side of the body. Listed below are the corresponding frontal fields of each of the Chakras:

1. Swadhisthana: tail bone
2. Manipura: navel centre
3. Anahata: heart centre
4. Vishuddhi: throat pit
5. Ajna: eye brow centre
6. Bindu: soft spot on head
7. Sahasrara: crown of the head

Symbolism of Chakras

Each Chakra is represented as a lotus and has a fixed number of petals as well as a specific colour as given below:

1. The Mooladhara Chakra: Four petalled deep red lotus flower
2. The Swadhisthana Chakra: Six petalled vermilion lotus flower
3. The Manipura Chakra: Ten petalled bright yellow lotus flower
4. The Anahata Chakra: Twelve petalled blue lotus flower
5. The Vishuddhi Chakra: Sixteen petalled purple lotus flower
6. The Ajna Chakra: Two petalled maroon lotus flower
7. The Bindu Visarga: Full moon
8. The Sahasrara Chakra: Thousand petalled multi-coloured lotus flower

These petals of each Chakra represent the Nadis that stem from that Chakra. There are letters on each of the petals of all the Chakras, which represent the fifty letters of Sanskrit. In the dormant state, the petals of all the Chakras are turned downwards, facing the Kundalini Shakti at the Mooladhara Chakra. After the Chakras are awakened, the petals turn upwards to face the Sahasrara Chakra.

The Mooladhara Chakra

The Mooladhara Chakra is located at the base of the spine and lies between the genitals and the anus. At the Mooladhara Chakra, the Serpent Energy, the Kundalini, rests. It is the most important Chakra because it distinguishes man from animals. It is the last Chakra for animals and the first Chakra for the higher evolution of man as it is linked with the higher consciousness in man. Below it, the Chakras in the legs and several other Chakras, which are present in animals too, can be found. These deal with the natural lower instincts of eating, sleeping and sex.

The Mooladhara supports all the other Chakras that come after it. Hence, it is also known as the Adhara (support) Chakra. Mooladhara is a conjunction of 'mool' which means root and 'adhara' which means support. It is directly connected with the Ajna Chakra located at the centre of the eyebrows. For the young practitioners, the mind may get distracted due to the stimulation of these instincts. It will be beneficial for you to hold this higher connection of the Mooladhara Chakra in mind while concentrating on it.

To get a clearer picture of the location of the Mooladhara Chakra, let us compare it with its gross counterpart, the cauda equina.

The spinal cord extends from the brain to the end of the spinal column where it tapers off into fine silken threads. Before it terminates, it separates into innumerable fibres crowded into a bunch of nerves. This bunch of nerves is called the cauda equina. In Yoga, this centre is recognized as kanda, which stands for 'bulb' and is known as the Brahma Granthi. It plays an important role in clearing the way for the awakening and ascent of Kundalini. Scientific research have discovered that this tiny knot possesses infinite energy and the ability to induce psychic experiences. There are three important Granthis that will be discussed in a separate section later.

The kanda is just above the Mooladhara Chakra. In the subtle body, all the Nadis spring from the kanda. It is the junction where the Sushumna Nadi is connected to the Mooladhara Chakra. The four petals of the Chakra are on the side of the kanda.

From this Chakra, four important Nadis emerge which appear like the four petals of a lotus flower. The subtle vibrations which are made by these four Nadis are the four Sanskrit letters—vam, sham, sham and sam.

Symbolism of the Mooladhara Chakra

The illustration of the Mooladhara Chakra will make it easy to visualize it and understand the symbolism associated with it. Moreover, it will assist you in focusing on its meaning, inherent quality and its manifold purpose and possibilities at the gross, subtle and causal levels.

It is depicted as a four petalled deep-red lotus flower inside a golden rectangle which represents the Earth element of this Chakra. An elephant, which symbolizes the heavy Earth element, is at the base with its seven trunks representing the Sapta Dhatu, the seven basic elements of our body and building blocks for all-life (as explained in the chapter on creation). At its centre is a black Shiva Lingam with the serpent-like Kundalini Shakti, coiled around the lingam in three and a half rounds with its head poised upward. The three rounds are symbolic of the Triguna—Tamas, Rajas and Sattwa; the serpent's head is poised upwards to unite with pure consciousness at the Sahasrara Chakra.

The sense organ linked with the Mooladhara Chakra is the nose and the tanmatra is smell. Its element is Earth which signifies its basic, gross character. At the psychological level, it controls our passions, attachments and sexual drive. Its karmendriya, organ of action, is the anus. Therefore, the awakening of Mooladhara Chakra sometimes results in the sharpening of the sense of smell. It may also result in itchiness or other sensations around the anus.

The Mooladhara is associated with the Bhur Loka, that is, the Earth and its inhabitants. Its presiding deities are god Ganesha and the goddess Dakini. Its *Beej* (seed) Mantra is 'lam'. (Just as a seed holds within itself the potential to grow into a whole tree, a Beej Mantra holds the full potential of the Chakra.) Chanting the mantra repeatedly, with awareness focused at the Mooladhara Chakra, is a beautiful practise of awakening this Chakra. Its Vayu is 'Apana', with a downward movement. It belongs to the Annamaya Kosha, the food body.

Nadis and the Mooladhara Chakra

The two Nadis, Ida and Pingala, have a special connection with the Mooladhara Chakra and play an important role in the awakening of the Sushumna Nadi. We have discussed how the three Nadis, the Ida, Pingala and Sushumna, emerge from this Chakra. Sushumna Nadi functions partially in most people because of imbalance between the Ida and Pingala Nadis. With practise of Hatha Yoga and Kundalini Yoga, balance between these two Nadis results in the awakening of the Sushumna Nadi. This is one of the first important steps in your Kundalini practise. It opens the pathway for the Kundalini energy to awaken and move upwards. Awakening of Kundalini without the opening of Sushumna Nadi will be futile.

Basic instincts and the Mooladhara Chakra

Sex has been considered a social and cultural taboo that manifests as schizophrenia, perversion and neurosis at the individual level and gender issues, rape, domestic violence and more at the social level. In nineteenth century Europe, when even table legs were considered too obscene to be left uncovered, Sigmund Freud became the first to address this taboo topic in his studies. He said everything in life was influenced by our sexual awareness or the lack of it. The present-day sex positive society is a far cry from the sexually repressed times in which Freud conducted his research. However, the world still shies away from the activity that is the source of all life. Sex continues to evoke feelings of guilt and shame and is still the subject of social, cultural and moral taboos.

Tantra addresses this issue directly by giving it its rightful place in the scheme of human life. The sexual drive is accepted as a part of human biology and psychology. How can the very source of life on Earth be shunned? In fact, it is looked upon as a divine act representative of the union of Shiva and Shakti. Therefore, the state of complete bliss and loss of self-identity that is experienced for a few seconds during an orgasm is but a glimpse of the eternal bliss that one achieves with the union of Kundalini Shakti with Shiva at the Sahasrara Chakra. The only adjunct is to use sexual union as a beautiful expression of love to transcend it instead of indulging in it only for the sake of pleasure. The Kundalini practice is so devised that the sexual energy is directed back upwards to the brain to awaken its dormant centres connected with the Mooladhara Chakra.

Kundalini practise neither prohibits sex nor does it advocate for celibacy. You can be married and can continue your conjugal life with your partner. The only advice is to sublimate the sexual energy for higher awakening. It is also, after all, a kind of energy. Once this is internalized, then every sexual act becomes a divine act of union of Shiva and Shakti or unity of Cosmic Consciousness with universal

Energy. A combination of this awareness with your Mooladhara awakening practise will surely purify your baser instincts and free up your mind for the rousing of the Mooladhara Chakra.

When Mooladhara Awakens

The awakening of the Mooladhara Chakra can be likened to a volcanic eruption. Just as a volcano throws up fire, lava and molten earth from the depths of Earth's belly, the awakening of the Mooladhara Chakra releases deep seated fears, desires and suppressed emotions. You confront your samskaras, hidden memories of this and past lives, that influence your present behaviour and attitude. For example, some people have irrational fears that they can't explain; some people have sexual fantasies or trauma related to sex that they involuntarily bury deep in their psyche because of cultural taboos and the feelings of guilt and shame associated with the subject.

All such repressed emotions, passions and memories create a knot, a blockage, which prevents the free flow of energy in your body and over time manifests in the form of physical ailments or mental disorders. You have been learning, from the beginning of this book, about the importance of removing all mental, physical and emotional stress and blockages from your entire body-mind system so that prana can flow freely through the Nadis. Starting with awakening the Mooladhara Chakra is the best way to handle those conscious and unconscious issues connected with the primordial nature of your being.

It is always advisable to practise under the guidance of an experienced Guru. As you break free of the animal instincts you may experience many things. Since the awakening involves breaking free of the pull of Earth's gravity, you may get a sense of lightness and levitation. But as this happens to your astral body, it does not mean actual physical levitation of your gross body. Some people may experience clairvoyance and clairaudience; some may experience a feeling of warmth in the perineal centre or a sensation of something moving up through the spine; others may experience mood swings or disturbed sleeping patterns.

These are signs of awakening of the Chakra and upward movement of Kundalini. Thus, it is important to practise regularly and, if possible, seek expert advice too.

Practise for Mooladhara

While all the aspects of the Chakra are fresh in your mind, it will be beneficial to discuss some of the asanas, pranayama, mudra and bandha (please refer to Section VII) that help arouse the Mooladhara Chakra from its slumber.

One of the easiest and most effective practises which directly impact the Mooladhara Chakra is Vajroli for men and Sahjoli for women. It involves the alternate contraction and relaxation of the perineal centre. This has to be done with awareness focused on your Mooladhara Chakra and movement of breath.

The other practise which directly affects the Mooladhara Chakra is the Maha Vedha Mudra.

Shambhavi Mudra and Nasikadrishti activate this Chakra. Since the nose is the jyanindriya which is directly connected with the Mooladhara Chakra, practise of staring at the tip of the nose with open or closed eyes helps awaken it. Similarly, since there is a direct connection between the Mooladhara and Ajna Chakra, trying to look at the eyebrow centre helps activate both of these important Chakras.

The Swadhisthana Chakra

The Swadhisthana Chakra is located where the spine ends in a tiny bulb at the tail bone. The word is a combination of 'swa' means self and 'adhistana' means dwelling place. It is located close to the Mooladhara Chakra and is associated with it in several ways. It can also be located by its kshetra, the frontal field at the pubic bone. Hence, both its kshetra and actual positioning are determined with the help of its physiological and frontal field. It controls the reproductive and urinary systems, that is, the prostate and utero-vaginal nerves.

Symbolism of the Swadhisthana Chakra

The Swadhisthana Chakra is depicted as a six petalled vermilion lotus flower. Its element is water. Within this lotus flower, the water element is symbolized by two crescent moons as two circles within each other. The outer moon has petals turned outward which symbolize consciousness. The outward turned petals carry the sound vibrations of six Sanskrit letters—bam, bham, mam, yam, ram and lam. The Beej Mantra of the Swadhisthana Chakra is 'vam'. This Chakra is the seat of past karma.

The inner moon's petals are turned inward and represent the unconscious in every individual. These two moons are separated by a crocodile. One can imagine this crocodile as black or white depending on how you visualize the unconscious state. The crocodile symbolizes the subterranean nature of the unconscious. Above the crocodile, inside the inner moon, is the Beej Mantra 'vam' which, like the crocodile, may be visualized as black or white.

The presiding deity of this Chakra is god Vishnu who is depicted with four arms and the goddess Rakini, resplendent and holding weapons in her uplifted arms. She is the Goddess of the vegetable kingdom which is why a vegetarian diet is recommended while awakening this Chakra. The Swadhisthana Chakra exists in the Bhuva Loka, the second plane of existence.

The tanmatra of this Chakra is the sense of taste; therefore the jnanindriya is the tongue and karmendriya consists of the sexual organs, the kidneys and the urinary system. The Vayu which rules this Chakra is 'Vyana', which moves in the whole body and the subtle body is Pranayama Kosha, that is, the energy body.

Swadhisthana and Your Unconscious

The Swadhisthana Chakra is connected to our unconscious mind and, like the Mooladhara Chakra, is a storehouse of mental impressions or samskaras. It would be fallacious to think that the unconscious is dormant in humans. On the contrary, it controls a lot of our strange behaviours, fears and thoughts. The Swadhisthana Chakra is the storehouse of all events from this life and past lives, not just as memories but as samskaras that influence your mind and emotions. Upon awakening it, one frees the subconscious linked with our evolution as cerebral and emotional human beings. Psychoanalysis is the method of exploring and understanding our deep unconscious mind. But it is a lengthy process and its success depends on the expertise of the psychoanalyst. But in Kundalini awakening, the process is faster and your practise and efforts determine the results.

Awakening of the Swadhisthana Chakra

At this stage, in addition to your daily practise, you must develop attitudinal self-awareness and detachment to be able to handle the effects of awakening of the Swadhisthana Chakra. Crossing this barrier will result in pleasant as well as unpleasant manifestations. Lethargy and excessive sleeping, nightmares or obsessive thoughts and dreams of sexual fantasies may manifest. You must keep in mind that the benefits of overcoming Swadhisthana far exceed the side-effects experienced as a result of its awakening. These benefits include wiping your slate of past karmas clean and getting rid of deep psychological problems.

As water is the element of the Swadhisthana Chakra, you may get the power to walk on water, but as discussed earlier, these powers are neither for practical use, like crossing a river, nor for egoistic demonstrations.

Having awakened the Mooladhara and the Swadhisthana Chakras, you move from the gross level to a more refined level of energy.

Practise for Swadhisthana Chakra

Amongst the various practises described in the practise section, Ashwini mudra is the most effective at rousing the Swadhisthana Chakra.

The Manipura Chakra

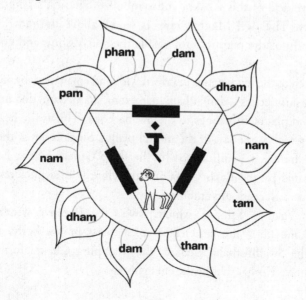

The Manipura Chakra is located inside the spine behind the navel centre. The simplest way to find its location is to stand sideways in front of a mirror, place the middle finger of your right hand on the navel centre and with your left-hand thumb, try to feel a point inside the spine directly behind the navel.

The navel is the frontal field, the kshetra, of the Manipura Chakra. It is associated with the solar plexus. In Yogic physiology, it represents dynamic energy akin to the Sun. Just as the Sun energizes all life in our planetary system, the Manipura Chakra provides succour, vitality and drive to the entire body. It controls our digestive system and the organs associated with it.

Symbolism of the Manipura Chakra

The Manipura Chakra is depicted as a ten petalled bright yellow lotus flower. Its Tattwa, element, is fire. This is symbolized as a blazing fire inside the red inverted triangle at the centre of the lotus. The triangle is enclosed by three bhupuras (T-shaped gates) on each side. At the apex of the triangle is the ram, the animal that is the vehicle of this Chakra and symbolizes vitality, strength and tenacity. The Beej Mantra 'ram' is seated above the ram. Inside the bindu of the mantra 'ram' reside the god Vishnu and goddess Lakini.

Each of the ten petals is inscribed with and emanates vibrations of the Sanskrit letters—dam, dham, nam, tam, tham, dam, dham, nam, pam and pham. It belongs to the Swaha Loka. This is the heavenly abode which is the last of the mortal planes. Since it lies within the mortal frame, it is influenced by the three Gunas. Swaha Loka is dominated by the Rajas Guna and therefore it is characterized by dynamism, success and ambition.

Its Vayu is 'Samana' which powers the digestive system and carries nutrition and sustenance to all parts of the body. Along with the Swadhisthana Chakra, the Manipura Chakra forms the Pranamaya Kosha, that is, the energy body.

In the macro world, the moon secretes nectar, Amrut, which is consumed by the Sun. At the micro level, the moon at the Bindu Visarga, at the soft part of our head, drips nectar which is consumed by the Sun at the Manipura Chakra. Awakening of the Manipura Chakra reverses this flow of nectar back to the higher Chakras to prevent its destruction at the Manipura Chakra. This reversal of flow prevents old age and diseases and aids in the preservation of youth and vitality.

Manipura awakening marks a significant milestone in your journey because once this Chakra is crossed then the Kundalini does not slip back to the lower Chakras provided that you continue your practise with the same intensity, regularity and sincerity.

There is another phenomenon which takes place during the Manipura Chakra awakening. It is the fusion of the two vayus, Apana and Prana at the navel centre. Let us understand how this happens.

Prana Vayu moves between the navel and the throat. When you inhale, it ascends from the navel to the throat and when you exhale, it descends from the throat to the navel.

Apana Vayu moves between the perineal centre and the navel centre. When you inhale, it ascends from the perineal centre to the navel and descends from the navel to the Mooladhara as you exhale. Swami Satyananda describes it as two trains coupled at the navel centre. As you inhale, both Prana and Apana trains move up and as you exhale, both move down. This has to be visualized, with eyes shut, in the frontal field of the Chakras.

The goal is to fuse Apana and Prana Vayu at the navel centre with Samana. Then the Apana stops descending from the navel to the Mooladhara upon exhalation. This fusion at the frontal field sends blasts of heat and energy to the Manipura Chakra in the spine, awakening the Chakra as Kundalini moves up from the Mooladhara and makes the Manipura Chakra its base.

Awakening of the Manipura Chakra

So far, you have been like satellites circling earth's orbit in the Bhu and Bhuva Lokas; you are still affected by the pull of gravity, desires, passions and subjected to the limitations of the sense organs and the mind. When Kundalini enters the Manipura Chakra, you enter the Swaha Loka, the abode of heavenly bodies and last of the mortal planes. We get a glimpse at the possibility of knowing other planes and dimensions of existence.

This coincides with the sharpening and scaling up of your daily practise of pratyahara.

Pratyahara practise involves shutting down your sense organs. If there are no inputs from the sense organs to the mind, the mind will not be subjected to their distractions. The mind becomes quieter and achieves a state of single-mindedness. In Ashtanga Yoga, in Patanjali's eight steps to Samadhi, Pratyahara is just before you enter the regions of Dharana (concentration) and Dhyana (meditation). You are just about getting ready to cross the boundaries of Maya to experience existence beyond the three Gunas, your limited senses, mind and mortality. Thus, once you've crossed the Manipur a Chakra, the Kundalini does not descend to the Swadhisthana and Mooladhara Chakras.

Since the Manipura Chakra is associated with the digestive system, you feel invigorated and experience freedom from disease. As Fire is the element of this Chakra, you do not feel afraid of it. Awakening of the Manipura Chakra will bring you wealth and prosperity.

Practise for the Manipura Chakra

Dhanurasana, Kandharasna, Chakrasana and Ushtrasana are some of the asanas for rousing the Manipura Chakra. Udiyana Bandha also stimulates the Manipura Chakra. These asanas are explained in the practise section later.

The Anahata Chakra

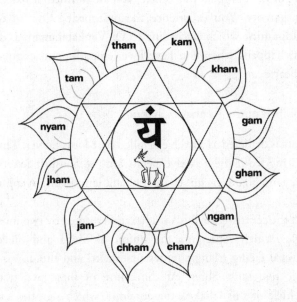

The Anahata Chakra is located behind the centre of the chest within the spinal cord. To locate it—place a finger of your right hand at the level of your heart but at the centre of your chest, then place a finger of your left hand at the back, touching a point on the spine directly behind the right hand's finger. The heart area is the frontal field, the kshetra, of the Anahata Chakra. Anahata literally means '**unstruck sound**'. This is appropriate because the heart beats from birth to death. At the cosmic level, the 'heart' of the universe has been beating with a transcendental sound which is unbroken since the beginning of time.

The Anahata Chakra corresponds to the cardiac plexus in human physiology. But in Yogic physiology, it assumes greater dimensions than just the functioning of the organs. The Anahata Chakra is the seat of creative abilities and finer sensibilities of the heart. The Kundalini at the Anahata Chakra awakens compassion, love and the finer emotions in humans which activate the creative centres of the brain. At this centre, you are purified of hate, jealousy and negativity. You experience the unimpeded flow of **oxytocin and dopamine** which, according to Dr Venkataraman, as discussed earlier, happens when you have love, empathy and compassion in your heart.

Symbolism of the Anahata Chakra

Anahata is depicted as a twelve petalled blue lotus flower. The sounds emanating from these twelve petals are the Sanskrit letters—kam, kham, gam, gham, ngam, cham, chham, jam, jham, nyam, tam and tham.

At the centre of the lotus is a hexagon formed by two intersecting triangles which represents the union of Shiva and Shakti. The downward facing triangle represents Shakti and the upward facing triangle represents Shiva. At the centre of these two triangles is the vehicle of this Chakra, the antelope, which signifies speed and alertness. Above the antelope is the Beej Mantra 'yam'. Inside the bindu of the Beej Mantra are the presiding deities of this Chakra, Isha and Kakini, benefactors of all.

At the core of the lotus is an inverted triangle within which burns an eternal fire. This fire symbolizes the jiva atma, the soul of the individual. Below the blue lotus is a smaller, red petalled lotus, within which is the kalpavriksh, the wish-fulfilling tree. Air is the element of this Chakra. We can observe that as we scale up along each of the Chakras, every aspect of each Chakra becomes more refined with energy evolving from the gross to the subtler states.

At the Anahata Chakra, you enter the Maha Loka, the first of the immortal planes. Prana is the Vayu which powers and controls all the functions related to the Anahata Chakra namely, respiration, heartbeat and blood circulation. Its gyanendriya is the skin, tanmatra is touch and karmendriyas are the hands. This explains the origin of the phrase 'he touched my heart'.

The heart space of the Anahata Chakra is also known as the Hridyakash. It is a point of meditation for awakening the Anahata Chakra. The second Granthi, that is, the Vishnu Granthi resides here. It presents the second knot to be unravelled in our journey towards ascending to the higher Chakras.

Awakening of the Anahata Chakra

An egotistical and selfish attitude can be the biggest obstacle you face at this stage. The irony of it all is that most egotistical people feed their ego by genuinely thinking that they have achieved it. Same goes for selfishness. Those engaged in social services like to believe that they are doing it with no ulterior or selfish motive. There is no point in berating this as it is all a part of our Antahkarna. We have seen in the process of creation that our ego and sense of individuality are integral to our existence.

There is a recourse for surmounting the two usurpers—ego and selfishness. Karma Yoga and Bhakti Yoga help in subsuming the ego and self-centredness. Karma Yoga practises action without attachment to the fruits of your actions. This message was relayed to Arjun by Lord Krishna in the Bahgwad Gita. This leads to disassociation of your ego from your actions. Bhakti Yoga is dissolution of the self in devotion to the supreme. Kalidas and Meerabai are supreme examples of the practise of Bhakti Yoga. The Hare Rama Hare Krishna (ISKCON) movement is also based on the Bhakti path.

As you add meditation to your practise, you climb another rung in self-awareness by observing the nature and flow of your thoughts. It helps tremendously if you have also internalized the message and logic contained in the Upanishads, Yoga Sutras, Samhitas and other yogic and scriptural texts. A combination of theory and practise are like the two wings of the bird that will help you fly to the higher states.

You become aware that a large chunk of your mind is occupied with ego and self-glorification. Awareness brings correction. Thus, your yoga practise starts affecting more than your bodily or psychological problems. You become aware of all your actions and mental processes as well as your emotional state. To maintain and further your progress in this state, you must surround yourself with people who have positive, healthy and happy dispositions. In the absence of a Guru, books, discussions and accessing talks by spiritual leaders like Ramana Maharshi, Ramakrishna Paramhansa, Vivekananda, the Swamijis of Divine Life Society lineage and so many others should become a part of your practise.

At this stage, it becomes possible to practise Karma and Bhakti Yoga with self-awareness of your hidden, inner motives of the ego and continue to look for things that benefit you. In this way, you discover the Guru and guiding light within you.

As you get closer to the higher Chakras, you do gain some powers, siddhis. You must remember to not only side-step them but also be aware of them. The Kalpavriksha at the Anahata Chakra, will make your wishes come true. But if you have not purified yourself of ego and selfish propensities, you may end up wishing for things that can destroy you.

The Greek legend of King Midas, who wished that all he touched turned to gold, turned not only his daughter into gold but also his food and that ultimately killed him. If you have not purified your heart of hatred, greed, jealousy and negative thoughts, you may wish something terrible for another in anger. This is why you must ensure that you've freed yourself of uncontrolled desires and negative thoughts and emotions as you awaken this Chakra.

As the lotus at this Chakra opens, you may feel pain in the heart region along with heart palpitations. Additionally, you will feel invigorated and experience an uplifted state of being. You will benefit from engaging in artistic and creative activities. You feel a sense of lightness and freedom as you get detached from worldly matters.

The Vishuddhi Chakra

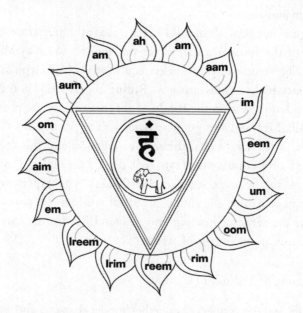

The Vishuddhi Chakra is situated at the base of the throat. It is easy to locate; simply place a finger on the throat pit and find the spot directly opposite to it inside the spine. Its frontal field is the frontal neck area. Physiologically, it corresponds to the laryngeal and pharyngeal nerve plexus. The word 'vishuddhi' means purification. At this Chakra, the nectar dripping from the Bindu Visarga is collected and split into amrut and poison, which represents the duality of life. This nectar flows down to the various Chakras and fills your lives with duality. When you start to your reverse journey by awakening each Chakra to reach Vishuddhi, this duality is harmonized and purified. The poison is discarded. You receive health and long life.

Symbolism of the Vishuddhi Chakra

The Vishuddhi Chakra is depicted as a sixteen petalled purple lotus flower. These sixteen petals are inscribed with the Sanskrit vowels—

am, aam, im, eem, um, oom, rim, reem, lrim, lreem, em, aim, om, aum, am and ah.

The element of Vishuddhi is ether, aakash. Therefore, at the centre of the lotus is a pale silver full moon, which symbolizes ether. The vehicle of this Chakra is a snowy white elephant that represents higher consciousness. Riding on its back is the Beej Mantra 'ham'. Within the Bindu of this mantra are the presiding god Sadashiva and the goddess Sakina. The Vishuddhi Chakra belongs to the Jana Loka, the seed of creation and the abode of the sons of Brahma. Its Vayu is 'Udana', the upward moving Vayu. With the awakening of this Chakra, you experience the Vijnanmaya Kosha, the subtle sheath of wisdom. Its tanmatra is shabda, the sense of hearing and gyanendriya are the ears. The vocal cords are its organs of action.

Awakening of Vishuddhi Chakra

As purity and the vastness of the ether are the character and element of this Chakra, you will experience them in yourself. Like a cut diamond, you have been cleansed of your impurities. You are free of all that keeps you bound to the false illusions of Maya. You are the seer of the play of duality. You are a detached witness of the ceaseless workings of desire, the limitations of your senses and the incessant workings of the mind. You are a witness to the unity in all things. You experience freedom from never ending desires. The greater mind works on extra-sensory powers and helps you experience the higher dimensions and planes of existence.

At this Chakra, your speech is purified by the state of your consciousness. Whatever you say has the power of *vak shuddhi*, that is, the power of speech and will have a tremendous impact on everyone around you. This is the direct result of the purification of your senses, mind, thoughts and actions. Everything that you do or say comes from a higher awareness. You will experience longevity, youthfulness and peace at the Vishuddhi Chakra.

The Ajna Chakra

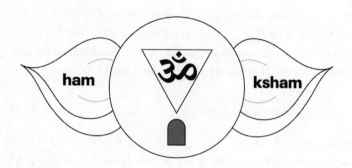

The Ajna Chakra is one of the most significant Chakras for Kundalini awakening and connecting with our physiology. The word Ajna means to obey or command. This is relevant both spiritually and physiologically. Spiritually, when you arrive at the Ajna Chakra you have gained command over all that was an obstruction in your journey towards the last and final step to the Sahasrara Chakra. Physiologically, it is connected to the pineal and pituitary glands. These glands, as discussed earlier, produce hormones that assist in not only gender distinction but also take us to higher states of joy and bliss.

The Ajna Chakra is located right behind the centre of the eyebrow, at the end of the spinal column, inside the medulla oblongata in the brain. It is easier to focus on its kshetra, the frontal field, at the centre of the eyebrows. Indians are familiar with this point as traditionally, the teeka, a red dot, is put on this spot. They are also familiar with portraits of Lord Shiva that depict his third eye at the centre of the eyebrows.

Symbolism of the Ajna Chakra

The Ajna Chakra is depicted as a two petalled deep-maroon lotus. On its petals are inscribed the Sanskrit letters ham and ksham.

Enclosed within the lotus leaves is a circle which symbolizes shoonya or nothingness. Within this circle is an inverted triangle that represents Shakti. Above the triangle is a well-defined Shiva Lingam, over which is an 'Om', the Beej Mantra of the Ajna Chakra. The deities who preside over the Ajna Chakra are god Paramshiva and the goddess Hakini. It is associated with the Tapa Loka.

Awakening of the Ajna Chakra

Awakening of the Ajna Chakra can be likened to standing at a height and viewing everything that is below you. Imagine you are on a hill-top with a vantage view of all that's happening below. You can watch two cars approaching each other round the bend and can anticipate if they are going to collide, which is something the two drivers at the ground level cannot know. Similarly, you are at a higher level of awareness which receives inputs from extra-sensory powers. You are a part of all that is happening to you and around you but your view of it is free from the limited, egoistic and self-centred understanding and cognition. From your vantage point of the greater mind, you know and understand the cause and effect behind the flow of events. You are no longer maddened by questions like, 'Why is this happening to me? What did I do to suffer this?' Or the opposite, 'How come that vile person has so much wealth? Where is justice in this world if the good suffer and the evil revel?' You are no longer bothered by these seemingly irreconcilable dichotomies of life.

When you have reached this stage of awareness and discrimination, it is but natural that your thoughts and actions now flow from the knowledge of the inexorable laws of cause and effect, your karmas, your samskaras and your prarabdha. In this state of being, you will go through the flow of the good and the bad without being affected by either, because you know the raison d'etre of it all. You are free from the errors caused by a lack of judgment. It is not difficult to visualize the wonderful state of your being at this juncture. You are one step away from merging with the origin of it all. Freed from the limited and limiting world of Maya, you are ready to unite with the source, the womb of creation, the hiranyagarbha.

Bindu Visarga

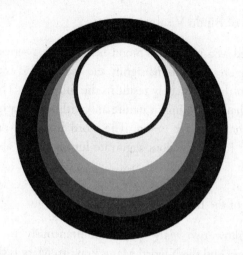

The Bindu Visarga is located at the anterior fontanelle, at the back of the head. It is the soft spot on the head of a newborn baby. At this spot, bald Brahmins leave a tuft of hair tied in a knot to always stay aware of this Chakra. Muslims also wear their skullcap over this spot. The Pope and the Bishops too wear their caps over this spot.

'Bindu' means a dot. Visarga in Sanskrit stands for 'sending forth' or 'discharge'. So literally, it means the dot that discharges the nectar, the amrut of life. The nectar flows into the Lalana Chakra and then the Vishuddhi Chakra. Therefore, as you will notice in our practises of Chakra awakening, you keep moving your awareness between Bindu and Vishuddhi. The Bindu is the spot from where the nectar drips down to the Vishuddhi, where it splits into amrut and poison, thus starting the duality of all creation.

It is also called the Brahmarandhara, meaning the hole of Brahma. According to the scriptures, life and illumination enter and leave the body through the Bindu. A Yogi who practises kalpa moksha, separates himself from his physical body at the time of death, by the Sushumna Nadi bursting forth from the Bindu Visarga. Such a Yogi attains immortality (from the Kathoupanishad).

Symbology of Bindu Visarga

It is depicted as a pearly full moon held within a series of crescent moons. The crescent moons signify the waning and waxing phases of the moon that ultimately result in the full moon. Thus, it is not surprising that everything in nature and within us is affected by the changing phases of the moon. The word lunacy is derived from 'lunar'. The full moon does aggravate lunacy but it also results in illumination.

Awakening of the Bindu Visarga

You can follow two *marg* (path) simultaneously to evolve—the Pravritti Marg and the Nivritti Marg. Pravritti Marg is the evolution of the individual by understanding the world outside of himself. Nivritti Marg is the involution when an individual looks inward to understand the world within. Both paths are necessary to complete the full cycle. Purushartha is what you must experience to know your potential against the dynamics of the world outside of yourself. Having explored this, the person becomes ready to involute to understand the dynamics of the world within himself.

It is advisable to make both of these paths a part of your daily life. The Pravritti Marg is necessary as we have seen from the life of the great spiritual master, Adi Shankaracharya who had to experience the worldly life of a householder to win the debate on the ultimate tenets of spirituality (see section I). Pravritti Marg leads you away from Bindu as extroversion. Nivriiti Marg takes you back to Bindu as introversion. The Bindu Visarga is the point from where the process of division of Shiva and Shakti begins, and also the point to which you return as your Kundalini Shakti unifies with Shiva at the Sahasrara Chakra.

The Bindu Visarga can be looked upon as what the scientists have termed as the Big Bang, the origin of the Universe or the process of fusion and fission in which infinitely small sub-atomic particles explode into nuclear and atomic energy. Since the macro exists in the micro and visa-versa, the Bindu is the Big Bang of the world within us; a tremendous amount of energy is released when the Kundalini Shakti returns to the Bindu to finally unite with Shiva at the Sahasrara Chakra. If black hole is where dissolution happens, then Bindu is the white hole where creation happens.

Hence, the awakening of the Bindu Visarga is the final annihilation of duality and the dawn of universal consciousness. This is a stage of super consciousness beyond language, words, form, time and dimensions.

The Sahasrara Chakra

Awakening of the Sahasrara Chakra is an experience beyond description. It is at once everything and nothing. The Sahasrara Chakra is the final destination of Kundalini as it awakens from the Mooladhara and travels up along the six Chakras through the Sushumna Nadi. It is situated at the crown of the head.

Symbolism of the Sahasrara Chakra

The Sahasrara Chakra is depicted as a thousand petalled multi-coloured lotus flower. The fifty letters of Sanskrit are inscribed repeatedly on these petals. At the centre of this multi-coloured lotus is a crystal lingam that signifies glorious illumination. Symbolism associated with this Chakra is sparse as all attributes are inexpressible. Its Loka is Satya. All Chakras are intimately connected with this Chakra. All other Chakras are only switches. All the potential lies in the Sahasrara.

Awakening of the Sahasrara Chakra

When the Kundalini awakens at the Sahasrara Chakra, the practitioner loses their individuality and becomes one with Sat-Chit-Ananada or Existence-Knowledge-Bliss. It is the culmination of the journey of a practitioner seeking answers to his existence and its purpose. It is the culmination of all the vibrations of sound into the silence of Shoonya. It is the dissolution of all forms into nothingness. The past, present, future and time itself become motionless here. Energy with its full potential to create rests here in seed form. The five elements—earth, water, fire, air and ether, the Antahkarna—Manas, Buddhi, Chitta and Ahankara are all dissolved, as Kundalini Shakti embraces Shiva, the super consciousness.

The sutras 74–76 of the Yogakundaliniupanishad describe the union of Kundalini with Shiva at the Sahasrara Chakra as follows, The Kundalini then goes to the seat of the Sahasrara giving up the eight forms of the Prakruti (earth, water, fire, air, ether, the Manas, Buddhi, Chitta and Ahamkara) and after clasping the eye, the mind, the prana and the others in her embrace goes to Shiva and clasping Shiva as well dissolves herself in Sahasrara. So the next moment, the Rajas, (solar and born of Prakti, the Jiva Tattwa) and the Shukla (lunar, of the Ishwara) these two dissolve themselves in Shiva (seated in the Bindu of the Sahasrara). The very next moment thereafter the breath dissolves itself; the Prana and the Apana born together do likewise, having reached an equipoise condition (no longer going up and down). Then (with the Prana spread outwards) in the form of attenuated elements or (in the mere remembrance of it) the mind reduces to the form of faint impressions and speech remaining only in the form of recollection, the Yogin thrives. All vital airs then spread themselves outright in his body, even as gold in a crucible placed on fire.

What remains of you? What becomes of you then? Though you in your body are still earth bound, your being is hitched on to the super-consciousness. Your ego, the tether for your individuality and point of reference, has been sublimated. Your senses and your mind have dissolved. Can you still carry on your business with all its worldly demands of material success? Can you still be a part of competitive sports? Can you still relate to your family and be caring and loving?

It is not unusual for the worldly to be wary of the path of spirituality. It is regarded as something that will rob you of your capacity to enjoy the pleasures, attachments and successes of normal life.

Let us examine and understand from your present perspective of who and what you become once your Kundalini is awakened. Perhaps, the simplest answer was given by a Zen Master when asked what happens after Enlightenment. He said, 'Cut wood, fetch water'.

Precisely, everything goes on as usual. It results in the sublimation of ego, your most basic point of reference; it is now devout, not burdened with I, me, mine. Freed of its many complexes carried forth from many lives, it assesses, reacts and perceives things as they are without the distortions of an ego working with a lesser mind that sees things with inputs from lower senses and mind. Great swaths of energy are not wasted in comparison, jealousy, envy, hatred, emotional swings and useless meanderings of the mind. You conserve this energy for creative thinking and, most importantly, use it in the right way now that your mind is calm and collected.

Simply put, you are suited for a more awesome world, which powers this little world of ours. As you become a part of the reflection of that universal source, navigating this world is child's play.

Swami Sivananda answered with a simple mantra, 'Serve, love, give, purify, meditate, realize, be good, do good, be kind, be compassionate.'

For those interested in reading about a personal account of experiences related to the awakening of each Chakra, I recommend Dr Hiroshima Motoyama's book *Theories of the Chakras: Bridge to Higher Consciousness* in which such experiences have been detailed in the chapter on 'Experience and Experiments of the Chakras'.

Section V

HATHA YOGA AND RAJA YOGA

There can be no perfection if Hatha Yoga is without Raja Yoga or Raja Yoga without Hatha Yoga. Therefore, through practise of both, perfection is attained

—Sutra seventy-six, Chapter two, Hath Yoga Pradipika

You have now reached an important juncture. If you have sincerely internalized the theory, you are ready for your Kundalini Yoga practise. You will grasp the import of the above sutra at the intellectual and experiential level and know how both Hatha Yoga and Raja Yoga become a part of our practise.

1

HATHA YOGA

Hatha Yoga is one of the most popular terms in yoga today. It was popularized by Yogacharya B. K. S. Iyengar. He was born sickly because his mother had contracted influenza when she was pregnant with him. His poor health often made him wonder if life was worth living at all. But life had different plans for him. He was introduced to yoga by his uncle, the Hatha yogi, Krishnamacharya, who lived in Mysore. Through his practise of yoga, B. K. S. Iyengar became the apostle of health and vitality and founded his own style of yoga, popularly known as Iyengar Yoga.

Originally, the purpose of Hatha Yoga was to cleanse the body. It comprised of the Shatkarmas, the six cleansing methods. Some of these cleansing and balancing methods which can be practised easily by anyone at home have been described in the practise section detailed later in this book.

It was only later that the Nath School of Yogis started regarding Hatha Yoga as an independent and complete practice instead of mere cleansing methods. The *Hatha Yoga Pradipika* by Yogi Swatmarama, *Gheranda Samhita* by Sage Gheranda and *Hatharatnavali* by Srinivasa Bhatta Mahayogindra are some of the important texts of Hatha Yoga. Thus, Hatha Yoga became a complete system of realizing a practitioner's full potential. Through the practise of Hatha Yoga, a person gains health with youthfulness, mental efficiency with peace and joy and creativity without restlessness.

The word 'Hatha' is a union of two words, 'Ha' which stands for the solar or the Pingala Nadi and 'tha' stands for the lunar or the Ida Nadi. Hatha is the union of these two Nadis so that the Sushumna Nadi can awaken and pave the way for the Kundalini Shakti to travel up to the Ajna Chakra at the eyebrow centre. To accomplish this, Hatha Yoga enlists practises that have been described in great detail in the practise section.

Hatha Yoga is partially *Bahiranga,* external yoga. It starts with tackling the physiological problems and malfunctions of the gross body through the practises of asanas and pranayamas. This is only the beginning of Hatha Yoga, though most yoga teachers and their students are content to achieve this minor goal. Once this preliminary stage of Hatha yoga is achieved, then they start the higher practises. For the world, the advanced asanas like Shirshasana, Mayurasana, Hanuman asana are the talking points. Contorting your body into difficult postures is what wins the admiration of all. However, these are the easier practises in comparison with higher practises, which involve merely sitting in padmasana for large swathes of time maintaining Shambhavi mudra with mantra chanting. These are part of Antaranga yoga. Hatha yoga is complete when both the Bahiranga and Antaranga yoga are accomplished.

People see an ocean as a mass of water in constant tidal motion with unceasing waves. There are but a few to dive into it to find the pearl hidden in its depths. One can say that Hatha Yoga is like a preparation for the sea diver who is learning the technique, the vigour, the preparation of body, mind and breath required to dive into the depths to find the pearl. Raja Yoga takes on from the point that he finds the pearl and becomes one with it.

The 196 sutras of Patanjali Yoga help you understand how to reach the depths of your being by observing the workings of your mind and developing a single-minded concentration to finally achieve that state where you are pure, unwavering awareness itself.

It is my firm belief that to understand the cryptic and complex Patanjali yoga sutras, you must first progress through the various stages of Hatha Yoga. The name Patanjali is being used by various schools and institutes teaching yoga. However, Patanjali's yoga sutras have not much to do with the practice of asanas and pranayama. His is a treatise on the mind and consciousness and how to achieve Samadhi after you have perfected your preliminary yoga of getting your body free of all problems. Later, in the next chapter you will see this is clarified in his very first sutra.

You must attempt to submerge yourself into Patanjali's sutras after you have advanced to the fifth step of Ashtanga ('Ashta' means eight and 'anga' means parts) Yoga of Patanjali through the Hatha Yoga practices.

The eight steps of Patanjali's Yoga are:

1. Yama (personal code of conduct)
2. Niyama (social code of conduct)
3. Asana (postures)
4. Pranayama (breathing practices)
5. Pratyahara (withdrawal of the senses)
6. Dharana (concentration)
7. Dhyana (meditation)
8. Samadhi (Enlightenment)

Hatha Yoga takes you up to the fifth stage. The journey to the final stage is explained in Patanjali's Yoga sutras. His sutras are devoted to breaking up the functioning of our mind to help understand it.

2

RAJA YOGA

Raja Yoga, Ashtanga Yoga or Patanjali Yoga are all names for the 196 sutras of Sage Patanjali. Sutras are aphorisms which consist of very few syllables and words to state the essence of the subject under consideration. The beauty and perfection of the Sanskrit language lend itself to the brevity and rhythm of Patanjali's sutras. Most of the sutras are no more than three to five syllables long but it takes pages of commentaries to explain and extol each one of them.

While these lead you to an understanding of the expansion of consciousness leading to Samadhi, these same can be related to aspects of everyday life. All things sublime also carry some useful everyday guide. And so do Patanjali's sutras.

At the outset, let me acknowledge that my total understanding and reading of Patanjali's Yoga sutra are based on Swami Satyananda Saraswati's lucid unravelling of the sutras in his book, *Four Chapters on Freedom* (Yoga Publications Trust, Munger, Bihar, India).

The very first sutra of Patanjali's yoga sutra, begins with the three words:

'*Atha Yoga anushasanam.*'

The three words literally mean, now (atha) Yoga discipline (anushasanam).

As clarified earlier, Patanjali himself says that now that you have accomplished the discipline of yoga, let us advance further. By this he means, now we have to move from the body to the mind. Hence, the second sutra dives into what must be done to the mind now.

The second, third and fourth sutras explain in a nutshell what yoga accomplishes. These three sutras form the foundation of the whole treatise of Patanjali's yoga sutras.

The second sutra is:

'Yoga chittavritti nirodhaha.'

In just three words, Patanjali has compressed all that yoga is. He says, yoga is stopping (nirodha) of all mental modifications (chittavritti). We have been seeing how this happens with our successive yoga practice. How else can we develop the witness attitude that reflects what the supreme consciousness is, that is, a detached witness?

The third sutra is:

'Tada drashtah swarupeyavasthanam.'

As a follow up on the second sutra, this sutra says that when you have blocked all the mental modifications, then (tada) the perceiving consciousness (drashta) is settled (avasthanam) in its own nature (swarupe).

The fourth sutra is:

'Vrittis swarupyam itaratra.'

This sutra illustrates the state of a person without the practise of yoga. It states that otherwise (itaratra) the perceiving consciousness is in conformity with the mental modifications (vrittis swarupyam).

A Hatha Yogi, who has reached the state of dharana and dhyana will have experienced the two states Sage Patanjali is referring to, that is, the ever-changing modes of the mind and the state without the mental modifications of the mind.

It is essential for a Hatha Yogi to wade into Patanjali's treatise to observe, internalize and plan the way they will accomplish the final goal of yoga. It is like an engineer working on the drawing board and building what he is drawing on paper.

Having summed up the basic nature of yoga, Patanjali goes on to
unravel the workings of one's mind. He defines the nature of asana,
pranayama and Kriya Yoga. There are just a few sutras on God or
Ishwar, the creator. The majority of these sutras take you step-by-
step, or rather sutra-by-sutra, through the process of qualitative
changes that your mind and consciousness will undergo as your
dhyana deepens.

For a serious practitioner of Kundalini Yoga, internalizing
Patanjali's Yoga sutras is a must. It is not the purpose or scope of this
book to unravel the whole of Patanjali's sutras. But, since the book
is for the amateur Yogi too, I will go into some details of the sutras
numbered five to twelve. This is because these can be applied to your
everyday life to help bring about clarity of thought and action.

The fifth sutra is:

'Vrttayah panchatatyaha klishta aklishtah.'

Patanjali says that mental modifications (vrttayah), some are
pleasant (aklishtaha) and some unpleasant (klishta). In this sutra,
Patanjali says that mental modifications are of five kinds; some are
pleasant and some unpleasant. For example, when you think of an
upcoming holiday, it makes you happy. But when you think of an
impending unpleasant confrontation in your workplace, it makes
you tense and unhappy.

The sixth sutra is:

'Praman viparyay-vikalpa-nidra-smrityaha.'

In this sutra, he says that right knowledge (praman), wrong
knowledge (viparyay), imagination (vikalpa), sleep (nidra), and
memory (smrityaha). It means that generally these five-fold mental
modifications are—right knowledge, wrong knowledge, imagination,
sleep and memory.

One has to simply observe the patterns of their thought process
or analyse the contents of their mind to find that they can be
categorized into one or a mix of these parameters. It's fascinating to
realize how most of our mental or thought processes can be simply
categorized.

It is a good exercise to check your thought process or your decisions against these five parameters. When arriving at any decision or to check if your thoughts are on the right track, this simple set of five parameters can be used to ascertain the basis for one's thoughts and determine if it is right knowledge, wrong knowledge, fancy (imagination), sleep or memory.

But there is no way for you to know if your parameter is right knowledge or not. So, in the seventh sutra he defines right knowledge. The sutra is:

'*Pratyakshanumanaha pramanani*'

This sutra means that direct cognition (Pratyaksha), inference (anumana), testimony (pramanani). This sutra means that direct cognition, inference and testimony are the sources of right knowledge.

It may seem like simplistic deduction. But if you apply them to any situation, you find that most of your thoughts are based on hearsay, your own imagination, the influence of past memories or your subconscious or unconscious, which manifests in dreams. Rarely do you put a brake to this never-ending thought process to ask yourselves, 'What are my thoughts and decisions based on? How can I know that I am moving in the right direction? How can I know that I am not deluding myself, or believing and acting on half-truths, imagination, false knowledge or unchecked facts? Am I influenced by my past memories?'

Hence, if you were to find some way out of this trap of typical human thinking, then Patanjali's seventh sutra makes a lot of sense. For sure, the best basis for any knowledge and therefore thinking is to have direct cognition—*ankhon dekhi* (eye witnessed).

But that is not always possible. However, you have to arrive at some decision or knowledge base. The next best option is inference. Where there is smoke, there is fire, is the simplest of such examples. If that is also not possible, you must turn to someone you can rely on. Therefore, you rely on a knowledgeable and trustworthy source.

Sometimes it can be mix of these parameters. For example, take the Coronavirus pandemic. Since the subject is complex and you could not have direct cognition of what was unfolding, a mix of the above three safeguards was what you could use to get the right knowledge on the subject to ensure your safety.

It is equally important to know when you could be relying on false or wrong knowledge which could create a host of problems. This was observed in abundance during the pandemic. There were some babas, quacks, mercenaries and the like, who misled the people into believing they could be safe from the virus if they ate the leftovers of the baba's food or drank a concoction of herbs and followed other baseless superstitions.

Let us see how Patanjali classifies and breaks down wrong knowledge in the next two sutras. In the eighth sutra he says,

'*Viparyoyo mithya-jnanam atadrupa-pratistham.*'

This means that distorted perception (viparyoyo), false knowledge (mithya jnanam), which is not based on fact (atadrupa-pratishtham).

The ninth sutra talks about fanciful thinking as one of the elements which lead to wrong knowledge.

'*Shabda-jyananupati vastu-shoonya vikalpaha.*'

This literally means having a host of thoughts (shabda-jynanupati) whose corresponding object (vastu) or subject are non-existent (shoonya) is imaginary or fanciful (vikalpaha). This malady afflicts a lot of people and is the root cause for many problems in the world. Many a time, we imagine things that don't have a basis which leads to poor decision-making and actions. This is the nature of fanciful thinking.

The tenth sutra deals with sleep. Patanjali defines it as:

'*Abhava-pratyayalambana vritti nidra.*'

Patanjali classifies sleep (nidra) as a mental modification (vritti) in which there is content (pratyayay) which has no support (alambana) and is non-existant (abhava). You must notice that he is talking about sleep and not dreams. Sleep is a state which is akin to samadhi but the two are different. During sleep, all support of the senses and therefore the external world is concealed. Swami Satyananda, in his commentary on the yoga sutra writes, 'He (Patanjali) says that in sleep there is no object before the mind--it does not see, hear, touch or feel anything. Every form of knowledge, every content of mind becomes silent.' It is an unconscious state of mind. In samadhi, there is awareness although there may be absence of vrittis or consciousness.

The eleventh sutra is about memory:

'*Anubhuta-vishayasampramoshaha smrtihi.*'

Lastly Patanjali has classified memory (smriti) as content (Vishya) that is a collection of a whole range of experiences through perception, apprehension, (asampramoshaha).

The cause of sorrow, pain and suffering in life is ignorance or negligence in examining your perceptions and watching the workings of your mind or your own mental modifications. Therefore, if you can learn how to perceive your thoughts through some Yogic techniques, then you will, as Patanjali advises, learn to block unnecessary and baseless thoughts. This, in turn, helps in stopping the re-manifestation of further useless thought processes and actions based on them.

You can see that once you have become accomplished at the practise of asanas and pranayama, using Patanjali's techniques and theory can help you scale the higher rungs of Chakras by making the mind quiet and getting rid of baseless and false misconceptions and thoughts.

3

HATHA YOGA PRACTICE

All the organs and systems in our body work round the clock, without a break and with the extraworkload of coping with a sedentary lifestyle, unbalanced diet, erratic sleep quality and chronic stress. This sets into motion a vicious cycle of an imbalanced lifestyle that results in overall poor health. Therefore, you must start with the Shatkarmas practise of Hatha Yoga to cleanse your body and mind and bring balance to all your bodily systems. The Neti and Dhauti (Kunjal and Shankprakshalan) methods cleanse your body of toxins and relieve blockages in the respiratory, circulatory and energy systems.

This is an important step because there should be no blockages due to impurities, toxins and tension in body and mind as you awaken their energy. It will impede your practise and frustrate you.

Let us first acquaint ourselves with the cleansing methods that can only be found in a few texts. The asana, pranayama, mudra and bandha practises of Hatha Yoga have been detailed later (see Section VII).

Shatkarmas

The Shatkarmas remove toxins and imbalances from the three bodily humours—mucus, bile and gas. Excess mucus can block the respiratory tract, gas can affect smooth functioning of the alimentary canal and excess bile can affect the functioning of the visceral systems. Cleansing the body and removing imbalances is essential for preparing the body for best results in the practise of asanas and pranayama, which in turn, help you progress to the more advanced practises of mudra, bandha, dharana and dhyana. Just as a musical instrument must be tuned first to produce good music, your body has to be in fine fettle to tune in to the universal vibrations.

The Shatkarmas Practice

This chapter is designed for beginners, but even experienced yoga practitioners must go through the Hatha Yoga techniques of body cleansing. Starting your practise with a detoxed body helps you in setting new parameters of diet and lifestyle. Having experienced a clean body, you will not pollute it with junk again. We aim to achieve Purity or Sattwa at all levels—physical, mental, emotional and spiritual.

Your Kundalini journey must begin with practising the Shatkarmas. Just as you service your cars and machines, your body also needs to be serviced and cleansed every now and then. In fact, it's not just your body that needs to be serviced; your mind also accumulates impurities, toxins, stress and tension. So, there are all kinds of impurities that must be cleansed from the body, mind and emotions. In short, your whole being needs periodic cleansing. This is especially true for those who are not living in controlled atmospheres like an ashram.

Once the body is cleansed, asana and pranayama bring about balance in the whole body-mind system. Thus, you will set forth a virtuous cycle of body, mind and emotions influencing each other in a healthy and positive way.

The best part of Hatha Yoga is that it does not lay down any moral or ethical codes of conduct nor does it expect you to control or subdue your mind. Instead, it makes use of your body to control the rest of your being.

The Rishis and Yogis realized that a person's mental and emotional states can be affected vicariously through the body. Just as chronic pain or illness is bound to affect the mental, emotional and psychological states of a person, a finely tuned body that is free of toxins, imbalances and disease will have a positive effect on these states. This can be observed in the case of B. K. S. Iyengar himself. When he was riddled with health issues, life held no charm for him. Later, when he gained health, strength and vigour through yoga, he became a beacon of light for people all over the world.

Hatha Yoga begins with the following six (shat) cleansing methods:

1. Neti
2. Dhauti
3. Nauli
4. Basti
5. Kapalbhati
6. Trataka

The first four are for cleansing our physical body but have concomitant effects on the mind and emotions too. The last two are specifically for cleansing our mind, emotions and the more subtle aspects of your being such as blockages in the smooth flow of prana and awakening dormant centres of the brain.

For the purposes of our Kundalini journey, you have to incorporate Neti, Dhauti (Kunjal Kriya), Kapalbhati and Trataka in your practise. Additionally, there is the Varisara Dhauti, also known as Shankprakshalan, which literally means water being poured on top of a conch (Shankh), travelling through the contours of the conch and coming out through the other end. Your body can be likened to a conch which is cleansed by this hydro-therapy of making water pass through the body, thus cleaning both the small and large intestines. The intestine cleansing is followed by Kunjal Kriya, which is a kind of stomach wash. It ends with Neti, which cleans out the Ears-Nose-Throat (ENT) system.

Neti

Neti practise has gained popularity because of increase in pollution levels as well as the recent Coronavirus pandemic. It is a simple practise that can be done in several ways. For our purpose, we will learn the practise of using water to cleanse the nasal tracts with the help of a special instrument known as a Neti pot.

You will need a Neti pot. It is available for purchase online and in many stores.

Steps:

1. Fill the pot with lukewarm saline water.
2. Bend over a wash basin with the Neti pot in your left hand.
3. Tilt your head to the right so that you are looking diagonally up to some point on your left. Fix the spout of the pot in the left nostril.
4. Breathe through the mouth and tilt the pot so that water flows from the left nostril and comes out through the right nostril.
5. Continue this till the pot is half-empty.
6. Then, keeping your head tilted to the right, close the right nostril and blow gently through the left nostril so that any remaining water clears off.
7. Repeat the same process with the left nostril by tilting your head to the left, holding the now half-empty pot in your right hand and pouring water from the right nostril so that the water flows out through the left nostril, all the while breathing through the mouth.
8. Clear the nostril by keeping the head titled, closing the left nostril and gently blowing through the right nostril.
9. Finally, keep your head straight, bend over the wash basin and blow gently through both nostrils.

Neti may be practised every day for a whole month in the beginning and reduced to twice a week later. Those who suffer from sinusitis, colds, nosebleeds, headaches or strained eyes may practise Neti everyday till they get some relief.

Kunjal Kriya

This practise involves drinking water and then regurgitating it. I'm putting this out in the beginning because vomiting tends to be unsettling for a lot of people. This is a mental block formed in childhood due to the unpleasant memories associated with vomiting, such as its smell, aftertaste, vomiting because of poor digestive health and more. However, this method involves practising on an empty stomach after you have cleaned your intestines. Thus, only water, mixed with bile or mucus from the stomach or the oesophagus, is vomited. After practising the Kunjal Kriya, you feel light and relieved. Kunjal Kriya can be practised to get relief from problems like indigestion or acidity.

Steps:

1. Stand near a wash basin.
2. Make at least six glasses worth of warm, saline water and keep it near the basin in a jug.
3. Drink four to six glasses of this water in a row.
4. At some point, you will feel nauseous and will not be able to drink anymore. You will feel the pressure of the water and spontaneously vomit it out. If you still feel full but are not able to vomit more, you may put your fingers into the throat to induce vomiting.
5. This can also be done to check whether you have vomited all the water.

Besides cleaning the stomach, this exercise activates the vagus nerve and releases pent up emotions. You should rest and have light, non-spicy food on the day you do this cleansing practise.

Varisara Dhauti or Shankprakshalan

Shankprakshalan is a three-in-one cleansing technique for the whole body. It incorporates the cleansing of both the intestines with hydro-therapy followed by the Kunjal Kriya and Neti. Those who are launching themselves into the world of Kundalini awakening must adopt this full body cleansing method as a monthly practice. However, you must keep some restrictions in mind. It must not be done during the monsoon season or extremely warm or cold weather. Any extreme climate is not the right time to do this practice.

If you are suffering from ailments like cough, cold, fever, or upset stomach, you must wait for it to get resolved. This practice must not be done by pregnant women or people with high blood pressure, heart problems, ulcers or kidney problems. You must do this practice on such a day when you can control your diet and schedule. Thus, doing it on a Sunday or a day off makes the most sense.

Once you start the cleansing process, you must complete it entirely without getting distracted. There should be no breaks once you start drinking the water and doing the sets of asanas. If you stop at any point, you may end up digesting the water which will defeat the purpose of the practise. This does not mean that you should hasten or rush through the practise. It is essential that you do it in a relaxed manner.

Steps:

1. Prepare at least eight to ten glasses of warm saline water.
2. Drink two glasses of this water, then do five to seven rounds of the following asanas in the order mentioned below:

   - Tadasana
   - Triyak Tadasana
   - Kati Chakrasana
   - Triyak Bhujang asana (Bhujang asana with body twisting)
   - Udarkarshasana

(For the asanas, see Section VII)

3. Repeat the process of drinking water and doing the sets of asanas till you feel the urge to have a bowel movement. At this stage, you can stop drinking water and doing the asanas.
4. Keep going to the loo till your bowels are empty and only clear water is expelled. This indicates that any waste matter stuck to the intestine walls has been excreted.

As cautioned above, you should only have moong dal khichdi, seasoned with the least bit of salt but a lot of ghee. You should avoid all other kinds of foods and only consume this khichdi for all meals. You must avoid alcohol and spicy, non-vegetarian or acidic foods. Shankprakshalan is a demanding practice, which is why you must not strain yourself with too much physical activity or by going out in the sun.

Those who find it difficult to drink two glasses of water at once can drink one glass between the sets of asanas. The quantities of salt in the water may also be reduced.

Once the practice is over, do the Shavasana but make sure that you don't drift off to sleep.

The asanas are so designed that performing them regulates the various digestive organs, stimulates intestinal peristalsis, opens the different valves, like the pyloric and ileocecal valves at the outlet of the stomach and of the small intestine respectively and finally the sphincter at the anus.

The benefits of this full body cleansing are manifold. It clears the digestive tract and rejuvenates the entire digestive system. This practice is used to control diabetes. It expels excess mucus and purifies the blood. These benefits ultimately strengthen your immune system.

The benefits of this cleansing can also be felt at the subtle level. It removes blockages from the Nadis which results in better pranic flow in the body. Energy which is spent in managing an unclean and imbalanced body is used for more constructive work. This directly impacts the functioning of the brain, which not only gets charged with greater energy and pranic flow but also becomes calm and peaceful.

Kapalbhati

Kapalbhati is one of the most enjoyable pranayamas. It shows the ingenuity of the yogis who devised a mere breathing process that is not only energizing and soothing but also comes with quite a few therapeutic benefits.

Let us first understand the technique required to practise Kapalbhati properly, followed by the effects it has on the brain and body. Kapalbhati is a combination of two words—'Kapal', which means forehead or frontal brain and 'bhati' means bellows. Basically, with the help of this practise, you will stimulate and awaken dormant centres of your brain.

For the practice:

Kapalbhati is a pranayama which involves repeated, forceful exhalation with short, passive and involuntary inhalation. Initially, to ensure that you are doing it correctly, place the left hand on the navel area and feel its sudden inward compression with every forceful exhalation and its return to its normal state with the passive inhalation. It helps to know that you are exhaling properly. People who have faulty breathing patterns inflate the stomach with exhalation and deflate with inhalation. They have to be taught to do the reverse which is the correct way. After you have corrected your Kapalbhati technique, you may stop putting your hand on the navel area.

When you breathe normally, inhalation needs effort while exhalation is automatic. In Kapalbhati, you reverse this process. André Van Lysebeth's book *Tantra: The Cult of the Feminine* is a classic in the sense that it took him thirty years to write it. In it he says that when we inhale, the cerebrospinal fluid in the brain is compressed and when we exhale, it is decompressed. When we breathe normally, this happens about fourteen times per minute. But with Kapalbhati, the rate at which the brain gets decompressed increases due to increased forceful exhalations.

As a result of practising Kapalbhati, you expel more carbon dioxide from the lungs and waste gases from the cells.

You may start your practise with a small number of rounds and gradually increase it to fifty. Three rounds each of fifty counts are good. After gaining some experience, you may take it upto 100 counts and increase it to five rounds.

The best time to practise Kapalbhati is immediately after asanas and Shavasana. You can sit in any of the meditative asanas, placing the hands in Gyan or Chin mudra on the knees. Keep your spine upright and make sure that there is no tension or tightness in any part of the body. Begin a few rounds of your normal, natural breathing and then start the Kapalbhati practice.

Once you've become proficient at Kapalbhati, then after every round, you will feel a sort of suspension of breath and blankness of mind as well as an emptiness, a completely different feeling that you may not have experienced before. As soon as breathing resumes, it is best to perform Kumbhak with complete exhalation and holding the exhalation as long as you can. This is called the Kumbhak practice.

Although Hatha Yoga classifies it as one of the techniques for cleansing and balancing the body and mind, Kapalbhati must be performed as a part of the Bandha practice in your daily Kundalini practice. Both Kapalbhati and Bhastrika achieve the twin objectives of energizing the body and mind. At the same time, they are tranquilising practices which help you achieve a quiet and calm state and arrest the constant wavering of the mind. They help you slip into a meditative state which is why they must be a part of your daily practice.

Trataka

'*Looking intently with an unwavering gaze at a small point until tears are shed is known as trataka by the acharyas (teachers).*'

—*Sutra Thirty-one, Chapter two,*
Hatha Yoga Pradipika

Trataka is the most subtle of the six Shatkarma practices. You know very well by now that the more subtle the practice, the more powerful are its results. We have seen how gross matter is Energy in condensed form. When gross matter explodes, a massive amount of energy is released, like in atomic fusion. Similarly, through these subtle practises, we uncover powerful sources of energy within our gross being.

Trataka and Khechari Mudra have always held a special place in my practise. It is wonderful to observe how from the strenuous and dynamic practice of pushing the boundaries of physical endurance, you realize that as you progress to the higher practises, what truly matters is stillness of not just posture but also the mind.

Once you have cleansed and brought about balance in your bodily systems, the last two cleansing practises, Kapalbhati and Trataka, clean up the subtle systems of your being such as the neurons in the brain and the thought factory of the mind. The Trataka practise is beautiful in its concept of achieving *ekagrata,* that is, focusing on a single point.

Steps:

1. Sit in any meditative pose. Relax your whole body.
2. Keep your back straight and centre yourself by observing the natural inflow and outflow of your breath. Your hands must rest in Gyan or Chin Mudra.
3. Keep the symbol that you want to focus on at eye level and at arm's length or two feet away. If your symbol is a candle flame, ensure that there is no breeze and that the candle flame is steady. For those suffering from eye ailments like a developing cataract or astigmatism, it is better to focus on a black dot.
4. Focus on your symbol, without blinking, for as long as you can. Ensure that you do not strain the eyes or try too hard to focus. This may prove tiresome and you might even get a headache.
5. Keeping your eyes relaxed, stare at a point just above the wick at the centre of the flame. If your mind wanders off, gently bring

it back to gazing at the flame. When your eyes start to sting or water, gently shut them.

6. Then close your eyes and gaze at the space between the centre of the eyebrow. Most of the time you will see a blue light or an image of the flame going up and down. Try to steady the image and make it sharper. (You may not see anything in the beginning, but don't get disheartened by this. With practise, you will be able to see the image. The more relaxed and focused you are, the faster you will get the result.) This makes up the first round.

7. Rest for a bit and then resume the practise.

8. Do three rounds in the beginning.

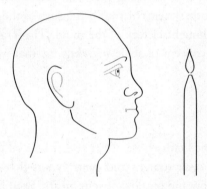

Later, you can take it up to five or however many rounds you are comfortable with. Trataka is best when practised at night before sleeping. It clears your mind and body of all the emotional ups and downs, stress and tension that you may have accumulated during the day. It improves the quality of your sleep by cleaning up the deeper levels of your subconscious and unconscious.

The other option is to integrate it into your daily practice and do it after finishing asanas, pranayama, mudra, bandha and mantra.

Trataka is a dharana, concentration practise. You need to remind yourself of Swami Satsangi's commentary on the 33rd sutra of Vijnana

Bhairava Tantra, 'not only the form of your symbol, but also the concept must hold steady.'

Let us understand through the example of a candle flame as your symbol. Besides focusing on the flame, you may focus on the steadfastness of the flame. Visualize that your mind is as steady and unwavering as the flame. Contemplate on the light of the flame and feel it stimulating and illuminating your mind.

Then visualize that your ego, greed, anger, vanity, jealousy and all such negative attributes are getting destroyed in the flame. This is just an example. You must independently explore your symbol and the concept you decide to focus on.

Hatha Yoga circumvents Buddhism's and Patanjali's yamas and niyamas, which are the fundamental practise in both. Hatha Yoga reasons that without a balanced, healthy body, you cannot have a mind and persona that will be able to follow the tenets of self-restraint, calmness and the various personal and social codes of conduct. Therefore, one can see why Hatha Yoga is one of the most popular forms of yoga. It gets rid of all kinds of aches, pains, discomfort and diseases which sets the stage for a harmonized persona with clarity of mind.

4

ASANAS

Asana has been described by Patanjali in just three words, '*Sukham Sthiram Asanam*', which literally translates to—asana is that pose in which you are happily comfortable and still. The fact is that most of us never sit or even sleep in a relaxed or comfortable way. There is always some kind of tension in the body or involuntary movements like shaking a leg, nervous twitches and more. To translate these three simple words of Patanjali into reality requires dedicated practise of asanas and purifying your body through the Shatkarmas.

This sutra of Patanjali also means that whatever the posture of your asana, whether bhujangasana, sirshasana or padmasana, once you get to the final posture, you must be completely relaxed and comfortable. In the beginning, you will find it difficult to get comfortable and would even be a little stressed as you try to perform those postures that your body is not ready for.

Attaining the final posture of any asana is not just about perfecting the pose. For example, paschimottanasa involves touching your toes while sitting with legs stretched out. Initially, you may only be able to touch your knees. It may be accompanied with some mental or physical stress and you may experience pain in the leg muscles or the back. But with practise you will be able to touch your toes. When you have perfected the pose and can easily touch your toes, then in this final position, you should be completely comfortable and feel relaxation in your whole body.

A focus on the spine is in-built in your asana practice. Getting the spine into a fine state is important for three reasons—firstly, your spine is the location of all the Chakras; secondly, the Sushumna Nadi passes through it and thirdly, it is the path along which Kundalini will ascend to reach the Sahasrara Chakra at the crown of the head. Therefore, your everyday practise must have asanas that target the spine.

The main emphasis, especially in the first and second stages of practise, is on the movements of the spine in five directions, namely—lateral, forward, backward, sideways and twisting.

Moreover, as you progress in your Kundalini practice, asana practise will become shorter. Pranayama and several kriyas that will require you to sit for an hour or more, will become the main part of your practise. How will you sit if your spine is not strong? In fact, not only your spine but your whole body should get into such a fine state that there are no energy blockages. When you have achieved that, even sitting for over an hour in padmasana, or Siddha yoni, siddhasana (for men) will not bother you. Your legs should not hurt or go to sleep. Even after more than an hour of sitting, without any movement and with complete concentration on the pranayama and Kriya practice, you should be able to get up and start walking normally after the practise is over.

The preparation and practise that goes into Kundalini awakening is as exhilarating as the experience of the end result, that is, the union of Kundalini energy with the super consciousness at the Sahasrara Chakra.

5

PRANAYAMA

Nowadays, asana and pranayama are household words. This means that the true import of their meaning, role and impact is not correctly understood. This is particularly true for pranayama. In fact, in many teachings of yoga today, the focus is only on asanas and on the fascination with getting into challenging poses of advanced asana practice. Pranayama is taught in a peremptory manner or not at all. This is a sacrilege in the practise of yoga.

The word *spirit* comes from the Latin word for 'breath'. Therefore, you can understand why pranayama is such an important link to all yoga practice. Prana is the umbilical cord between you and your Creator. A foetus gets its sustenance through the umbilical cord till birth which is then replaced by a special lifelong bond between mother and child. Similarly, prana is the cord which represents the special bond between you and the source of your creation. Pranayama which enters your being by riding on your breath is the way to explore your primordial link with your Creator.

Let's start with the etymology of the word pranayama. It is a combination of two words—prana + ayama. Prana is vital life force and ayama means to expand. Thus, pranayama is the practice of expansion of the vital life force within the framework of your mind and body. Through your breath, you get to know, feel and experience the presence of the pranic energy within you. Although prana is distinct from your breath, you do use your breath to know and regulate the prana.

Patanjali's cryptic definition of pranayama is just three words which hold a world of meaning within them.

'*Tasminsati shvasaprashvasayorgativichchhedah pranayama*'

Patanjali says, '*tasminsati,* which means, now that you have mastered asanas, then know that pranayama is the expansion of the gap between every inhalation and exhalation. Yes, it is not your breath but the attempt to expand the short almost imperceptible gap between every inhalation and exhalation, that is Pranayama.' This means shortening the breath and increasing the breathless state, also known as Kumbhak in yoga.

Let us proceed step-by-step to understand Patanjali's definition of pranayama. If pranayama means expansion of prana, then how can this be achieved by stopping our breath? Isn't our breath our life force and when it stops, life itself ends?

Yes, breath is what fuels our whole body-mind system. We normally breathe at a rate of fourteen times per minute which translates to around 21,000 times in a day. Creatures that have a longer lifespan, like tortoises, elephants, alligators or snakes, have longer breathing cycles than human beings. An elephant takes only four to five breaths per minute while an alligator may breathe only once in a minute in a relaxed state. The Giant Galapagos tortoises, that are said to live up to 400 years have breathing cycles similar to the elephant and during hibernation in winters it falls even lower. In contrast, animals with shorter breathing cycles, like rabbits, rodents or birds, have shorter lifespans.

The Yogis learned a lot from nature and its creatures around them. They realized that to increase one's lifespan, one must slow down their breathing speed. When animals hibernate, their metabolism drops dramatically. This state of hibernation can be likened to the Yoga Nidra state. This means that there is a difference between

sleeping and hibernating. While hibernating, like in the Yoga Nidra
state, you are in a deep, restful state but not asleep. In fact, some
birds and squirrels go into the hibernating state but remain active.
Yoga uses and integrates the knowledge of lower breathing cycles and
the state of hibernation to achieve not just longevity but also a state
of peak awareness and relaxation. Before we go into the dynamics of
pranayama, let us further understand yogic theories and methods.

There are as many paths to our final destination of awakening
the highest Consciousness and Energy as there are people with
varying personalities. But making the mind calm and one-pointed is
part and parcel of all forms of yoga. In this context, we can observe
an interesting interplay between Hatha Yoga and Patanjali's Yoga
Sutras. Hatha yoga achieves this calm, one-pointed state of mind
by using the body to influence the mind. Patanjali Yoga Sutra starts
where Hatha Yoga ends. Since this book is meant for 'All', the Hatha
Yoga path is better suited for those who are walking the thin edge
between the worldly and the Yogic lives.

In its most elemental sense, Pranayama is the slowing down of
your breath. For this, pranayama starts with the most basic lesson on
how to breathe correctly, something that most people do not know
how to do. Listed below are some faulty breathing patterns that you
can check for in yourself:

1. Shallow breathing: Many of us do not realize that our breathing
   is shallow. This is mainly because of stress, tension, anxiety or
   winding oneself up to a hyper-active state. Over a period of time,
   shallow breathing results in many physical, mental, emotional
   and psychological problems. Practising yogic breathing exercises
   can remedy shallow or incorrect breathing habits.
   The first step of yogic breathing is to lie down in Shavasana. As
   you breathe in, you balloon your stomach as if you are filling it
   up to its maximum capacity with your breath. As you breathe
   out, you deflate your stomach completely, pulling in the navel
   area towards your spine.

This is followed by concentrating your breathing in your chest area. Inhale deeply to fill up your chest area only. The stomach area now is passive. Feel your rib cage and chest expand as you inhale, filling your lungs to their maximum capacity. When you have reached the peak of inhalation, then slowly breathe out and feel your rib cage, lungs and chest area contract.

The third step of yogic breathing is to perform the two methods described above together. In one deep inhalation, first fill up your stomach area then your chest area. Then, as you exhale, first deflate your chest then your stomach area. You will feel your breath moving like a wave from the stomach to the chest and vice versa.

2. Movement of diaphragm and stomach with breathing: The movement of your diaphragm and stomach in tandem with your breathing is another problem that most people face. Most people take in the stomach while inhaling and push it out while exhaling. The opposite is what should happen. When you inhale, the diaphragm moves down and pushes the stomach out, thus maximising the space for the lungs to expand into. When you exhale, the diaphragm moves up, and the stomach contracts, thus squeezing the lungs to expel carbon dioxide. The yogic breathing practise will also help correct this error in breathing.

3. Irregular breathing patterns: In your natural and relaxed state your breathing is smooth, regular and rhythmic. As the pressures of life take their toll, you unconsciously adopt irregular breathing patterns. Irregular breathing disturbs the smooth functioning of the bodily systems as well as the brain. This manifests in the form of imbalanced personalities and lifestyle disorders. In contrast, regular, rhythmic breathing results in a calm mind and relaxed state of bodily systems, which manifests in organized lives internally and externally.

4. Awareness of your breath: Breath gives us the gift of life. But since breathing is controlled by our involuntary parasympathetic system, we are mostly unaware of it. Observing your breath and

becoming aware of every aspect of it is not only essential for pranayama but also for the higher practices of mediation. As discussed earlier in our study of the brain and the central nervous system, awareness of breath influences the RAS, the vagus nerve and the neurons in our brain and body.

Deep and controlled breathing is an established technique for managing your anger and emotional upheavals. Even an enraged person calms down the moment he starts to watch his breath. At the subtle level, becoming conscious of the mostly unconscious process of breathing builds a bridge between the conscious and the unconscious parts of our brain. This fosters the release of energy within you that is trapped in chaotic mental patterns. This energy and awareness can be redirected towards happy and creative activities.

By keenly observing your breathing patterns, you also learn to observe the pattern of opening of the nostrils. Since getting both nostrils equally open is a part of our pranayama practice, awareness of your own breathing becomes a must. When both nostrils are equally open, the Sushumna Nadi becomes active.

5. Breathing through the nose: There are people who unconsciously breathe through the mouth. In doing this, they deprive themselves of the benefits of breathing through the nose. When you breathe nasally, the fine nasal hair prevents impurities from entering your body through the breath and your breath gets warmed to the body's temperature and moistened by nasal mucus before reaching your lungs. Those who find themselves compulsively breathing through the mouth must visit a doctor to check if there is an internal defect preventing them from breathing nasally.

Rules for Pranayama

Time of practise: As with everything else associated with yoga practise, dawn is the best time to do pranayama, followed by dusk. Before going to bed at night, one may practise tranquilising pranayama, like Brahmari or breath awareness. It is also essential to maintain the same time and place of practise. Regularity and consistency are of prime importance to the practise of yoga.

Bathing and clothes: Having a bath or at least washing your face, hands and feet is advisable before you commence your practise. Loose and comfortable clothing is important. Tight clothing will prevent the easy flow of prana. Also, ensure that you wear clothes according to the season. The basic idea behind this is that discomfort due to clothing or climate should not hijack your awareness away from your practice.

Diet: Practise only on an empty stomach or at least three to four hours after having a meal. As discussed in the section on diet, try to maintain a light, nutritious and balanced diet.

General Instructions for Pranayama

It is advisable to get your body into a good shape with the help of your asana practise and detoxed through the Hatha Yoga body cleansing practices before you start with serious pranayama practices. Along with your initial practice of yoga, you must master all the simple stages of pranayama. There will not be extensive or intensive pranayama practice in the final stages of your Kundalini Kriyas. But for the Kriyas to be effective and to fructify, you must first awaken and tune your body with intensive pranayama practice.

As with everything related to your yoga practice, don't rush to reach higher practices, especially the ones related to breath retention. Take your time to learn these practices in a relaxed way. Practises like Kapalbhati and Bhastrika may heat up the body or effect changes in the mucus, air and bile proportions in the body. If you face any discomfort, slow down the practice or seek expert advice.

6

THE MUDRAS

The word 'Mudra' means a gesture. Mudras become part of our practice after we have cleansed and refined our gross body and mind through the practise of Hatha Yoga. Asanas work on the gross body and a combination of asanas and pranayama work on the body and the brain, taking the mind-body complex from gross to subtle state. Mudras uplift you further from the subtle to the casual state. Mudras can be a combination of asana, pranayama and even Bandha. Here we talk about Mudra practice that is distinct from the therapeutic practice of holding a mudra for extended periods of time to get rid of a headache and relief for other bodily discomforts.

The Mudra practice in Kundalini is to experience higher states of consciousness.

Mudras work at two levels:

1. Impact the brain by working on the nervous system.
2. Impact the brain through the prana.

There are various types of mudras which involve different parts of your body:

1. hastha (hand) mudra: Gyan, Chin, Yoni, Hridaya and many more
2. manas (head) mudra: Khechari and Shambhavi mudra
3. kaya (body) mudra: Prana mudra
4. bandha (locked) mudra: Jalandhara, Uddiyana bandha
5. adhara (perineum) mudra: Ashwini and Mool mudra.

Mudras are of three kinds: gross, subtle and casual. The bodily ones are gross mudras, the subtle ones are linked with mantra and when the meaning of the mudras is realized or revealed in the practise, it is the casual type which is the highest.

Let us start with the two most basic hastha mudras—the Gyan and Chin mudras. In most of your higher practices, when you sit in padmasana or any of the meditational poses, your hands will be in Gyan or Chin mudra.

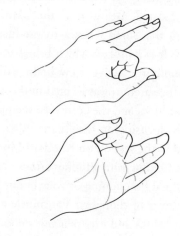

Place the back of your wrist on the knees. Curl the index finger so that it touches the root of the thumb. The other three fingers should be pointing outwards. This is Chin mudra. The same posture with the palm facing downward is Gyan mudra.

These mudras may seem simple but they manipulate important Nadis that connect the lungs to the thumbs. Dr Hiroshima Motoyama, a PhD in Psychology and Philosophy, in his book *Theories of the Chakras: Bridge to Higher Consciousness*, states that these two mudras redirect energy back into the body as the index finger and thumb form a closed circuit of Nadis, thus preventing the dissipation of energy. This helps in meditation.

We have already read about how Dr Motoyama scientifically proved the existence of Nadis and meridians of acupuncture through his experiment with the AMI instruments.

You may wonder how such a simple practise could hold the key to entering the subtle, sublime state. To answer this, let us understand the psycho-physiological effects of the mudras.

The cerebral cortex of the brain is the higher physical representation of the psyche. As we evolve, the cortex gets linked up with the deep, sensory structure of the brain; this is where the Soma Chakra is located. Below it is the Manas Chakra, which links the cortex to the Soma Chakra to produce a process called telencephalization. It is a process which brings into awareness what is instinctive. It links the active, new brain with the deep-seated instinctive brain. If awareness was located in the brain, we can say it is between the mid-brain and the cortex. In the practice of Khechari mudra, you will be focusing on the Lalana, Ajna, Manas and Soma Chakras described in the section on Khechari Mudra.

Sustained meditation with mudras brings about an interesting reversal in the normal functioning of your brain. Normally, you are flowing with the river of thoughts. You hurtle along hitting some rocks, falling over brinks and experiencing smooth as well as rough rides. You are not distinct from the river of thoughts. You are it.

But in your mudra practice, you follow the pattern of your thinking. You are still flowing in the river of thoughts. But you are aware that there is a rock ahead, there is a bend, a fall. You are not just flowing unaware but observing and safely cruising through the river of thoughts.

Mooladhara Chakra

Swadhisthana Chakra

Manipura Chakra

Anahata Chakra

Vishuddhi Chakra

Ajna Chakra

Bindu Chakra

Sahasara Chakra

Tadasana final pose

Triyak Tadasana final pose

Kati Chakrasana final pose

Backward bending pose

Forward bending pose

Makrasana—Folding one leg pose

Bhujang asana final pose

Pada Uthanasana—Both leg raising pose

Dynamic Halasana—Starting sitting pose

Dynamic Halasana—Backward swinging action

Pawan Muktasana final pose

Udarkarshasana—Final body twisting pose

Halasana final pose

Matsyasana—Fish pose

Ushtrasana full pose

Shashank asana full pose

Supta vajrasana final pose

Chakrasana

Dhanurasana

Ashtanga Namaskar asana

Sirshasana head stand final pose

This new awareness of the thought process breaks the normal and ordinary habits of the brain. It creates new pathways and refines the functioning of the brain.

While this is happening, there is another vital process which is set into motion.

The inverted awareness breaks the control of the senses over the thought process. This breaks another habitual link of the brain and results in Pratyahara, that is, withdrawal of the senses.

You can see how we are tracing backwards the steps to our creation. We are getting closer to the point of accosting the veil of Maya. Thus, we are getting closer to entering the other realm of existence where we have no use for our senses or the mind, which is dependent on information from the senses. Now we awaken the greater mind that possesses super sensory powers.

The Hastha Mudras activate certain meridians in the body-mind pathways. To experience this at the most basic level, you can sit in a meditation pose, centre your awareness internally and perform different hastha mudras such as the Bhairav, Bhairavi, Gyan, Chin, Hridaya or any other Hastha Mudra. Observe where most of your breath is centred while performing each mudra. You may experience that for some mudras, the breath seems centred in the stomach area, or in the chest areas, the throat or the nostrils. Each of you may experience it in different areas. Thus, one can experience the effect of these mudras in the physical body too.

There are subtler mudras like the Shambhavi Mudra in which you gaze at the eyebrow centre internally with your eyes closed. There are many aspects to this simple yet powerful gesture.

One aspect is watching the space at the eye-brow centre, your Chidakash or your mind (chitta) space (akash). From being a novice to steadily progressing in this practice, you will see different things manifest on this internal screen. The effort, however, is to see your favourite symbol, say, a beautiful candle flame or a golden rising sun, at the space at the eyebrow centre. Shambhavi Mudra, when combined with Trataka practice, helps you see the symbol at this space, which is also the location of the Ajna Chakra, which is directly connected with your pituitary and pineal glands.

Hence, you end up activating the pituitary and pineal glands. These are two important hormonal glands whose functions have been discussed earlier. Significantly, it is the awakening of the pineal gland which brings about dramatic changes at several levels of your being.

The Khechari Mudra, which may be classified as manas mudra, merits a detailed section on it.

Khechari Mudra

This mudra holds a prime position in the practises for Kundalini awakening. It happens to be one of my favourite practises. The great propagator of Hatha Yoga, Swami Swatmarama, devotes eighteen sutras (from sutra thirty-two to fifty-four, Chapter three) to Khechari Mudra in the *Hatha Yoga Pradipika*.

The Kechari Mudra is considered important as it impacts many powerful Chakras in the higher centres. Understanding the practice first will make it easier to follow its impact. In short, Khechari Mudra involves curling up your tongue and touching the tip of the tongue on the upper palate as far inside the mouth as possible. This is practised in conjunction with breath manipulation, Shambhavi Mudra (eyebrow centre gazing) and a mantra.

With dedicated practise of this mudra, you will find that the tip of the tongue touches a point in the opening of the nasal cavity, which is the confluence of four Chakras, namely, the Lalana, Ajna, Manas and Soma. Lalana is below the Ajna; Manas is above the Ajna and Soma is above Manas at the cerebrum above the sensorium, as detailed by Swami Satyananda Saraswati in his commentaries on the *Hatha Yoga Pradipika*.

The confluence of both the Chakras and the Nadis has an impact on the brain, the endocrine system and the nervous system that sets the stage for an overhaul of your whole being. And an overhaul it is, because we are getting closer to our final destination of awakening the Kundalini.

Let us follow step-by-step how physiological changes brought about by this mudra connect us to the extra-sensory which in turn connects to the super-mental, which ultimately connects with the Superconsciousness.

Khechari Mudra connects us to the Bindu Visarga. The Bindu Visarga is the white hole—the source of all creation. The Bindu Visarga, the soft spot on the top of our head, is not just symbolically depicted as a full moon, it is the place where your internal moon resides.

On a full moon night, the moon shines its golden, mellow light on the earth. Similarly, the Bindu Visarga drips its nectar down through the various Chakras to permeate our whole body. However, in the normal course of our existence, the Bindu Visarga remains inactive. The practice of Khechari Mudra, in conjunction with breath regulation, mantra and Shambhavi Mudra, generates heat within us, which melts the nectar within the Bindu Visarga. The melted nectar flows down from the Bindu Visarga to Soma, Manas, Ajna and finally to Lalana Chakra. This activates these four Chakras, which are connected to those vital centres of the brain that control most of the functions of the body.

The pituitary gland regulates the functioning of the thyroid, thymus, adrenal, mammary and reproductive glands. The Khechari Mudra also influences the hypothalamus at the brainstem, which is connected to the RAS and the thalamus which, as we have discussed earlier, is connected with our autonomic system of wake-sleep cycle and the cardio-vascular and respiratory functions.

The probing of the tongue also influences the salivary glands and the taste buds. It is said that, while doing this practise, if the salivary taste is sweet, it means the earth element is strong within you, which in turn means that the Mooladhara Chakra is active. If the taste is astringent, the water element, the Swadhisthana Chakra is active. Fire element, which is the element of the Manipura Chakra, is characterized by bitter taste. The air element of the Anahata Chakra is acidic and finally, the Ether of the Vishuddhi Chakra is pungent and hot.

When the tip of the tongue can reach right into the nasal cavity, it also influences the three main Nadis—the Ida, Pingala and Sushumna Nadis. This results in the opening up of the Sushumna Nadi.

Thus, you have learned that the cleansing and balancing of the body through the Shatkarmas, the asanas for therapeutic relief, the pranayama for activating and regulating the vital force in your whole body, the advanced practises of Mudra, Bandha, Mantra, Kundalini Kriya along with Khechari Mudra, result in an orchestrated finish to the finale of the crescendo to the awakening of the SuperConsciousness.

7

BANDHAS AND MANTRAS

The word 'Bandha' means 'to lock'. However, this practise does just the opposite. It relieves physical stress, tension and mental and deep psychological blocks. When you reach the stage of practising mudras and bandhas, you have resolved most of the bodily and vital energy problems of your mind-body system. In this practise, you deliberately create locks in your breathing and in other parts of the body to open some deep-seated blockages. The following are the three main Granthis or locks that the bandha practise releases:

1. Brahma Granthi at the Mooladhara Chakra released by Mool bandha
2. Vishnu Granthi at the Anahata Chakra released by Uddiyana bandha
3. Rudra Granthi at the Vishuddhi Chakra released by Jalandhara bandha.

According to the scriptures of yoga, these Granthis are blockages which prevent you from seeing and knowing your basic nature. They are the last obstacles in your journey towards awakening the Kundalini Shakti.

You must have observed that stress, tension and anxiety mostly affect the three areas associated with the granthis of your body. When you experience any distress, you tend to tighten the perineum area, pull in your stomach area or feel stiffness around the heart and shoulder areas. All these result in shallow, irregular or fast breathing. You tend to feel tension in the muscles and nerves of the various parts of your body such as the jaws, shoulders, neck, fingers, spine and perineal area.

All the bandhas, that is, the Mool Bandha, the Uddiyana bandha and the Jalandhara Bandha involve tightening up of all these areas which are points of accumulation of tension, stress and anxiety which results in energy blockages. Yoga removes these by consciously and deliberately creating locks in these areas with breath retention, which helps release the tightness at the physical level as well as clear the blockages at the unconscious and subconscious levels of our mind.

The second most important aspect of Bandha is manipulating the vayus to move in a certain way to clear the way for the Sushumna Nadi. It also makes use of the three pranic vayus, namely, Apana and Prana to unite with Samana at the Manipura Chakra and then makes these travel upwards. In fact, Bandhas are supposed to be an integral part of inducing Samadhi, that is, the ability to leave the physical body at will.

As we have discussed in the section of vayus, the Apana Vayu moves in the downward direction. It regulates the functions associated with the Mooladhara Chakra. When you perform Mool Bhandha, you tighten your perineum centre thus pushing the Apana Vayu towards the Manipura Chakra.

Similarly, when you perform Jalandhara Bandha by constricting the throat area, you force the Prana Vayu to move down towards the Manipura Chakra.

The third lock is Uddiyana Bandha at the Manipura Chakra where Samana Vayu unites with Apana and Prana and the three move upwards.

Thus, you can observe the manifold benefits of your Bandha practice. Firstly, it helps unlock the three main locks within the body. Secondly, it helps clear the way for the Sushumna Nadi which in turn allows Kundalini to move up along it. Thirdly, it manipulates the movement of vayus so that they are released from their restricting attachment to the Chakras. Lastly and most significantly, all this transports you to a meditative state, which is the aim of yoga and Kundalini awakening.

Although the sense you get is that you must use your will and apply force to tighten these areas, it is advisable to remember that the eternal principle of yoga, that is, relaxation, awareness and no stress and strain applies to this practise more so than ever. Also, the mind should be totally inverted inwards to follow the instructions and be ever alert of the attendant results of this practice.

Mantra

Mantra practice is the simplest and yet the most powerful of all practices. It can be practised at all stages of life, at any time and place and even by those who have been rendered feeble with age or ill-health. It does not require you to explicitly understand the meaning of the mantra. It is not specific to any religion, language or geography. Mantras may have meaning but there are some that sound just like the Tantric and Buddhist mantras. The effect of mantra chanting is universal. It is simply sound vibrations that have a specific effect on you and your surroundings. Mantras are not dependent on language but are the basis for all words and languages.

In my experience as a yoga teacher and a counsellor, I've observed how mantras can affect people in powerful ways. I've already recounted how mantras helped me overcome my fear of ghosts. A lady who lost her husband found equilibrium and internal strength through the chanting of Gayatri Mantra 108 times every morning and evening. Mantra chanting is found to work on depressed and even epilepsy patients.

For those who think of mantra as a religious or mystical practice, there is a plethora of research conducted by various universities and medical institutions which have tabulated the effect of mantras on the brain, the nervous system, the heart and on the general mental and emotional state of a person.

Their findings revealed that mantra de-stresses, relaxes and helps in gathering energy and attention to a focal point. Typically, this energy is dissipated or lost because of a perpetually wavering, anxious and stressful mind. Stress, anxiety and fears affect memory, concentration, judgement and decision-making. Without delving into the scientific explanations, let us focus on the yogic explanations because that's where we will find the answers and the guidance to reach our focal point, the Kundalini awakening.

Mantra, the word is a combination of two words, 'man' which means mind and 'trayate' which means liberation. Mantra is what helps liberate the mind from its limitations, impurities and vacillations. From Patanjali to Hatha Yoga to Kundalini Yoga, the recurring emphasis has been on how to deal with the wavering mind, the pull of desires, and the hold of the senses, all of which delay you from realising your highest potential. All the yoga practises, starting from the asanas, are but a series of steps towards maximising your creativity and potential in every respect.

Let us first look at the techniques of mantra practice. There are four methods of mantra chanting:

1. Baikhari: In this method, the mantra chanting is audible. It lays emphasis on chanting the mantra with a focus on the pronunciation and meaning, if any. This is usually taken up in the initial stages of mantra chanting. You may chant with a rosary of prayer beads to keep count, or synchronize it with the breath or even with some activity, like chanting the Surya mantras with Suryanamaskar, or chanting or singing out loud with a group of people.

2. Upanshu: The word Upanshu means whispering. As you advance in your mantra chanting, you will find yourself repeating the

mantra softly. It is the intermediate stage between Baikhari and Manasi systems. Your mind still wanders away from your mantra.

3. Manasi or pashyanti: Manasi means mental and pashyanti means when you see through your mind's eyes. This stage of mantra chanting is reached when the mind is relatively still and mere mental repetition is enough for you to experience the state of something close to thoughtlessness. In this method, besides the string of beads or the breath, you begin to focus on specific regions like the heart area and visualize symbols associated with the mantra. For example, when you chant the Gayatri mantra, you may visualize a beautiful golden rising sun at the eyebrow centre or with Om chanting, a beautiful candle flame or the Om symbol at the Ajna Chakra; with the mantra, 'Om Namah Shivaye', you may visualize a Shiva Lingam at the heart centre, the Anahata Chakra.

4. Para: This is the last stage of mantra chanting. This is the stage at which you experience Ajapa Japa. In this stage, the mantra remains with you even when you stop saying it consciously. This is similar to a song or a piece of music which keeps repeating in your head all day long or for some time after you hear it. While the song or music may keep playing mechanically, with the mind going about with its usual distractions and worries; but mantra affects your state of mind by keeping it quiet and calm.

Mantra will play a significant role as you enter the Stage III of your Kundalini practice. Once your gross body has been brought in balance and cleansed of all impurities through Hatha Yoga, you need to clean the deeper psychic levels of your unconscious and subconscious mind. This cannot happen without the subtle practice of mantra.

We have noted in the chapter on Creation that the first movement towards creation was the birth of nada (vibration), followed by bindu (particle) and kaala (wave). Vibration is the beginning of creation and is associated with the Vishuddhi Chakra. Wherever there is movement or vibration, there is sound. Thus, mantra becomes a part of your daily practise as you ascend each Chakra from the gross earth element of the Mooladhara Chakra, to the water element of the Swadhisthana Chakra, to the fire element of the Manipura Chakra to the air element of the Anahata Chakra, you are moving to the increasingly subtle elements and the higher Chakras associated with each of these elements until we reach the Vishuddhi Chakra, which is associated with sound vibrations and the element ether.

Because of their innate vibrations that have their origins in the building blocks of creation itself, Mantras carry within themselves the power to dive deep into your being. After all, sound is one of the first elements to manifest in the creation of the universe. As we retrace our steps back to our union with our Creator, our practice incorporates those sounds that vibrate in consonance with our state of being.

Mantra is a sound vibration that has been divided into fifty sounds or the letters of Sanskrit. The Sahasrara Chakra is a thousand petalled multicolour lotus with each petal representing a combination of these fifty sounds. There are different types of mantras. For instance, the Mahamrutnjaya mantra is for healing, immunity, good health and strength. The Gayatri mantra is for brain power, memory, intellect and brilliance. Like Om, these mantras are also universal.

The Mandukya Upanishad lays down the meaning, significance and impact of chanting the Om mantra. It delineates the three letters of A-U-M to the three states of the mind; the syllable A is associated with the conscious state, O with the subconscious and M with the unconscious. The ardha matra, the half-moon and bindu above the letter Om, is connected to the turiya awastha, or super consciousness. One can see that chanting this mantra connects you to the three important states of your consciousness and the transcendental state.

In the awake, conscious state, you are part of the external world using all the twenty-five elements that are a part of our creation. The dream state is one in which the eyes are closed but you can still see, feel and experience everything related to the external world in a way that is similar to the awakened state.

In deep sleep, everything is shut down and none of the twenty-five aspects of your being are active. Everything is in a state of rest with the external and internal worlds withdrawn into a state of nothingness. When you emerge from this state of deep sleep, you have no recollection of it. But you feel wonderful after deep sleep. Do you know why this state of deep sleep is so precious? Or why it is so rare for people to have a good restful, dreamless sleep? Why does no sleeping pill or any other aid help us get that deep, restful sleep? While the natural deep sleep results in a feeling of rejuvenation and energy, most aids leave you with side effects and a dependency on them.

This is because of the simple reason that most of us have the threefold aspects of our consciousnesses—the conscious, subconscious and the unconscious—in a state of flux with unresolved conflicts, deep-seated fears, accumulation of stress and tension. These result in fitful sleep with disturbing dreams or an inability of the body and mind to let go and slip into deep sleep.

The mantra Om, being a primordial sound, has the power to clean up your deeper psyche because each of the letters of the sound, as we have learnt from the Mandukya Upanishad, is connected to our different states of consciousness. Therefore, chanting of Om before sleeping helps overcome insomnia and assists in experiencing deep, restful sleep.

Traditionally, the Gayatri mantra and Suryanamaskar are taught to children before they enter puberty. This helps in managing the rather drastic transition into adulthood, when hormonal changes wreak havoc on the emotional and mental states of the children. Unfortunately, people have either forgotten this age-old system or they have no faith in it.

8

SHAVASANA AND YOGA NIDRA

Shavasana and Yoga Nidra are phenomenal contributions of yoga to the modern world. Ironically, the more we have advanced scientifically and in the materialistic world, the further we have moved from the simple ability to relax and be happy. The assault on your ability to be happy and relaxed starts at a young age through the pressure to perform well in school from parents. This pressure persists throughout life in the form of different goals such as financial stability, a good reputation and fame to be achieved. This not only leads to a decrease in your natural capabilities and potential, but also makes for fertile ground for a life riddled with diseases.

The profound principle of Yoga Nidra is a reminder to all parents, schools and workplaces that a relaxed state is more conducive to learning, retention and performance than tension, anxiety, fear and stress. Dr Esther Sternberg, MD, in her book, *The Balance Within: The Science of Connecting Health and Emotion* gives the physiological explanation of the disastrous effects of prolonged stress, anxiety and tension.

She says, 'Some stress is good, but too much becomes bad. Under stress, the nervous system secretes more and more stress hormones, like cortisol and adrenaline, as a bodily response to the stress. Cortisol increases the sugar in the bloodstream to draw on excess energy for the stress response. On the other hand, it suppresses other functions such as digestion, reproductive functions and even growth. It is, therefore, not surprising that working women are unable to conceive these days. Just two generations ago, women had to look for ways and means to not get pregnant. It spawned an industry of copper tube, abortion, birth control pills, etc. Now, it is the reverse.' Now we have IVF, Test Tube babies and surrogacy.

Dr Sternberg says that this release of hormones in response to stress increases performance but sustained stress becomes harmful because of the difference in speed of response to stress by the nervous system and the immune system.

She writes, 'The nervous system and the hormonal stress response react to a stimulus in milliseconds, seconds, or minutes. The immune system takes parts of hours or days. It takes much longer than two minutes for immune cells to mobilize and respond to an invader. So, it is unlikely that a single, even powerful, short-lived stress on the order of moments could have much of an effect on immune responses. However, when the stress turns chronic, immune defences begin to be impaired. As the stressful stimulus hammers on, stress hormones and chemicals continue to pump into the body. Immune cells floating in this milieu of blood, or passing through the spleen, or growing up in thymic nurseries never have a chance to recover from the unabated rush of cortisol. Since cortisol shuts down immune cells' responses, shifting them to a muted form, less able to react to foreign triggers, in the context of continued stress we are less able to defend and fight when faced with new invaders. And so, if you are exposed to, say, a flu or common cold virus when you are chronically stressed out, your immune system is less able to react and you become more susceptible to that infection.'

One can imagine progressive damage to our body's eco-system with the constant unabated bombardment of stress. Therefore, yoga lays stress (pun intended!) on relaxation. Relaxation is part and parcel of the practice of yoga. Shavasana, Yoga Nidra and conscious relaxation of the body throughout the yoga practice get rid of accumulated stress in the body and instil in the practitioner the ability to relax. Gradually, the habitual stress orientation is replaced by a habitual relaxation orientation.

The fascinating story of how Swami Satyananda Saraswati stumbled upon the secret of Yoga Nidra, which illustrates that relaxation is the bedrock of performance.

Here is the story in Paramahamsa Swami Satyananda Saraswati's own words as reproduced in the Introduction of his book '*Yoga Nidra*', published by the Yoga Publication Trust, Munger.

'*When I was staying with my Guru, Swami Shivananda, in Rishikesh, I had a very important experience which triggered my interest in developing the science of Yoga Nidra.*

I had been appointed to watch over a Sanskrit school where small boys were learning to chant the Vedas. It was my duty to remain awake all night to guard the school while the Acharya was away. At three a.m., I used to fall into a deep sleep, and at six, I would get up and return to the ashram. Meanwhile, the boys got up at four, bathed and chanted Sanskrit prayers, but I never heard them as I was fast asleep.'

'*Sometime later, my ashram was holding a large function, and the boys of the Sanskrit school were brought to chant the Vedic mantras. During the function they recited certain shlokas which I did not know, yet somehow, I felt I had heard them before. As I listened, the feeling grew stronger and I tried in vain to remember where and when I had heard them. I was absolutely certain that I had never read or written them, yet they sounded so familiar*'.

Finally, I decided to ask the boys' Acharya, who was seated nearby, if he could explain the meaning of this. What he told me changed my entire outlook on life. He said this feeling of familiarity was not at all surprising, because my subtle body had heard the boys chanting the same mantras many times while I was sleeping in their school (in the wee hours).'

This was a great revelation to me. I knew that knowledge is transmitted directly through the senses, but from this experience I realized that you can also gain direct knowledge without any sensory medium as well. That was the birth of Yoga Nidra.

From that experience further ideas and insights came to my mind. I realized that sleep was not a state of total unconsciousness. When one is asleep, there remains a state of potentiality, a form of awareness that is awake and fully alert to the outer situations. I found by training the mind it is possible to utilize this state.'

Swami Satyananda conducted many experiments to validate his idea. He writes that he tried it on children as well as an Alsatian dog! It is said that Swami Satyananda used Yoga Nidra techniques to teach scriptures to Swami Niranjanananda Saraswati, who, as a child, had been a handful. He writes, 'I began by chanting the fifteenth chapter of the Gita to him about three minutes after he had fallen asleep. Then when he got up in the morning, I would have him read through the chapter, which he would do, of course, mindlessly. After one week, he was able to recite the whole chapter by heart. This way I managed to teach him Shrimad Bhagawatam, Upanishads, Bible, Koran, English, Hindi and Sanskrit.

Swami Niranjanananda Saraswati, besides being an authority on scriptures, is fluent in fourteen foreign languages.

Shavasana is a shorter practice than Yoga Nidra. It can be included in your daily practise and done immediately after the Suryanamaskar and before you start Pranayama and other higher practices. About five to seven minutes are sufficient for your daily practice.

Yoga Nidra is a much longer practice of minimum twenty to maximum forty-five minutes to even an hour. It can be practised two to three times a week in the beginning and then tapered off to once a week. You are the best judge of the frequency and timing of practising as you progress in your practice.

You must understand the unfolding of the subtle but powerful effects of Yoga Nidra practise. One of the earliest references to Yoga Nidra is in the Bhagwat Puran; in the chapter on how Lord Vishnu created the world, it says, 'he lay down in Yoga Nidra. In this state Lord Brahma emerged from his navel on a lotus flower. Then through Brahma, Lord Vishnu created the universe.' This illustrates the importance which is given to yogic relaxation and its link with the ultimate potential of creation.

Do not confuse relaxation with going out, travelling or partying. In all these activities, the lower self, the ego and things connected with it are active. They provide temporary enjoyment, pleasure, joy and even relaxation to some extent. But such activities do not address the long-term solutions to deep-seated tensions, conflicts and fears. These continue to fester and further complicate our psyche.

Since yoga aims to awaken your psychic powers, how will it ever be possible if your psyche itself is a problem? What is the solution? Yoga Nidra, along with your other daily practises, is not only a powerful but also simple and enjoyable practise. My students wait for the weekly Yoga Nidra class like little kids waiting for candy. After all, it means no strenuous yoga practise; they just have to lie down, hand over the reins of their minds to the teacher and drift into the beautiful world of deep relaxation. A significant part of Yoga Nidra are the symbols which are used to evoke response from the deep psyche of the practitioner.

Carl Jung classified this as 'the archetypes'. In the development of the human psyche, most of these symbols are common and universal. These are what Jung called a part of the collective consciousness. When these standard symbols are invoked in our imagination during Yoga Nidra, it is brought to the conscious level and gets converted back to its original state of content. Anything that is brought to your consciousness from your deep-seated subconscious and unconscious psyche no longer remains as a part of your dark complexities. Surely but slowly, these complexities like bubbles in a pond, rise to the surface from the depths and are released. You become free from shackles that you didn't even know bound you.

For example, some people suffer from frigidity because of trauma from their present or past lives. Its cause may be related to a traumatic event which one may bury deep within oneself. Any unresolved complex in the psyche will manifest in the physical body.

Since there are no ostensible symptoms of the malady, it becomes difficult for the medical world or the person himself to understand the mystery behind his problem. This causes unhappiness, shame, guilt and a whole lot of other responses which complicate the matter further.

Therefore, there isn't a better way to solve these psychological problems than a combination of Yoga Nidra, mantra chanting and your daily yoga practice. In the practice of Yoga Nidra, you make a resolve, take a Sankalp, something good and positive for yourself. A resolve made in the course of Yoga Nidra becomes a reality, it is asserted by Swami Satyananda.

I have included some samples of Shavasana and Yoga Nidra practice. You will find many on YouTube too. I've also put some on my YouTube channel by my name, Kamini Bobde.

Section VI

PREPARATION AND PRACTICE OF KUNDALINI YOGA

1

PREPARATION FOR PRACTICE OF
KUNDALINI YOGA

The practice of Kundalini Yoga is divided into four stages. The first stage deals with preparatory practice for those who have no experience in the practise of yoga of any kind. After a month of practise, they can move on to the secondary stage which is for those who have practised some form of yoga before. The third stage is a preparatory stage before you start your Kundalini practice. Finally, the fourth stage is the practise for Kundalini awakening. Before we dive deep into these stages, there are some rules and guidelines that must be observed.

Commercially, yoga is sold in many forms and formats; there is Power Yoga, Hot Yoga, Cold Yoga, White Tantra, Black Tantra, Beer Yoga and what not. In our practise, we will stick to the time-tested methods handed down by generations of Yogis and realized souls.

Time of Practice

Unfortunately, the best time to practise yoga clashes with the hectic schedules of householders and working people. It is Brahmamuhurta, that is, during the wee hours, when night meets day, around 3.45 a.m. The reasons for this timing are pretty clear. There is an aura of peace and calm and the best of divine forces are at play at this hour which provide the most powerful backdrop for your practise. You may go back to sleep at around 6 a.m., for an hour or two, depending on your schedule.

Sunrise, which is usually at around 6 a.m., is the next best option. If this is also not feasible, sunset is another good time. Despite the time you choose, you must ensure that you always practise on an empty stomach. Once you have decided on a time, try to stick to it. You will need to set aside one hour for Stage I and II and thereon increase it to an hour and half for Stage III and finally to two hours every day as you reach Stage IV. This commitment of time is non-negotiable.

The Place of Practice

The place of practise must also be fixed as far as possible. Do not get caught up in romantic ideas of retiring to a cave in the mountains to do your Kundalini awakening. You can create a cave in your home by assigning a room or a place that is fairly quiet, not frequented by others, well-ventilated and free of mosquitos. You can decorate this place with inspirational pictures or statues of your favourite gods, saints or yantra and mandalas as per your personal preferences. You may light a lamp or burn incense if you would like to create an atmosphere of worship and devotion. If you are an atheist, you can devise your own system to orient your mind towards the practise and disconnect it from your surroundings.

Diet for Practise

Today's world is tormented by the act of deciding what to eat. Thanks to globalization, countless food choices are now available to everyone. Adding to this confusion, advice on diet has turned eating into some kind of fad. It has been reduced to drawing room conversations over meals which challenge the very subject under discussion. To make matters worse, moral and ethical overtones add inferiority and superiority complexes in people.

As Kundalini aspirant, you must pay no heed to such confusing advices. The foremost important and basic aspect to be followed is to keep your diet simple and light. Eating less is always better than overeating which puts the body under strain. You must try to eat generic and seasonal food. This saves you from the stress of procuring exotic and out of season food products. There is merit in eating generic, local and seasonal food because nature knows better than us where what should grow and when it should. Olive oil may be good but it's better if the natives of Eastern India use mustard oil, Southern India use coconut or sesame oil and Northern India use peanut oil.

There is debate over vegetarian, non-vegetarian and dairy products. To steer clear of all these confounding choices, the easiest and the best advice is to know what is good for you. Your body is the best dietician for you. Most people try to get dietary advice from several sources. What they should do instead is pay attention to the feedback given to them by their body. Even within a family, every member's system is distinct and has different requirements. For example, in a non-vegetarian family, there may be one whose body rebels against non-vegetarian food. In short, swadhyaya or self-knowledge, will help you follow an uncomplicated and wholesome diet.

The practice of Kundalini Yoga does not prohibit you from consuming non-vegetarian food or alcohol. But you must keenly observe if such consumption is, in any way, obstructing your practise. There is the left-handed tantra, vam margi tantra, that employs the consumption of meat, fish, wine and sex for yogic practises. This illustrates that yoga is all-inclusive. But, such practices are not only not easy but the person has to be following the rules in every aspect for spiritual awakening and not indulgence. For the worldly who face distractions as it is, yoga emphasizes the point that humans have longer intestines (thirty-six feet) than most carnivores. Longer intestines are likely to cause non-vegetarian food to ferment and putrefy in the guts; in comparison, vegetarian food can be digested with ease.

Care must be taken to not consume heat generating spices which also tend to excite the mind.

You must strive to eat food that is alive or, in yogic parlance, food that is amruta. Amruta is a combination of two words—'a' and 'mrutyu', which means not dead. In short, you should eat foods that are alive, not dead. The level of freshness of a fruit, vegetable or any other food item determines how alive it is with pranic energy. The older it gets, the more pranic energy it loses. Even if it's kept in the fridge, it may be safe to eat but it loses its life-force gradually before it decays. Thus, sugar, polished grains and other processed foods have such a long shelf life, because they are 'dead food'. It takes years for sugar to go bad. Such food products are merely fillers or indulgences and should be strictly avoided.

Foods with pranic energy fuel the brain and the nervous system. Foods without nutrition or Sattwa burden the digestive system and affect the working of the entire body. Hence, it is vital that you pay attention to what you eat.

You must always cook your food before consuming it. With the exception of fruits and dry fruits, most food must be steamed or lightly cooked so that it can be digested easily. You should avoid drinking cold or hot water; drinking room temperature water is the most beneficial.

Your diet should be light and easily digestible, which is why you should try to give up foods that are sour, pungent, bitter or spicy. Do not indulge in too much fasting either. Sage Gheranda says that the best rule for how much to eat is to fill your stomach to half its capacity, fill quarter with water and rest should be free for the circulation of air. The stomach should not feel heavy nor should the body feel lethargic after eating.

Occasional fasting will also help in cleansing and resting the digestive system. A balanced diet will be important for people engaged in demanding routines besides their Kundalini practice. This is because Hatha Yoga, which involves cleansing the body, will be a part of the practise. There is no point in cleansing the body with Neti, Kunjal or Shankprakshalan if you'll end up polluting it with junk food.

Kundalini practice is bound to change your bodily systems. With the awakening of pranic energy, your metabolism, need for oxygen and internal temperature may go down. You must remain sensitive to these changes as they will need concomitant changes in your diet.

Lifestyle changes

As you dive deeper into the Kundalini practice, you may undergo some lifestyle changes as a side effect of the internal changes taking place in your body. You may find yourself falling into a routine which complements the practise and its many requirements. Self-regulation through awareness is the best. You will need to alter certain aspects of your personality. These changes may involve practising sobriety in everything, including your interactions with others, exercising restraint while talking, avoiding ego clashes, practising silence and developing an awareness of your thought process and actions.

It is delusional to think that merely an hour or so of practising asana, pranayama and dhyana will awaken Kundalini. You are seeking a multi-dimensional change in yourself, therefore, it will require a multi-dimensional effort from your end. If you practise the physical exercises but spend the rest of the day gorging on processed foods, getting into vexatious conversations over a debate, trying to appear wise and worldly, trying to dominate a conversation with an attitude of superior knowledge, it will be counter-productive. What makes it difficult is that most of us lack the ability to self-appraise. People swing from self-deprecation to self-indulgence in the blink of an eye. A balance is possible only through self-awareness. Therefore, the topic of self-awareness warrants a more detailed section.

2

SELF-AWARENESS

Self-awareness is life's strangest paradox. The self is the all-consuming aspect of life but the subject, more often than not, ends up as the object. People go through life without even realising this, much less correcting it. This has become the fountainhead of a myriad of problems faced at the individual as well as the global level. The era of consumerism and materialism has fostered a social compulsion of assessing oneself in the eyes of the world. This propels an individual and their life. German philosopher Arthur Schopenhauer summed up succinctly, 'Materialism is the philosophy of the subject who forgets to take account of himself.' This objectification of the self has engendered manifold distortions and suffering.

Experience is the process of the inside and the outside. The present market-driven world lays emphasis on the outside wherein the subject (the self) is merely aware of itself as an object. The subject never looks at itself minus the outside. We are given to looking at ourselves from other's eyes. Each real thing is, then, a subject because of the inside that goes along with its outside.

This is beautifully illustrated by Herman Hesse in a short story called 'Within and Without'. It is a story of two friends, Fredrick and Erwin. Fredrick is obsessed with the rational and logical. Erwin, with the occult and magical. When this difference in outlook becomes too deep for them to bridge, they agree to part ways rather than torment each other. As a parting gift that represented his conviction that all that is outside is within you and vice-versa, Erwin gives Fredrick a little statue with two heads that Fredrick instantly finds grotesque.

He tries to place the statue in different spots in his home to avoid its presence but it continues to torment him. He even starts travelling to avoid being at home. Once, upon returning from his travels, he finds that his maid had accidentally broken the statue and thrown away the pieces. He is relieved that the statue is finally gone from his life.

But the statue keeps popping up in his head and continues to torment him. Frustrated and wondering if Edwin had cast a spell of magic on him through the statue, he accosts his friend one night. Fredrick accuses Erwin of using magic to torment him. He relates how he is not able to stop thinking about the statue despite its destruction.

Erwin calmly explains to Fredrick that there is no distinction between the outside and the inside. A fragmented mind doesn't know this. Whatever is outside is within you and whatever is within you is outside you.

Yoga tries to break this chain of subject and object through pratyahara. Pratyahara practice involves withdrawal of the senses and cutting off all external inputs so that the self remains engrossed. This breaks the dichotomy of the subject and object. The seer and the seen become one. The oscillations stop and the mind crosses over from one dimension of consciousness to another.

Sustained pratyahara practice leads to dharana or concentration.

Swami Satyasangananda Saraswati, in her commentary on the thirty-third sutra of Sri Vijnana Bhairava Tantra, writes, 'Dharana means holding something in the mind, so along with concentration on one object or point, conceptualization is also dharana.'

Swami Satsangi elaborates, 'The quality of your conceptualization and your ability to hold that concept for a sustained period of time to the exclusion of all else also figure largely in determining your success . . . This is only possible when the mind is very sensitive and observant and is able to focus on the present moment without interruption.'

The above is a subtle but important point for you to internalize. This knowledge will come in handy when you start practices such as Trataka, Shambhavi and finally the meditation practises like Antar Mauna.

The object of your absorption is irrelevant; it may differ from a devout to a worldly person, from an agnostic to an atheist. It matters not.

This may seem too difficult to accomplish. But yoga makes it manageable by breaking it up into small daily practises. Initially, you may not even realize that you are taking baby steps towards the enormous achievement of awareness which precedes self-knowledge.

This can be understood with the help of an example. Even the simplest of asanas will involve postures that require you to be aware of your synchronized breathing and the impact of the postures on different parts of the body. In the practice of asana and pranayama, you are constantly advised to ensure that your thoughts do not hijack your awareness of your practice. You have to observe your breath and the impact of asanas on different parts of your body. This helps turn your gaze inwards. You become an observer of your breath and body. This dual action cuts you off from the external world.

Gradually, with sustained effort, you may experience moments or flashes when the external is cut off and the mind is quiescent; you get a taste of this alternate state of thoughtlessness. You experience an alternate state of being.

It is an alternate state because usually, with the exception of deep sleep, your cognition and experience are based on inputs from your senses. At this point, the cyclical process of subject-object-subject is broken. The subject becomes its own object and you realize that there is another Self watching this self. Thus, subject and object become one with this Self, which is the witness and you progress on the path to self-awareness.

However, this knowledge will remain clinical if your daily practise, along with your journey into yourself, is not accompanied with compassion, humility and love. Indian mythology is full of stories about great practitioners, who practised hard asceticism and gained many powers and boons. But since they did not annihilate the negative and destructive attitudes of greed, violence, hatred, jealousy, with vanity and ego their sadhana, they did not know compassion and their hearts remained indifferent to human suffering. Spiritual practices deem such behaviours as dangerous to the practitioner as well as society at large.

3

TIPS FOR YOUR YOGA PRACTICE

How is yoga different from any other form of exercise done to attain a healthy mind and body? There are some distinguishing aspects that you must keep in mind otherwise you will end up doing some form of fitness regime but not yoga. To practise yoga, you will have to bear in mind the following four factors:

1. Do not practise yoga with a sense of competition or with the burden of failure. These two imposter have to be shrugged off before you roll out your yoga mat. They represent the engines of stress and tension instilled in you from a very young age. The aim of yoga is to banish these two enemies from within you. These must be replaced with humility and awareness of your own limitations and potential not only at that moment in a limited sense but also in life in a broader sense.

   For example, imagine you are in a group class practising forward bending. There will be some who will be able to rest the entire palm flat on the floor and others who will easily touch the toes while you may be struggling, only managing to take your fingers a few inches below the knee. Do you think it's shameful? No! While doing yoga, begin with the affirmation that you will do your best that particular day, compete only with yourself and accept your limitations in a relaxed, comfortable way. Know that with sincere practise, you will be able to perfect any posture.

2. Maintain internal awareness on breath and body. The second tip for your practise is to maintain awareness of your breath and on how the body is affected by the practise. You have read that one of the goals of yoga is to draw you inside and away from the outside world. Through your microcosmic within, you will become one with and know the cosmic macrocosm. Can you write poetry without learning the alphabet? No. Similarly, these brief lessons are essential for your transformation into a composite Yogi. Awareness of when to inhale and exhale is important during asanas as it helps in getting the maximum benefits from a posture. This works on the principle that whenever the posture involves opening up of the body, you inhale and when you close or contract your body, you exhale.

3. Be ever relaxed during your yoga practise and thus move to making relaxation a default setting for yourself. As children we are mostly relaxed, and stress, tension, fear of failure or pressure of success are yet to be part of our lives. Later, for most people, a gnawing sense of restlessness, stress and tension become the norm. However, for your yoga practise it is imperative that your body is completely loose and relaxed.

Yoga helps you achieve this by taking small steps in your daily practise towards complete relaxation. The instructions of your yoga practise will repeatedly tell you to keep your body relaxed. A relaxed body engenders a relaxed mind. Thus, your whole mind-body complex learns to be relaxed. Gradually, it becomes a part of you. In the beginning, you may involuntarily tense up your back, neck, jaws or other parts of the body that are prone to tense up. Thus before the start of any asana or pranayama you are repeatedly told to relax your whole body. This you will notice in the practise instructions too.

4. You spend a large portion of your lives working so that one day
    you might purchase your own home. Sadly, you do not bother to
    spend as much time or energy caring for the home you are born
    in, your body. You are almost never aware of the inner workings
    of your bodily systems.

    A huge part of asana practice is to become aware of every part of
    your body. Bhujangasana is an asana that affects the spine, the
    digestive system, the thyroid gland, the lungs and the muscles of
    your arms. When you practise this asana, you can focus on the
    various parts of the body that this asana affects in each round.
    You must do this with every asana practise. Thus, awareness will
    gradually become a part of you.

Section VII

PRACTICE BEGINS

1

STAGE I

It is essential to tune into your body and mind for your practise. There is nothing that can achieve this better than the age-old short invocation. Every practise session must begin with an invocation to dedicate your practise to the Cosmic Consciousness and Energy and specifically to Kundalini Shakti with a firm resolve to achieve your goal of awakening Kundalini. Depending on your personal propensities and personality, you may include the evocation of your *ishta devta* (your favourite god) or if you are agnostic or atheist, you can focus on a symbol and any mantra of your choice.

You have to do all these movements neither in a hurried nor a very slow motion. However, these simple practices can be used as awareness intensifying practices by deliberately doing them slow and all the while keeping your awareness fully focused on the movements and their impact. Usually the Sukshma Vyayam takes 7 to 10 mins to complete. The day you decide to do the slow, intensive practice, it may take you up to 20 minutes. This can be applied to all the various practices. I do not want to specify a time frame because each one has a different body flexibility. If you go on my YouTube channel, you will find this practice. Just type Kamini Bobde among the several videos is the Sukshma Vyayam which I have called, 'Limbering up Practise'.

Also, when you start with your asanas practice, you will have to determine your pace of practise. It is good to vary your practice by doing dynamic (faster) practice some days—slow and deliberate on some days—holding in the final position for counts varying from 10 to 20 counts on some other days. The counting must be done to the rhythm of seconds. When you hold in the final position, at that point see that your whole body is relaxed and run your awareness on the various parts of the body that you feel the impact of the posture. This also brings variation in your practice depending on time available and your disposition on any particular day.

The shoulder joint rotation and neck movements, I find my students simply enjoy it, as instantly you feel the tightness, tension around the shoulders and neck areas getting freed up.

Practice for Beginners—Sixty Minutes

Invocation:

Sit comfortably in any one of the meditative poses described below. Close your eyes gently. Become aware of your surroundings, your body and the purpose of your practise. Focus on the part of body where there is tightness or tension and try to relax that part. Make sure that the whole body is loose and relaxed. Your spine should be upright but relaxed.

Take awareness to your own normal, natural breathing. Observe its natural flow for three to five rounds. Then hitch your awareness to the centre of your eyebrows, inhale deeply and as you exhale, chant the Om mantra three times. You can do it out loud or internally depending on what feels more suitable. As you chant the mantra, try to visualize a candle flame, the Om symbol, your favourite god or any other symbol which may appeal to you at the centre. After the chanting, rub your palms and place them on your eyes. Repeat this three times.

You may use Aim, Ahmen or any other mantra chanting that you would prefer over Om. However, in yoga 'Om' is not a religious mantra.

Sukshma Vyayam—Body Limbering up

In the following practises, you will learn about the Sukshma Vyayam asanas, which are also known as the Pawan Mukta asana series which has been thoughtfully categorized by Swami Satyananda Saraswati in the book *Asana, Pranayama, Mudra, Bandha*. Those who are starting out with their yoga practice must treat this book like the Bible for the practise of Shaktkarmas and Hatha yoga. Swamiji has expertly divided the Pawan Mukta asana series into three parts, with the first part dealing with warming up, the second with the digestive system and the third with releasing energy blocks in the neuro-muscular system and improving the functioning of the heart, the lungs and the endocrine system.

I have incorporated the part of this practise that helps the body limber up. It is an unbeatable combination of some simple postures and movements to limber up the body. It frees up the joints, gets the muscles into action, improves blood circulation and limbers the body from the toes to the top of your head. Make sure to do the eye movements. It is the least you can do to protect your eyes from the damage sustained due to staring at all kinds of screens. People who suffer from chronic body aches, general tiredness, cramps, accumulation of stress and tightness around the shoulders, jaws, neck and other bodily problems will get quick relief from this simple and short practise. It can be discontinued once you move to higher practices, although I have practised this without a break and still begin my yoga practise with it.

It is advised that you read the instructions more than once to get them right. There are some pointers you may miss in the first reading, especially when you get to the Kundalini practices. The instructions are as follows:

1. **Toes bending**: The steps are as follows:

   • Sit comfortably on the mat with both legs stretched out in front of you.

- Place both hands behind you with palms resting on the floor and fingers pointing away from the body. The back should be upright and relaxed.
- Inhale and pull the toes of both legs towards yourself and as you exhale, stretch them away from yourself. See that only your toes are moving and rest of the body, from the ankle joint upward, is in a completely relaxed state. This completes one round.
- Do a minimum of five to a maximum of ten rounds.

Focuses on: The toes and joints of the toes and your breathing rhythm.

2. **Ankle joint movement:** The steps are as follows:

- Continue to sit in the same base position.
- Inhale deeply and pull your ankle towards yourself.
- Exhale and move them away from your body.
- Again, only the ankle joint must move and the rest of the body should be still and relaxed. This completes one round.
- Do a minimum of five to a maximum of ten.

Focuses on: On the ankle joint.

3. **Ankle joint rotation**: The steps are as follows:

- Sit comfortably in the base position. Relax your whole body and ensure that your spine is straight but relaxed.
- Rotate your right ankle joint first in a clockwise motion for five to seven rounds and then in an anti-clockwise motion for another five to seven rounds.
- Repeat the same with your left ankle joint.
- End with rotating both ankle joints together, first in a clockwise motion and then an anti-clockwise motion for five to seven rounds.

Focuses on: The ankle joints, the heels and the calf and thigh muscles up to the hip. Breathing is normal.

4. **Flexing the knee joint**: The steps are as follows:

   - Continue to sit in the base position.
   - Move your awareness to your knees and keep your body relaxed.
   - Take a deep breath in. Squeeze and tighten your knee joint and watch and feel the kneecap moving up.
   - Exhale and relax your knee. This makes one round.
   - Do this for five to ten rounds.

   Focuses on: The knee joints and breathing.

5. **Hip Joint Rotation**: This asana and the following Butterfly asana are good for relaxing the hip and the knee joints. It releases tension from the thigh muscles and removes tiredness in legs caused by standing or walking. They are preparatory practises for sitting in meditative poses. Hip joint movement regulates the prostate glands and the butterfly pose is a mood elevator. The steps are as follows:

   - Sit comfortably with the legs stretched out in front of you.
   - Fold your right leg and hold it with both hands around the ankle and place your right foot on the left leg's thigh as high and close to the groin as possible.
   - Hold the right leg's toes with your left hand and place your right hand on the right knee.
   - Straighten your back, relax your body and rotate your hip joint, first in a clockwise motion for five to ten rounds and then in an anti-clockwise motion for another five to ten rounds.
   - Repeat the same with the left hip joint. Maintain normal, natural breathing.

Focuses on: The hip joints, the knees, the calf and thigh muscles. These are the most neglected parts of the body.

6. **Half Butterfly**: The steps are as follows:

    - Sit comfortably in the base position.
    - Fold your right leg at the knee and place your right foot on the left thigh.
    - Hold the toes with both hands and pull up the foot as close to the groin as is comfortably possible.
    - Hold the right foot or ankle with the left hand and lightly hold the right knee with your right hand.
    - Flap the right knee up and down just like the wings of a butterfly. Do ten to twenty rounds of this. Repeat the same with the left leg by folding it up.

    Focuses on: The mental and emotional states. This exercise releases stress, uplifts your mood and is used to treat depression.

7. **Full-Butterfly**: The steps are as follows:

    - Continue to sit with your legs stretched out.
    - Hold the toes of both legs by folding the legs at the knees.
    - Pull your feet up close to your groin and place the soles of both feet so that they touch and face each other.
    - Holding the feet with both hands, start flapping your knees up and down as if they are the wings of a butterfly. Do ten to twenty rounds of this.

    Focuses on: Same as for Half-Butterfly.

8. **Finger joints**: The following movements release stagnant blood in veins and arteries, which are directly connected with the heart. The present-day usage of mobile phones, computers and other

electronics makes it necessary for you to do these practices to release stiffness in the fingers, elbows and shoulders. The steps are as follows:

- Sit cross-legged or in the base position.
- Ensure that the spine and the head are in a straight line and relaxed. Stretch both hands in front of you, at shoulder level, with palms facing down. Keep awareness on your fingers.
- Inhale and stretch all your fingers as much as possible and then exhale and close the hand to make a fist with the thumb placed inside the fist. Do ten rounds of this.

Focuses on: The finger joints and the effects on all the joints and muscles right up to the shoulder joint.

9. **Wrist joint**: The steps are as follows:

- Sit cross-legged or in the base position.
- Stretch your hands out in line with your shoulder.
- Hold the right wrist with the left hand. With awareness on your right wrist, make a fist with the fingers circling the thumb and the fist facing downwards.
- With normal breathing, rotate the right wrist first in a clockwise motion and then anti-clockwise motion. Do five to ten rounds of this. Repeat the same with the left wrist.

10. **Elbow joint**: The steps are as follows:

- Continue sitting in the base or cross-legged position.
- Stretch your arms out at shoulder level with the palms facing up.
- Maintain awareness on the elbow joints.

- Inhale and fold the elbow joints of both arms with the fingertips resting on your shoulders.
- Exhale and stretch your arms again to the starting position. This makes one round. Do five to seven rounds of this.

11. **Shoulder Joint**: This simple practice releases stress around the neck and shoulder area. It is a prescribed practice for spondylitis and cervical problems.

- Sit cross-legged or in the base position. The steps are as follows:
- Ensure that your spine is straight. Relax your whole body.
- Fold the right hand and place the fingers on your right shoulder and your elbow should point outwards at the shoulder level.
- Rotate the shoulder in a clockwise motion. As you bring your elbow in front of the body, exhale and inhale as you pull it back.
- Repeat the same in an anti-clockwise motion.
- Do five to ten rounds of this. Repeat the same with the left shoulder joint and with both shoulders together.

Focuses on: In all the above asanas, the awareness must be on the related joint and your breathing pattern. Feel all tightness, stress and tension getting released from the upper back, shoulder blade and neck area.

12. **Neck Backward and forward bending:** The following movements of the neck are simple yet powerful practises because all the important nerves, veins and arteries connecting the brain to the body pass through the neck. Present-day lifestyle accumulates a lot of stress and tension at precisely this area. Therefore, practises in the morning prepare you for the day's work and other activities. Please be aware that those suffering from cervical issues or spondylitis must avoid forward bending of any kind, including neck movements. The steps are as follows:

- Sit cross-legged or in the base position. The spine and head should be in a straight line but relaxed.
- Take a deep breath and slowly throw your head back and fully stretch your neck.
- Exhale and slowly drop your head until the chin touches the chest. Do five rounds of this.

13. Sideways bending of neck: The steps are as follows:

- Centre your head, inhale and as you exhale, drop your head to the right, bringing the right ear close to your shoulder.
- Then as you inhale, bring the head back to the centre and as you exhale bend it towards the left shoulder.
- This makes one round.
- Do five rounds of this. Do not raise your shoulder. The movement should only involve the head and neck area.

14. Neck Twisting: This is a neck twisting movement. The steps are as follows:

- Inhale when the head is at centre.
- As you exhale, twist your neck to the right as much as possible.
- Inhale and come back to the centre and as you exhale, twist the neck to the left. This makes one round. Do three to five rounds of this.

15. Neck Rotation: This is the last of neck movements. The steps are as follows:

- Sitting in the same base position or padmasana.
- Keep the head at the centre, then rotate the head first in a clockwise motion for five to seven rounds and then in an anti-clockwise motion for another five to seven rounds.
- Inhale when head is thrown back and exhale while the head is bent forward.

Focuses on: Awareness must be inside the neck area and with focus on release of stiffness, on the thyroid glands and on the veins and arteries passing through the neck area.

16. **Eye Exercises:** It is sad to see children under the age of six wear spectacles nowadays. Staring at electronic devices such as televisions, phones and computers for long intervals of time weakens the eye muscles. Eye exercises can help strengthen the eye muscles. Some of them are mentioned below.

You can finish off the Sukshma Vyayam practice with eye movements: sideways movement, up and down movement and rotating the eyeball in circles, first in a clockwise motion and then in an anti-clockwise motion. One of the most relaxing and effective eye exercises is palming of the eyes. Initially, have someone check if you are moving the eyeballs correctly in all directions because you cannot see it yourself.

You will be able to finish the above practice in ten minutes. This practice is suitable for people of all ages. These are specially good for old people and infirm people.

Practise of Some Meditational Poses

Padmasana: This universal meditation pose prevents the wastage of energy as, in this pose, all ends of the body create a circuitous loop. The spine is firmly supported and the flow of energy within the body is balanced. It also activates the Mooladhara Chakra. This posture exerts pressure on the lower back and spine which has a relaxing effect. The relaxing effect helps lower your heart rate and blood pressure. With the effect of gravity no longer pulling blood towards the feet, this blood is directed to the digestive system. This posture induces calmness, makes focusing easier and also helps in inducing meditational states. This is also known as the Lotus pose. The steps are as follows:

- Sit with your legs stretched out in front of you.
- Relax your whole body and visualize the padmasana pose.

- Then place your right foot on your left thigh. Let it rest there comfortably, feeling a slight pressure of the right heel on the pubic area.
- Fold your left leg and place it on your right thigh so that your posture is kind of locked.
- Stay in that position as long as it is comfortable.

In the beginning, you may struggle to get in this position or there will be those who will manage to get into the posture but will find it difficult to maintain it beyond a few seconds. This is not a problem. Just keep trying every day and, slowly but surely, you will get to that position. Also, your daily asana practise will free up your body of stiffness and soon you will find it easier to get into this pose. This posture is universal and is also one of the best meditational poses.

Siddhasana: In addition to all the benefits of Padmasana, Siddhasana has the benefit of stimulating both the Mooladhara and the Swadhisthana Chakras. In activating these two points by exerting pressure on them, impulses are sent to the brain, which help control reproductive hormones. This helps in controlling sexual impulses and is beneficial for people wanting to adopt Brahmacharya as a part of their practise.

This is a posture for men. Subtle changes are made to the Padmasana posture to get to Siddhasana. The steps are as follows:

- Sit comfortably with legs stretched out in front of you.
- Fold your right leg and place the sole of right foot against the inner side of the left thigh such that the right heel presses against the perineum (point between the anus and the genitals).
- Bend the left leg and press the toes in the space between the right thigh and calf.
- You will know your posture is correct when the left ankle bone and the right ankle bone are touching each other. The left heel now is pushing against the pubis and the genitals now rest between both the heels.

- Grasp the right toe and pull it up through the space between the left calf and thigh. See that finally, you are sitting on the right heel.
- Adjust your whole body so that it is upright and the knees are flat on the floor with legs locked. Place your hands on the knees with the fingers in Gyan or Chin Mudra.

Focuses on: On the pressure exerted on the pubic area by the heels of your left and right foot and on the Mooladhara and the Swadhisthana Chakras.

Siddhiyoni asana: This posture is for women. The benefits are the same as Siddhasana. The steps are as follows:

- Begin by sitting with legs stretched out in front of you.
- Fold the right leg and place the foot against the inside of the left thigh such that the heel presses against the groin.
- Bend the left leg and press the left foot in the space between the right thigh and calf.
- Grasp the right toes and pull them up from the space between the left thigh and calf.
- The left heel is above the right heel and presses lightly against the pubic area.
- Adjust your whole body. The knees will be flat on the floor.
- Place your hands in Gyan or Chin mudra.

Focuses on: It is similar to Siddhasana.

Asanas for the Spine

There is no way you can do Kundalini Kriyas without first strengthening your back. Your spinal cord is the highway along which the Kundalini will move towards the Sahasrara Chakra at the crown of the head. Any kind of blockages in the spine will make

Kundalini return to the base of the spine. Therefore, you will find that the practice covers all five movements of the spine, namely lateral stretch, sideways bending, twisting, forward and backward bending. I have mentioned the Chakra to focus on for each asana. However, initially, just focus on getting the right pose with breath awareness and the body parts being impacted. Once you have perfected the poses, then you can focus on the Chakras.

People with back issues must first address the problems and then start these practises. People with cervical issues, vertigo and spondylitis must avoid forward bending asanas. A few sessions with a yoga teacher will remove all back issues.

The later stages of your practise will require you to sit still in a meditational pose. Again, this will not be possible unless your spine can hold you in that position for long intervals of time. As you progress in your practise, you will be the best judge of how many of these asanas you should practise daily.

Tadasana (Lateral stretch of spine): This asana helps bring all parameters of your body in balance which is essential for your Kundalini practice. It stretches the vertebrae, the abdominal muscles and the intestines. It clears up the congestion of nerves along the spine. It tones muscles and ligaments in the legs, arms and along the back. It is one of the asanas practised during the full body cleansing, that is, Shankprakshalan, which is included in the Hatha yoga practice. The steps are as follows:

- Stand with your feet together or a few centimetres apart with arms hanging by the side of the body.
- Feel the balance and equal distribution of body weight on both legs. Relax your whole body.
- Fix your gaze at some point a little above the eyes. This is important as it will help you maintain balance as you come up on your toes.
- Raise your hands over your head, interlock your fingers and place your interlocked hands on your head with palms turned upward.

- Inhale and stretch your arms over your head and simultaneously come up on your toes to experience a full body stretch, from the fingers to the toes. Hold the position while maintaining internal breath for as long as it is comfortably possible.
- Then, as you exhale, lower your whole body, come back to the starting position and relax your body. This is one round. Do five to seven rounds of this.

You may change this asana by looking at the interlocked hands over your head or closing your eyes in the final position, which you will be able to do after some practise.

Focuses on: On maintaining balance, on the stretch in the entire body from the toes to the tip of your fingers. Spiritually, on the Mooladhara Chakra initially and later, on the Ajna Chakra.

Triyak Tadasana (Sideways bending): It stimulates the intestines and also helps massage the liver and pancreas with the alternate stretching and compression of the muscles around these organs. It is one of the asanas included in the full body cleansing, that is, Shankprakshalan. The steps are as follows:

- Stand with your feet about shoulder-width apart from each other.
- Interlock your fingers and raise both hands above the head with palms facing upward; elbows should be straight.
- Feel balance and steadiness. Relax the body in this starting pose.
- Inhale and then as you exhale, bend your top torso to the right without bending from the hips, keeping the body and face forward.
- Bend as much as you can. Hold for a few seconds.
- Then as you inhale, come back to the centre. Exhale and bend your torso to the left. This makes one round. Do five to seven rounds of this.

Focuses on: On bending as much as you can while keeping the elbows straight and seeing that you do not bend forward because this will prevent the real benefits accruing to the body. Awareness spiritually on the Manipura Chakra.

Kati Chakrasana (Spine twisting): This asana is a full body twist. It executes twisting in the neck, the spine, the stomach and the hip area. It relieves tightness and tension and at the same time, stimulates the thyroid gland, all the digestive organs and the urogenital organs. It releases tension along the spine and loosens up the vertebrae. It is one of the five asanas for the Shankprakshalan practice. The steps are as follows:

- Continue in the same starting position as in Triyak Tadasana, with legs shoulder-width apart and arms by the side of the body.
- Inhale and raise both hands to shoulder level with palms facing downward.
- Exhale and twist the body to the right with the right hand circling the waist and the left hand resting on the right shoulder.
- Twist as much as you can and try to look at the back. Hold the final position for a few seconds or as long as you can hold in exhalation.
- Then as you inhale, come back to the centre.
- Without lowering your hands, exhale and twist to the left side with your left hand circling the waist and the right hand resting on the left shoulder.
- Hold for a few seconds. Then inhale and come back to the starting position. This makes one round. Do five to seven rounds of this.

Some days you can stop every time you come back to the Centre, some days just do it in one motion from one side to the other, enjoying the swinging motion.

Focuses on: On the twist in the neck, stomach and spine. It stimulates multiple Chakras—the Vishuddhi, the Manipura and the Swadhisthana.

Backward and Forward Bending: The benefits of backward and forward bending are manifold with this asana affecting the spine, the digestive system, the thyroid gland and all the lymph nodes in the body. This is even more relevant in the presentday due to the extensive usage of mobiles and computers, which leaves one in an unnatural position for long stretches of time. The opposing movements stretch and then compress the stomach and neck areas, thus stimulating all the digestive organs and the thyroid gland. The steps are as follows:

- Stand with legs together or just a few centimetres apart.
- Relax the whole body and feel your body weight distributed equally on both legs.
- Take a deep breath, lift both arms above your head and bend them behind and over the head as much as possible.
- Then exhale and drop your whole body slowly and bend forward with the hands reaching for your toes.
- Then inhale deeply and slowly raise your arms and straighten your body and finally bend back as much as possible.
- Then exhale and again bend forward to touch your toes. This makes one round. Do five rounds of this.

This asana is a combination of two asanas—first is backward bending and then gradually forward bending. The whole movement has to be done smoothly and slowly. You should avoid any abrupt or fast movement. Also, do not exert to touch the toes. Both backward and forward bending must be done according to your body's limits and without any discomfort or aches and pains.

Focuses on: On the cycle of inhalation and exhalation. On the spine and each vertebra as you bend backward and forward. On the alternate stretch and compression of your stomach area and the digestive organs as you bend both ways. Similarly, feel the opening and closing of the chest area, the rib cage and the lungs. Lastly on the neck area, thyroid gland as it gets regulated, massaged with the backward and forward bending.

Paschimottanasana (Spine stretching pose): As the name indicates, this asana massages and stimulates the entire spine. As you practise it, you will notice that it stretches the hamstring muscles, increases flexibility in the hip area and helps remove excess weight from the stomach area. It tones up the liver, pancreas, spleen, urogenital system, kidneys and adrenal glands. The steps are as follows:

- Sit on the mat with legs stretched out and hands resting on the knees or by the sides of the body. This is your base position. Relax your whole body.
- Take a deep breath and as you exhale, place the hands over your knees and start bending forward from the hips with your fingers reaching for your toes while your head moves towards the knees.
- Stretch as much as is comfortably possible and hold this position for a few seconds.
- Then inhale and come back to the base position. This makes one round. Do five rounds of this.

At first, you may not be able to touch your fingers to your toes nor your forehead to the knees. With practise, you will get there. Remember to relax the body and imagine the final position and then start bending forward.

Focuses on: On your back, stomach and hip area. On your breathing cycle. On the sweet pain all along the under side of the legs right up to the spine as all muscles and ligaments are stretched along the underside of the legs and all vertebrae are pulled in the spine. It activates the Swadhisthana Chakra.

Vajrasana: This asana can be practised at any time of the day and the only asana that be done after a meal. Sitting in this posture after a meal aid digestion. Until you reach the Chakra practises, this posture can be used for pranayama and mediation. As you advance, it is better to adopt any one of the three meditational postures mentioned earlier. It provides a therapeutic cure for lower back problems, hydrocele in men, menstrual problems in women, sciatica, acidity and peptic ulcers. The steps are as follows:

- Begin with kneeling on the mat, keeping the knees together.
- Bring the toes together and separate the heels.
- Slowly lower your buttocks on the heels so that they rest on the inside of the feet.
- The heels are much like a cushion for your buttocks. The back should be upright and whole body relaxed. Hands should be on the legs in Gyan or Chin Mudra.

Focuses on: It helps awaken Sushumna Nadi for our Kundalini practice. It also helps activate the Manipura Chakra.

Makrasana: This asana helps relieve lower back problems like sciatica or a slipped disc by relieving the pressure on the nerves between vertebrae. It alleviates asthma as it helps increase oxygen in the lungs. For asthma, the entire emphasis should be on the lung areas and slow, rhythmical breathing. One may or may not give emphasis to the movement of the legs. The steps are as follows:

- Lie down on your stomach with feet together and toes stretched out.
- Stretch your arms out and place your forehead or your chin on the floor. Relax your body in this position.
- Feel this relaxation spreading to all parts of your body, from the tips of the fingers to the tip of your toes.
- Then gently raise your head and cup your chin with your hands. You will feel a gentle pressure on your lower back.
- As you inhale, fold your right leg at the knee so that your heel touches your right buttock or at least move towards it as much as is comfortably possible.

- Exhale and straighten the knee and lower the leg to the ground.
- Do the same with the left leg and then with both legs together. This makes one round. Do five rounds of this.

Focuses on: On lower back and the curve of the spine. Spiritually on the Manipura Chakra.

Bhujangasana: This asana helps in strengthening the spine and making it supple. For treating all kinds of back problems, it is beneficial to introduce this asana after a few days of Makrasana practise. It helps in resolving all digestive and urogenital problems. It also resolves menstrual problems. The steps are as follows:

- Continue lying on your stomach with your forehead or chin on the floor, hands stretched out in front of you, toes together and also stretched out.
- Place your palms along the shoulder, a little away from the body while keeping the elbows close to your body and fingers pointing ahead. This is the starting position.
- Relax your whole body, take a deep breath, slowly raise your chin off the floor and begin to tilt your head backwards creating compression in the back of the neck while stretching it in the front.
- Simultaneously raise your body till your navel is just about two to three centimetres off the floor so that your spine is curved as much as possible.
- Hold the final position in inhalation as long as possible.
- Then as you exhale, come back to your starting position and relax your whole body. This makes one round. Do five rounds of this.
- As a progression, you must try to hold the final position in the beginning for ten seconds and then progress to holding it for one to five minutes. You may breathe normally in the final position.

Focuses on: On the curve of the spine and each vertebra. On the thyroid gland, and stretching of the neck area. This asana exerts pressure on the Swadhisthana Chakra. However, as an alternate practise, you can focus on each of the Chakras on the spine. When you reach your final Bhujangasana pose, then as you inhale and exhale, you move your awareness up and down the spine, stopping at each of the Chakras. As you inhale, you start with awareness on the Mooladhara Chakra, then moving up to focus on the Manipura to Anahata to Vishuddhi to Ajna. And then as you exhale, move your awareness from the Ajna to the Mooladhara Chakra with awareness of each of the Chakras in between.

Asanas Lying Down on the Back

Body Twisting Asana (Supta Udarkarshasana): As you do this practise, you can feel the various parts of the body and the organs in those parts getting massaged and regulated. It alleviates constipation and other digestive problems. It's a must for the present-day sedentary lifestyle. It helps remove stiffness in the different body parts caused due to prolonged sitting. All twisting asanas regulate the pancreas and are used for managing diabetes. The steps are as follows:

- Lie down on your back, keeping the spine and the head in a straight line. Relax your whole body.
- Fold your knees and bring your heels as close to the hips as possible, keeping your feet flat on the floor.
- Your knees and feet are together throughout the practise. Interlock your fingers and place the hands under your head resting on your palms and elbows touching the floor.
- Inhale deeply and as you exhale, drop your knees to the right towards the floor and turn your head to the left, exerting a full body twist.
- The arms and elbows remain flat on the floor.

- Hold in exhalation as long as possible and as you inhale, come to the starting pose at the centre.
- Repeat the same on the left side of the body. Both sides make one round. Do five rounds of this.

Focuses on: On the twist in the body along the spine, in the stomach area and the throat area. It stimulates the Manipura Chakra.

Leg Raising Pose: It influences the digestive system and helps prevent prolapse. Good for toning up stomach muscles. The steps are as follows:

- Lie down on your back with your spine and head in a straight line.
- Keep the whole body relaxed and your hands by the side of your body with palms turned upwards.
- Relax your shoulders and arms and keep them like this throughout the practise. You are not supposed to take support of your upper body and your arms for raising your legs. Let your stomach muscles do the work.
- Inhale deeply and as you exhale, lift your right leg up, keeping the knee straight. Lift as high as you can without any discomfort or pain.
- The final position is to hold the leg perpendicular to your body. Hold this position for as long as you can, then as you inhale, slowly lower the leg, keeping it straight. Do not make any fast or jerky movements.
- Relax your whole body, then repeat the same with the left leg.
- Finally, repeat the same with both legs together. This makes one round. Do five rounds of this.

Focuses on: It must be on your stomach muscles. Feel them tighten as they take the entire weight of lifting your legs. Awareness on the Manipura Chakra.

Pawan Muktasana: As the name suggests, this asana will mainly help you get rid of flatulence, gas and constipation. It loosens the vertebrae and strengthens the lower back. The steps are as follows:

- Lie down on your back with your head aligned with the back. Relax your whole body. Keep your arms by the side of your body.
- Inhale deeply and lift your right leg straight up at ninety degrees to the body while keeping the knee straight. The left leg remains flat on the ground.
- Then exhale and fold your right knee, clasp your knee with both hands, lift your head and try to touch your nose to your knee.
- Hold in exhalation for as long as you can, then slowly lower your head to the floor, raise the leg to ninety degrees and then slowly lower it back to the floor.
- Repeat the same with left leg and then both legs together. Do three to five rounds of this.

Focuses on: Awareness must be on the stomach area, the back and the pelvic area.

Dynamic Halasana: It is a suitable preparation practice for beginners who cannot get to Sarvangasana, the inverted body pose or Halasana, the plough pose. The steps are as follows:

- Lie down on the mat with your legs stretched out and arms by the side of your body. Inhale and take the arms over your head behind your head until they are straight and resting flat on the floor with palms facing upward.
- Then with a push of the arms, sit up so that in one movement your hands reach for your toes, head moves towards the knees.
- Then holding your toes, with a swing, roll over back on your spine so that your toes are now touching the floor behind your head with you continuing to hold the toes.

- Then almost instantly, give a push and with the same rolling movement swing back to the sitting position with head near the knees and hands holding the toes.
- Thus, you keep rolling forward and backward on the spine for five to seven rounds.

Be careful and in the beginning, do as many back-and-forth swinging movements as possible. Initially, don't force your hands to hold the toes or the head to move towards the knees. Do whatever is possible. I've given what you have to finally target. In the beginning, if you cannot come up to the sitting position, then start with sitting up with hands towards your toes and roll back on your spine and with the momentum roll back to sitting position.

Focuses on: On your spine with full enjoyment of this motion.

Shavasana: I have also given a sample practise at the end of Section VII.

Asana practise must always end with minimum 3-5 minutes of Shavasana before you move on to Pranayama.

Pranayama Practise

Kapalbhati Pranayama: It massages the abdominal area and activates and revitalizes the digestive system. It helps still the mind, cleanse the Nadis and brings balance between the Ida and the Pingala Nadis. It is prescribed for asthma as it helps clean up blockages right up to the alveoli in the inferior lobes. It overall brings about alertness and improves mental capacity as it charges the frontal lobe. This practise involves emphasis on forceful exhalation. The steps are as follows:

- Sit comfortably in any of the meditational poses (already described in the previous section in this chapter).

- Close your eyes and watch your natural breathing for a few rounds. Your head and spine must be in a straight line. Keep your face and the rest of your body relaxed.
- Close your eyes and exhale forcefully through both nostrils simultaneously. The stomach will be drawn in with the contraction of the stomach muscles.
- The next forceful exhale must follow immediately, giving barely any space for inhalation as such. In this way, you do rapid exhalation.
- After a fixed number of rounds, watch your normal breath and feel the effect of your Kapalbhati practice.
- Then start the next round. As you get proficient, you may sometimes feel like there is no breath left after doing say, fifty rounds of Kapalbhati.

Initially, you can start slowly and build it up to rapid exhalation. Start with ten rounds and build the practise up to twenty, then thirty and finally fifty rounds. On a good day, you may even do up to 100 rounds, especially before you start your Kundalini Kriya practices of Stage IV.

Focuses on: On your breath around the nostrils and the stomach and facial muscles, which must remain relaxed. You should not contort your face or knit your eyebrows. As you become proficient, awareness must be on the frontal lobe as Kapalbhati, as the name indicates, is for charging the frontal lobe. In between each round of Kapalbhati, you must pause and observe your breath and feel the effects of your practise on your whole body, especially your breath. It will become subtle and very thin and sometimes it may disappear, making you experience calm and stillness.

Awareness may be on the Ajna Chakra at the centre of the eyebrows.

Bhastrika: This pranayama is beneficial for your physical, mental and psychic states. Besides affecting the respiratory and digestive organs, it creates heat, which activates the metabolic rate and helps flush out toxins and waste matter. It also brings the *kapha, vata, pitta (phlegm, wind, bile)* in balance. It helps induce tranquillity and increases concentration, which are crucial for inducing meditative states. In this pranayama, you inhale and exhale forcefully in rapid succession. The steps are as follows:

- Sit comfortably in your preferred position. Your spine and head must be in a straight line. Keep your whole body relaxed.
- Watch your breath for a few rounds and centre your mind on your breath.
- Start with forceful exhalation, as in Kapalbhati, and immediately follow it up with a forceful inhale.
- Continue this practise of forceful exhalation followed by forceful inhalation for a few rounds.

Concomitant with this exercise will be the movement of your stomach, diaphragm and chest area. With every exhalation, the stomach muscles will pull the stomach in; the diaphragm will move up, squeezing the lungs. As you inhale, the stomach muscles will push the stomach out; the diaphragm will move down, giving space for the lungs to expand to the fullest.

Start with ten rounds and build it up to fifty or even 100 as per your own personal preferences. Like in the practice of Kapalbhati, you rest between each round and observe your normal breath and the effects of the practise on the state of your breath, and mind as well as your whole being. Often people take in their stomach on inhalation and expand it on exhalation. This is wrong breathing and over a period can result in health problems. Bhastrika helps in correcting this defect.

Focuses on: Same as Kapalbhati. Keep the cycle of breathing rhythmical with inhalation and exhalation being equal in proportion. Awareness can be on the Manipura Chakra.

Anulom Vilom: The benefits of this pranayama are manifold. Breath is the umbilical cord that connects you to the source of your creation. With Anulom Vilom, you can hold this cord by which you will slowly ascend to the dimensions of a higher world. This is the most important aspect of this pranayama as you start on Kumbhak practice.

It is also a practice that balances the Ida and Pingala Nadis. This makes you aware of the changing patterns of the breath that flows through the nostrils according to the phases of the moon or changes in your diet, sleeping patterns and lifestyle. Be sure that the amount of awareness you bring into this practice will determine the speed with which you move closer to your Kundalini practice.

This pranayama must follow the earlier two pranayamas. Through the practice of Kapalbhati and Bhastrika, you awaken and rejuvenate your whole body as well as the nervous system and the brain. Through Anulom Vilom, you assimilate and distribute this awakened energy throughout your whole body-brain system and get it in balance. Most importantly, this pranayama gets your Ida and Pingala, the sympathetic and parasympathetic systems, in balance so that the Sushumna Nadi becomes active for Kundalini to pass through it as it ascends each Chakra.

- Sit in any of the meditational postures with the body erect but relaxed. Close your eyes. Observe your normal breathing.
- Then take your right hand towards your nostrils. Place the middle and forefinger at the eyebrow centre, use the ring finger to close the left nostril and the thumb to close the right one. Keep the left hand in Gyan or Chin mudra.
- Close your right nostril and breathe in through the left nostril as deeply as possible without straining, making a loud sound or pulling up your body. The inhalation should happen inside the left nostril.
- When you have reached your maximum capacity, close the left nostril and slowly breathe out through the right nostril.

- When you have exhaled completely, inhale through the right nostril and exhale through the left. This makes one round. Do five to seven rounds of this.

As you advance in the practice, you can count the seconds as you inhale and exhale so that you know how much time it takes you to do both. Initially, it is good to keep equal balance between the two. As beginners, you may comfortably start with anything between six to fifteen rounds of this practise. The effort should be that before moving on to Stage II, you should be able to do twenty-four counts/seconds inhale and twenty-four counts/seconds exhale. This will help you in moving into Kumbhak, the breath retention practise, in the next stage.

In the second stage of practice, Kumbhak or breath retention will be introduced in the Anulom Vilom practice.

Focuses on: This is a subtle practice. Awareness must be continuously inside both nostrils, on the flow and every other aspect of the breath. Observe if it is rhythmical, fast or slow, sharp or soft, cool or warm. Observe days when your mind is distracted does it shorten the inhale and exhale and when mind is focused does it result in deeper and longer breaths.

Ujjayi Pranayama: This is a simple pranayama which calms the mind and is beneficial in managing blood pressure. It is yet again a pointer towards how the yogis, through experiential and intuitive knowledge, controlled the various systems of the body.

There are carotid sinuses on both sides of the main artery in the throat through which blood flows from the heart to the brain. These sinuses regulate the blood flow and pressure. Whenever there is a fall or rise in the blood pressure, these carotid sinuses send a message to the brain to increase or decrease the blood pressure. The brain reacts by increasing or decreasing the heartbeats and narrowing or dilating the arterioles to manage the blood pressure. This pranayama is practised with Khechari Mudra for greater impact and benefits of

Ujjai pranayama. Ujjai may be performed in any position, sitting, standing or lying down in Shavasana. Sustained Ujjai in shavasana is a good antidote for insomnia.

The steps are as follows:

- Sit in a meditational pose with body relaxed and awareness on the rhythmical flow of your breath.
- Then consciously make your breath deep and slow.
- After a few rounds, slightly contract your glottis so that you can hear your own breathing like gentle snoring and feel the breath inside your throat area and not inside your nostrils.
- Apply compression on the throat area just enough to put mild pressure on these sinuses.

Mudras

Ashwini Mudra: This practice prevents and cures incontinence. It's a good preparatory practice for Kundalini as it redirects energy from the Mooladhara to the higher Chakras. It activates this base Chakra. Ashwin means horse in Sanskrit. This practice takes inspiration from a horse's compulsive contraction of its anal region. The steps are as follows:

- Sit comfortably in any meditational pose, leaving your whole body loose and relaxed. Gently close your eyes.
- Observe your normal, natural breathing for a few rounds.
- Then shift your awareness to your anus.
- Alternately contract and relax the anal muscles in a continuous rhythmic manner.
- At first, it may be difficult to get into a rhythm. With practice, you will be able to do ten to twenty counts in one go. Practise three rounds of twenty counts each.

Focuses on: On the Mooladhara Chakra.

Shambhavi Mudra: This is a powerful mudra which will be incorporated with several other practises like pranayama, mantra, dharna and dhyana. This practice will stay with you till the end of your Kundalini journey. When Paramhansa Yogananda left his body, his eyes were hitched on to the eyebrow centre in Shambhavi mudra. He was speaking at the conclusion of a banquet in Los Angeles in the presence of Indian Ambassador Bina Ranjan Sen and other dignitaries. It is a known fact that his body remained without any signs of decay for three weeks after his death. This was attested by those working on the embalming process, who called it an unparalleled phenomenon in the history of mortuary science.

The practice of Shambhavi mudra benefits the body in a number of ways. It makes the nerves and muscles around the eyes stronger. It awakens the Ajna Chakra, which activates the pituitary and pineal glands.

It gets you into a meditative state almost instantaneously. The eyes are the primary source of distraction for the mind; when they are locked in Shambhavi mudra, your mind becomes still and calm.

Shambhavi mudra is focusing with open or closed eyes at the eyebrow centre. The mind is ever following the eyes. It goes where they go. As the eyes focus on the eyebrow centre, so does the mind. Shambhavi mudra brings about one-pointed concentration. It is one step away from meditation. Sustained practise leads to dharana (concentration) and sustained dharana leads to dhyana, that is, meditation. The steps are as follows:

- Sit in any meditational pose. Relax the whole body and keep the spine erect.
- Ensure that your whole face is relaxed along with the eyes and all the nerves around them.
- Close your eyes and watch your breath for a few rounds to get yourself centred.
- Then open your eyes and gaze at some point ahead.
- Slowly raise your gaze to your eyebrow centre.

- Though your eyes are open, you are actually looking inward at the center of your eyebrow.
- Hold for a few seconds and then slowly release the Shambhavi mudra.
- Close your eyes and relax them. Become aware of the state of your mind and gaze at the darkness before your closed eyes. You may see patterns, colours or images; whatever you see before your closed eyes, just watch it. You are now trying to open and see through what is known the Third Eye.
- As you sit in a meditational pose later, you will visualize your chosen symbol for concentration and meditation in the same spot.

The space at the eyebrow centre is known as your Chidakasha, your psychic space. Shambhavi mudra achieves the twin objectives of shutting down your lesser eyes to open up your Third Eye, so that you can see what manifests in your Chidakasha, the sky beyond your sky.

After some days of practising simply gazing at the eyebrow centre, you must synchronize your breath with your practise. Inhale and raise your gaze to the eyebrow centre. Hold the gaze and the inhalation in a relaxed way. Then as you exhale, release your Shambhavi mudra. Throughout the practise of this mudra do not strain the eyes. If there is any discomfort, just release your mudra and relax. Do not forge the practise against the feedback of pain and strain from your eyes. The goal of this exercise is to awaken your third eye without causing a retinal detachment.

Focuses on: On the Ajna Chakra.

Bandhas

All Bandha practises are meant to increase awareness. The yogis and rishis of yore discovered these practices to sharpen our awareness and concentration.

Mool Bandha: The steps are as follows:

- Sit in any meditative pose. Your back should be straight and the body completely relaxed.
- Close your eyes and watch your breath for a few rounds.
- Then take your awareness to your Mooladhara Chakra. Maintaining awareness there, inhale and contract the area around the Mooladhara Chakra.
- In the beginning, the anal and vaginal muscles will also contract. But with practise, you will be able to contract just the Mooladhara area. Hold the contraction for a bit and then release your Bandha.
- Relax the perineal area. You can do alternate contraction and relaxation and vary it with holding the bandha for extended periods of time.

Focuses on: This practice requires full and complete awareness on the Mooladhara Chakra. Besides activating the Chakra, it manipulates the Apna Vayu. The Apana Vayu's normal downward flow is made to turn upward. This helps in the advanced practises of uniting Apana with Prana Vayu and ultimately uniting both with the Samana Vayu at the Manipura Chakra.

Jalandhara Bandha: The steps are as follows:

- Sit comfortably in any of the meditational poses.
- Place your palms flat on the knees and straighten the elbows so that the knees are pressed flat against the floor.
- Take a deep breath, then simultaneously raise your shoulders up and forward and exert full pressure on the knees.
- Drop your chin to your chest and lock the inhalation inside the body. Hold for as long as possible, without strain or discomfort.
- When you feel like exhaling, relax the shoulders, then the arms and release the chin lock.

- Relax your whole body and observe the effects of your practice on your breath and body. Jalandhara bandha can be practised with external breath retention too. Do five rounds of this.

Focuses on: Physiologically, it stimulates the thyroid gland, which helps activate and regulate metabolism. Like all bandhas, this helps relieve tension, anxiety and anger, and makes the mind calm and quiet. It also helps in regulating blood circulation. The carotid sinus in the throat area, which controls the heart rate and blood pressure, is stimulated by the chin lock.

Spiritually, Jalandhara Bandha, as its name indicates, helps hold the Amrut which flows from the Bindu Visarga, at the Vishuddhi Chakra and prevents it from flowing down.

Uddiyana Bandha: The steps are as follows:

- Sit in any meditational pose with the spine erect and the body completely relaxed. Place your palms flat on the knees.
- Take a deep breath and then exhale completely.
- Push your hands on the knees, straighten your elbows and pull up the shoulders so that the spine is further stretched.
- Then lock your chin against the chest (Jalandhara bandha).
- Maintaining external breath retention, pull in your stomach and diaphragm and hold this position. This will create a cavity in the abdominal area.
- Hold for as long as you can without inhaling.
- When you feel like releasing the lock, inhale slowly, bend the elbows, lower your hitched shoulders and release the stomach lock.
- Relax for a bit and then start the next round. Do five rounds of this.

Focuses on: The Uddiyana Bandha activates all the digestive organs and the adrenal gland. Besides removing problems relating to the stomach, liver, pancreas and intestines, the regulation of the adrenal gland activates you and releases anxiety and tension.

This Bandha marks a milestone in our practice as it pushes the Prana Vayu down, pulls up the Apana Vayu so that both unite with Samana at the Manipura Chakra. From here on, through the Mahabandha and other practises, these three vayus move further up to the Vishuddhi and the Ajna Chakras. The Bandha activates the Manipura Chakra.

Mahabandha: The word Mahabandha means great lock. Mahabandha is a multi-dimensional practice; through its practise we can benefit from the effects of the three Bandhas simultaneously. It stimulates the pituitary and pineal glands that regulate the endocrine system. Its impact can be felt up to the cellular level and it arrests the aging process. It awakens the Vishuddhi, the Anahata and the Mooladhara Chakras. It unites the three vayus, Apana, Samana and Prana at the Manipura Chakra which is the prime motive for the practice of pranayama in conjunction with the three bandhas. Spiritually, it opens up the three locks: Brahma Granthi at the Mooladhara, Vishnu Granthi at the Anahata and Rudra Granthi at the Vishuddhi Chakra. The steps are as follows:

- Sit in any of the meditational poses. Keep the back straight and whole body relaxed.
- Close your eyes and stabilize yourself with simple breath awareness.
- Keeping the eyes closed, inhale deeply and then exhale completely.
- Simultaneously, lock your palms against the knees, hunch your shoulders and perform Jalandhara bandha first, followed by Uddiyana and finally Mool bandha.
- Hold for as long as possible without straining yourself.
- When you want to inhale and release the three locks, start with releasing Mool, then Uddiyana and finally Jalandhara.
- Relax and become aware of the state of your being, mental, physical, emotional, with eyes closed. Generally, a pleasant state of no-thought and expansiveness is achieved.

- Mahabandha is practised in conjunction with pranayama as you progress in your practice.

Focuses on: Awareness is on the three knots, the Granthis at the Mooladhara, the Anahata and the Vishuddhi Chakras.

Mantra Practice

Om chanting with Ajna Chakra awareness: The steps are as follows:

- Sit comfortably in your preferred meditational pose with the body straight but relaxed. Close your eyes.
- Internally take your awareness to the eyebrow centre and watch the space at the eyebrow centre. Do not strain your eyes.
- Inhale, and as you exhale, chant the mantra Om flowing from the first syllable A to O to M in one rhythmic flow, visualising your chosen symbol at the eyebrow centre.
- Continue to repeat this with full feeling and emotion.
- To begin with, you can chant eleven times, then increase it to twenty-seven, then fifty-four and finally to 108. You can increase this as you progress into the later stages too. Progress can be gradual. You may choose any other mantra depending on your religious faith.

So-Hum mantra with Nasikadrishti: The steps are as follows:

- Begin as above. Take your awareness to your nostrils.
- Watch the nose tip as you exhale and inhale. Do not miss even a single breath.
- Then as you inhale normally, internal silently, say the mantra 'So' and with every exhale, 'Hum'.
- Start with eleven rounds and gradually build it to twenty-seven, then fifty-four and finally to 108.

- As mentioned earlier, progress can be gradual. No stress of targets in your practise.

For both of these mantras, awareness must be on feeling the vibrations of the mantra in your entire mind-body frame, down to the cellular level. You may feel the vibrations entering you as cosmic energy and then going right down to your cellular level. At other times, you may feel the vibrations from your cellular framework going out through your body to the cosmic framework around you.

Bhramari Pranayama: It calms the mind and is good practise for inducing sleep. It activates the vagus nerves and helps all the functions of the body, which are controlled by vagus nerve, namely, digestives, respiratory and immune system.

Through this pranayama you create a humming sound in your head and which is why it is called Bhramari, which means 'humming like a bee'. The steps are as follows:

- Sit in any meditational pose. Relax your body while keeping the spine and head in a straight line. Close your eyes and watch your normal breath for a few seconds.
- Using your forefingers, plug both ears.
- Take a deep inhalation and as you exhale say Om, keeping the first two syllables, A and O, short and extending the last syllable M as long as you can exhale to create a humming sound in your head.
- The sound should be continuous, smooth and neither too soft nor too loud. This is one round. Do five to seven rounds of this.

Focuses on: Keep awareness inside the head and on the frontal lobe. You may end your daily yoga practise with this. It can also be done before going to bed as it helps alleviate sleeplessness.

Invocation for Ending the Practise

The steps are as follows:

- Continue to sit in the meditational pose. Watch your breathing and remain centred within yourself. Remember your Gurus and the Supreme and express your gratitude for their grace and blessings.
- Inhale deeply and chant Om three times.
- Rub your palms and palm your eyes three times.

This is the practice for beginners. You may practise it for fifteen days to a month. Measure your progress to decide for yourself when you will be ready to move on to the next stage.

2

STAGE II

Practise for Beginners—90 minutes

Needless to say, you must begin the practise with the same invocation as the one used at the beginning of Stage I. You should also be getting comfortable with sitting in one of the three meditational poses described earlier.

Start this stage with the Sukshma Vyayama or the body limbering up practise detailed in Stage I.

Practise for the Spine

You are the best judge of which of the asanas for the spine you need to keep doing. Some of the asanas in Stage II will also affect your back, along with providing other benefits. You can continue to practise some of the asanas from Stage I.

Advanced asanas

Yoga mudra asana: It makes the spine flexible and relieves pressure from the nerves between each vertebra. The heels press against the lower and mid-section of the stomach, thus massaging and regulating the lower and upper digestive systems. It relieves constipation.

Constipation is not just a physiological problem; it is often a manifestation of some mental or emotional problem. These problems can also manifest as acidity or ulcers. The removal of this physical manifestation also helps in removing the source of the problem; not fully, but in some measure. The steps are as follows:

- Begin in Padmasana. Relax your whole body by watching your natural breathing. Imagine your body relaxing with every inhalation; with every exhalation, all the stress and tension is flowing out of your body.
- Take both hands at the back and grasp one wrist with the other hand. Keep the body erect and relaxed. Relax your hands behind your back.
- Take a deep breath and as you exhale, slowly bend from the hips until your forehead is resting on the floor. Hold this position for a few seconds.
- Then inhale and come back to your starting position.
- Throughout the practise keep awareness on the spine and on each vertebra as you bend forward and rise back to the sitting position.
- Initially, it will be difficult for the mind to remain focused on the spine; your thoughts will try to distract you and interfere in the practise.
- Just be aware of this and gently bring awareness back to the spine. This is one round. Do five to seven rounds of this.

After a week of daily practise, you must do this same practise with awareness on the six Chakras along the spine, from the Mooladhara to the Ajna Chakra as you bend forward, feeling the exhalation passing through each Chakra and from the Ajna to the Mooladhara as you come up, feeling the inhalation flowing through the Chakras. The flow of awareness along the spine is smooth, with just a split second spent on each Chakra.

Focuses on: Awareness must be on the spine and on Manipura Chakra before you start the awareness on all the six Chakras from Mooladhara to Ajna.

Matsyasana: This is a counter-pose to the Yoga mudra asana. It affects the abdominal area and helps alleviate digestive problems. It removes constipation, especially if done after drinking two to three glasses of water. It removes the problem of piles. It also regulates the endocrine system, activates the thyroid and thymus glands and boosts immunity. The steps are as follows:

- Continue to sit in Padmasana. Relax your whole body.
- Drop your elbows to the ground behind you.
- Slowly bend back and support yourself with your elbows and arms.
- Lift the torso a little and slowly drop the crown of your head to the floor.
- In the final position, hold the toes with your hands. Ensure that your head rests in such a way that you are able to arch your spine to the maximum.
- Stay in this final position for as long as you can hold the inhalation. You could also hold the final position while breathing in and out.
- Then slowly, with the help of the arms, lift your body and come back to the starting position.
- Alternately, after resting the head on the floor behind you, place your hands under the thighs; with this support of the arms, lift the head and let it dangle behind you. This ensures maximum arch of the back and complete stretching of the neck and stomach area and opening up of the chest area.

Focuses on: Awareness has to be maintained on the various parts of the body this asana impacts in each round. Do five rounds of this practise. Keep awareness on the Manipura, Vishuddhi and Swadhisthana Chakra.

Ushtrasana: This backward bending asana is a counter pose to any forward bending asana like Shashank asana or Paschimmoattansana. This asana helps correct defects in posture and rounded shoulders. It helps alleviate asthma because of the full opening up of the chest and lungs. The steps are as follows:

- Begin by sitting in Vajrasana. Come up on your knees with hands dangling by the sides of the body. Balance the body and relax.
- Inhale deeply and move your left hand towards your left heel and let it rest there.
- Then take your right arm over your head and stretch it behind you as much as possible. Also throw your head back as much as possible.
- The left hand is like a prop for the whole body.
- Bend back as much as you can without experiencing discomfort or pain or losing your balance.
- Hold this position in inhalation for as long as possible and then as you exhale, come back to the upright sitting position.
- Repeat the same with the right hand resting on the right heel, the left hand raised up and back as much as possible and the head thrown back.
- Finally, repeat the same with both hands resting on the heels and the full body stretched back with the head thrown back. This makes one round. Do five to seven rounds of this.

Focuses on: On your breathing, on the arch both on the back and front of the body, right from the fingertips and arms to the torso and feel all the organs in the body being massaged with the alternate stretching and contraction of the body. Awareness should also be on the arch of the spine. Awareness, as for all asanas with multi-dimensional benefits, must be on the different parts that are impacted in every round, like the spine, the stomach and neck areas. This activates the Swadhisthana Chakra.

Shashank Bhujang Asana: This asana is a combination of two asanas, Shashank asana and bhujangasana. It combines the benefits derived from Shashank asana and bhujansana.

- Begin with sitting in Vajrasana as described in Stage I. Relax and ensure that the spine is straight.
- Inhale deeply and stretch your arms over your head with elbows and fingers straight and palms facing in the front.
- Exhale and lower your hands to the floor, with palms flat and the arms straight so that both the arms and the head touch the floor simultaneously.
- The head must rest a little before the knees on the floor. Relax in Shashank asana for a few seconds.
- Then begins the second part of the asana, that is, Bhujangasana.
- Inhale and slide your body along the floor, like a gliding snake, putting the full body weight on the arms, come up in bhujangasana.
- Straighten your legs and arms and arch your back fully. The body may lift off from the navel and some more.
- Then slowly slide back to Shashank asana by lowering the front of the body and finally slide back to sit in vajrasana.

Focuses on: On the breathing rhythm. On the smooth transition from one asana to the other without any jerky movements or losing balance. Attention on the Swadhisthana Chakra.

Dhanurasana (Bow Pose): The dhanurasana is one of the best asanas for the back, the digestive system and the reproductive organs. It regulates the liver, pancreas and kidneys. It releases stiffness in the back and alleviates cervical problems. It releases tension, stress and tightness accumulated in the back, neck, stomach and urogenital area. This is a huge benefit as stress and tension in the body are not only the primary cause of disease but also block the flow of pranic energy in the body and obstruct the rise of Kundalini energy. It also strengthens the arms and legs. The steps are as follows:

- Lie down on your stomach with your chin on the floor and arms by the sides of the body. Relax your whole body.
- Fold your legs so that you can hold both ankles with your hands. This is the starting position.
- Take a deep breath and lift your thighs and chest off the floor forming an arch with the back.
- In the final position, your head is tilted back, the arms are straight, and the body is resting on the stomach.
- Relax in this position and hold your breath.
- When you want to exhale, release and come back to the starting position.
- You may breathe in and out in the final position if you are comfortable in it, without experiencing any discomfort or strain. This makes one round. Do five to seven rounds of this.

Focuses on: Awareness on the Manipura Chakra.

Shav Udarkarshasana: It relieves tightness and tension in the body. It particularly helps in toning up the pelvic and abdominal areas. The steps are as follows:

- Lie down on your back. Relax your whole body.
- Stretch the arms out, keeping them level with the shoulders. This is the starting position.
- Take a deep breath, fold your right leg and place the right foot flat next to the left knee and place your left hand on the right knee. Relax in this position.
- Then exhale completely and slowly twist your body and pull the right knee close to the floor with your left hand while turning

your head and upper body to the right, looking at the middle finger of your right hand.

- The left leg and the right arm should remain straight and flat on the floor. Hold the final position for a few seconds, inhale and return to the starting position.
- Repeat the same by twisting the body to the right side with the right leg straight and the left foot next to the right knee. Doing both sides makes one round. Do five rounds of this.

Focuses on: On the twist in the spine. On the stretch in the underarms and along the whole arm that is stretched out. On the twisting of the neck, spine and stomach area. Emphasis on the Manipura Chakra.

Sarvangasana: This is an inverted pose. Those who have practised the Dynamic Halasana in Stage I will find it easy to get into the Sarvangasana pose.

Sarvangasana, being an inverted pose, benefits the body in several ways. It improves blood circulation in the legs, which rejuvenates the heart and the brain. It prevents prolapse and releases the gravitational pressure around the anal and genital areas, which is beneficial for the reproductive organs. It also rejuvenates the digestive, endocrine and respiratory systems as well as the thyroid and parathyroid glands. It induces relaxation in the nervous system and has a tranquilizing effect on the mind. It helps reduce emotional stress and tension. All of this helps in building up the immune system. Moreover, it helps the ENT area by stimulating the eyes, ears and the throat, which improves eyesight and alleviates ear problems. The steps are as follows:

- Lie down on the mat with your head and spine in a straight line.
- Keep your arms by the sides of the body, palms facing down and legs together and straight. Leave the whole body loose and relaxed.

- Inhale and contract your stomach muscles and raise both legs together until they are perpendicular to the body. Relax and use your arms to lift your torso with the spine rolling off the floor.
- Once the whole body is vertical, bend your arms at the elbow and place your palms under the back of the chest to support the whole body. The chin will be pressed against the chest in the final position by raising the chest by a little.
- Relax your legs, feet, toes and the whole body and remain in the final position for as long as you can.

Focuses on: On the smooth movement of the body. On the effects of the inverted position, on the reverse flow of circulation to the head and heart. On the Vishuddhi Chakra.

Halasana: This asana is best done either in conjunction with Sarvangasana or independently. This asana has multi-pronged benefits as it impacts the endocrine and digestive systems, thyroid gland, spleen, pancreas, liver and kidneys. It relieves constipation, dyspepsia and increases insulin production. It regulates the endocrine system and boosts immunity. It massages the muscles along the spine while stretching it. Finally, it regulates the thyroid gland, thus balancing the metabolic rate. The steps are as follows:

- Lie down on the mat with your whole body in a straight line. Keep your feet together and the body relaxed. Palms are flat on the floor by the sides.
- Inhale and tighten your stomach muscles.
- As you exhale, slowly raise your legs until they are perpendicular to the body.
- Then, with the support of the arms pressed against the floor, lift your buttocks off the floor and roll off the spine as if raising it vertebra by vertebra off the floor.
- Lower your legs over the head and try to lower your toes to the floor behind your head. Keep your arms flat on the floor with

palms facing down. This is the final position. Hold it as long as you can. You can breathe normally in the final position.

- To return to the original position, support the back as you straighten your legs and slowly roll down the back and then the legs.
- Relax for some time and feel the effects of your practise.

Focuses on: Your awareness must be on doing the exercise correctly because you may end up hurting your back if you make a wrong move. Awareness on the Vishuddhi Chakra.

Chakrasana: To get into this pose, it helps to first imagine yourself doing it. This is because there is a certain fear associated with this pose. In Chakrasana, your torso is fully arched which affects the front as well as the back of the body. The entire spinal column is curved which stimulates each vertebra. From the neck to the pelvic area, the digestive, respiratory, cardiovascular and glandular systems are regulated. It also strengthens the arms and legs. The steps are as follows:

- Lie down on your back.
- Fold your legs and bring your feet close to your buttocks. The legs should be at least thirty centimetres apart. Place the palms flat on the floor behind the head with fingers pointing towards the body. This is the starting position. Relax the whole body.
- Inhale and lift your body into an arch so that it is resting on the head.
- Then slowly straighten both arms and legs and lift your body and head off the floor to form a semi-circle. This is the final position.
- Rest in this position as long as it is possible. Some may skip placing head on the floor, instead with a push just raise your whole body with the legs and arms straightening up and the whole body making an arch.

- Then slowly lower your whole body and return to the starting position. Practise three rounds of this.

Focuses on: On the spine. On the Manipura Chakra.

Follow up these asanas with the '2 T's 1K'—Tadasana and Triyak Tadasana, and lastly Kati Chakrasana described in Stage I.

Suryanamaskar

Suryanamaskar is a full body practise, intense but necessary to prepare the body, mind and nervous system and to open up the energy flow in the whole body. It consists of twelve poses in half a round; repeating these twelve poses makes up one round. It is spiritually likened to offering prayers to the Sun God and invoking the energy and brilliance of the Sun within.

Starting pose: Stand with the feet together and the hands by the sides of the body. Close your eyes and feel the weight of the body evenly distributed between the two legs. Take your awareness through the body, relaxing each part as you run your awareness from the top of the head to the soles of the feet. Take your awareness to your heart or eyebrow centre and visualize a golden rising sun. This is the starting position. Beginners may keep their eyes open and slowly progress towards keeping their eyes closed throughout the practise with awareness at the heart or eyebrow centre.

Pose 1: Prayer pose—Pranam asana: Stand upright with your feet together. Keep the body relaxed. Close your eyes and join your palms together in front of the chest. Take awareness either to the eyebrow centre or the heart and visualize a beautiful golden rising sun. Mentally offer salutations to the sun within you. This is the first of the twelve poses of half a round of Suryanamaskar.

Focuses on: On the Anahata Chakra. On balance on both feet.

Pose 2: Backward bending—Hasta Uthanasana: The prayer pose flows smoothly into the next pose. Separate your hands and as you inhale deeply, raise them over your head, keeping them shoulder-width apart. Throw your head and upper torso back as much as possible and feel the front of your body stretch, your lungs open up and the spine slightly bend backwards.

Focuses on: On the Vishuddhi Chakra.

Pose 3: Forward Bending—Padahastasana: From the second pose, flow into forward bending by exhaling completely and bending from the hips, dropping your arms so that you can touch the toes or flatten the palms on the floor beside the feet. Do not strain. If in the beginning you are unable to achieve the final position, do not stress or force the body. With practise, you will be able to get to the final position.

Focuses on: On the Swadhisthana Chakra. Feel the flow of blood rushing to the head.

Pose 4: Horse riding pose—Ashwasanchalan: To flow into the next pose, inhale deeply, bend your knees, place both palms flat on the floor beside the feet, stretch your right leg behind you so that the knee rests on the floor and the toes are erect. The left leg remains in the same position with the feet flat on the floor and bent at the knee. The arms do not move and remain straight. Throw your head slightly towards the back to stretch the neck.

Focuses on: On the Ajna Chakra. On your thyroid gland, on the opening up of the chest area, on the stretch along the thigh of the right leg.

Pose 5: Mountain pose—Parvat Asana: To flow into the next pose, exhale slowly and then take your left leg back to join it with your right leg with the feet flattened on the floor. Straighten your arms without moving them, push your hips back as much as you can and dangle the head between the arms. Your body will be in a V shape, just like a mountain.

Focuses on: On the Vishuddhi Chakra. Feel the body stretch from your heels to the arms.

Pose 6: Ashtanga Namaskar: Ashtanga means eight body parts. This pose literally means doing Namaskar with eight points of your body touching the floor. You slide into this pose from the Mountain pose by exhaling and moving your body into a plank pose so that your whole body rests on your arms and toes. Then slowly drop your body so that first your chin, then the chest and finally the knees rest on the floor one after the other. Stay in this position as long as it is comfortable. You exhale in both the Mountain and the Ashtanga pose.

Focuses on: On the Manipura Chakra. On exhalation, the curve of the lower back and on the stomach region.

Pose 7: Cobra pose—Bhujangasana: From the Ashtanga Namaskar pose, you get into the cobra pose by first inhaling, then keeping your hands and feet fixed, slowly raise the upper part of your body and throw your head back. Raise and bend your body backwards until your arms are straight. Initially, because of stiffness in the back, some of you may not be able to straighten the elbows and arch the back fully. In such a case, you can bend the elbows.

Focuses on: On the Swadhisthana Chakra. On the arching of the lower back. On the stretching in the front of the body, massaging all the digestive organs, opening up the lungs and stretching the thyroid gland.

Pose 8: Mountain pose—Parvat asana: Exhale and keeping hands and feet in the same position, push your buttocks back and high, straighten your arms, position your head between the arms and flatten the feet on the floor. Follow the rest of the instructions as described earlier.

Pose 9: Horse-riding pose—Ashwasanchalan: Inhale and move the left leg forward bent at the knee and with the left foot in line with the hands, lower the right knee to the floor and get into the horse riding pose as described earlier.

Pose 10: Forward Bending—Padahastasana: Exhale and bring your right foot forward and place it next to the left foot. Bend forward simultaneously with hands touching the toes or the palms resting flat on the floor next to the feet. The rest is the same as described earlier.

Pose 11: Backward bending—Hasta Uthanasana: Inhale as you raise your hands from the forward bending position to behind the head simultaneously raising the whole body and bending it backwards with the head thrown back. The rest is same as described earlier.

Pose 12: Prayer pose—Pranam asana: Exhale and bring the hands together in front of the chest and join the palms in prayer pose.

This completes half a round of Suryanamaskar. Repeat the same poses but this time stretch back the left leg in the Ashwasanchalan and in the other poses too. Make sure to move the left leg in the second half of the round as you moved the right leg in all the poses in the first half.

Twenty-four poses make one round. In the beginning, do three rounds. Build it up to five and then gradually keep increasing it. After you've gained some practise with it, you can do a minimum of ten and a maximum of twenty-seven rounds. In the later stages, many variations of practising Suryanamaskar have been detailed.

Always follow up Suryanamaskar with Shavasana or Yoga Nidra practise (description at the end of practice).

Pranayama Practice

1. **Kapalbhati with Udiyana bandha:** Sit comfortably in any of the meditational poses.

Practise Kapalbhati for fifty rounds. After this, wait for some time and observe your normal breathing and feel the impact of the rapid exhalation practise. You will experience stillness of breath and mind. When your breathing is almost normal, exhale forcefully, emptying out your lungs completely and pull in your stomach so that the diaphragm moves up.

Then place your palms on your knees and straighten the arms, pulling up the shoulders and further contracting the stomach area. Lock your chin to the chest and perform Udiyana bandha as described in Stage I. Hold this position as long as you can hold external retention of breath. Do not strain your body. At the slightest discomfort or a feeling of dizziness, release your kumbhak and relax with inhalation. Do five rounds of Kapalbhati with external Kumbhak.

Dizziness happens only if the Kapalbhati has not been done properly. Seek expert guidance.

2. **Bhastrika with Internal Kumbhak with Mool and Jalandhara Bandha:** Sit in any meditational position with eyes closed. Straighten your back, relax your whole body and internalize your awareness.

Practise fifty rounds of Bhastrika, as described in Stage I. At the end of the practise, pause for some time and you may experience a sense of emptiness when there is no breath. When the breath returns, inhale deeply and let the breath gather in the stomach region. Then practise Mool bandha and Jalandhara bandha together. Maintain awareness at the Manipura Chakra and at maintaining the two bandhas. Hold for as long as it is comfortable, then exhale and relax by releasing Mool bandha first, then Jalandhara bandha. This is one round. Practise five rounds of this.

3. **Anulom Vilom with Kumbhak—Alternate nostril breathing with breath retention:** Sit in any meditational pose with eyes closed. Keep your head and spine in a straight line and relax the body. Keep both hands in Gyan or Chin mudra. In Stage II, incorporate breath retention in the practise of alternate nostril breathing.

Internalize your awareness and, with eyes closed, watch the normal flow of breath. Then position your right hand for alternately opening and closing both nostrils as described in Stage I Anulom Vilom practice.

After some time, you can mentally control alternate nostril breathing without physically closing them with your fingers. This is better because your arms may tire after some time.

Inhale deeply through the left nostril, counting to the rhythm of seconds. Inhale for a minimum of eight counts. Then close both nostrils and hold the inhalation inside for sixteen counts and exhale through the left nostril in eight counts. This is 1:2:1 practice.

Slowly take it up to 1:4:1 and then 1:8:2. As your capacity increases, you may increase the starting counts from eight to a higher number.

Dharana with Mantras

So—Hum with Nasikadrishti: The steps are as follows:

- Sit comfortably in Padmasana. Close your eyes. Internalize your awareness. Run your awareness throughout your body. Wherever there is any tightness or tension, relax that part of the body.

- Then move your awareness to your nose tip. Watch the flow of breath at the nose tip.
- As you watch each inhale and exhale, with every inhale, internally chant the mantra 'So' and with every exhale, 'Hum'. Do not miss even a single breath. Your mind will wander off or your awareness may shift from your breathing and the mantra.
- Keep bringing your awareness back to your breathing and the mantra. One inhale and exhale makes one round. Start with eleven rounds and build it up to twenty-eight rounds.

With practise, you will find that the spells of distractions are reduced. Also, the longer you keep awareness focused on breathing and the mantra, the more will be the different states of mind and body. The quality of breath changes dramatically and there are times when it disappears completely, filling you with an experience of nothingness and void. With the fall in breath, the flow of thoughts decreases and you feel an unusual relaxation and rejuvenation. You can also focus on the meaning of the mantra which is, 'I am that'.

Focuses on: This practice awakens the Mooladhara Chakra as it is directly connected with the sense of smell and the nose.

Shambhavi Mudra with Om chanting: The steps are as follows:

- Continue sitting in the meditative pose.
- Now, move your awareness to the eyebrow centre without opening the eyes. Try to visualize a beautiful candle flame or any of your favourite symbols at the eyebrow centre.
- Maintaining awareness there, inhale deeply and as you exhale, chant the mantra Om. This makes one round. Start with eleven rounds and build it up to twenty-eight rounds.

Focuses on: On the Ajna Chakra. On the vibrations of the mantra inside you and around you. On the various states that each syllable of this mantra represents.

Guru Mantra Chanting: You should end your practice with chanting any of the universal mantras like the Gayatri mantra, Om Namo Bhagate Vasudeva, Om Namah Shivaye or any mantra that you may have received from your Guru.

End the practise with chanting Om three times along with Shanti mantra.

3

STAGE III

Kundalini Kriyas practice—90 Minutes

Begin with invocation, relaxation and internalisation of your awareness.

1. Sukshma Vyayam: Body warming and limbering up as described earlier.
2. Spine movements and asanas for the whole body are the same as in Stage II practice. After the last asana of Stage II, Chakrasana, you should do the Sirshasana described below, then the 2 T's and Kati Chakrasana followed by Suryanamaskar.

Sirshasana

Sirshasana is one of the most powerful practices with manifold benefits. But it must be practised with caution. In the beginning, sufficient precautions must be taken. It is the king of all practices as it activates the Sahasrara Chakra.

Its fundamental impact is that it is anti-gravitational. Thus, it reverses the blood flow and redirects it from the legs and the abdomen to the head, which revitalizes the brain. In this practice, the stomach area exerts pressure on the diaphragm and contracts the lungs; this expels excess carbon dioxide from the body. It relaxes the spine and relieves anxiety and other psychological problems.

You must do this asana by following the instructions step-by-step. In the beginning, practise this asana against the wall. I do not recommend using props because you may end up getting too accustomed to them which makes them hard to get rid of. With practise, your neck and shoulders will become strong and you will be able to do this inverted pose comfortably and without the support of the wall.

1. The base position to start with is Vajrasana. Relax the whole body.

    Interlock your fingers and place your arms on the floor so that the elbows are close to the knees. Place your head between the palms; this will support the head so that it does not roll back as you lift your body.

2. Raise your knees and buttocks off the floor and straighten the legs so that your body makes a V shape.

3. Walk towards your hands and head so that the thighs press against the abdomen and chest while your back is almost straight.

4. Begin by lifting the right leg off the floor and keep the knee bent. Then lift the left leg to bring both legs together. The knees of both legs are bent.

    Slowly transfer the weight of the body to the head and arms.

5. Begin to straighten your knees so that your thighs are in line with your torso. At this point, most of your body weight has been transferred to your arms and head. The lower part of your legs is perpendicular to the thighs.

    Adjust the weight of the body on the arms and head. Try to keep the whole body balanced.

6. Straighten your legs so that your whole body is in a straight line and resting on your arms and head. This is the final position.

Close your eyes and balance the whole body. Then consciously try to relax it.

Returning to Base Position

Slowly bend your knees and lower your body in the reverse order until the toes touch the floor. Remain in the crouching position for some time.

Then return to Vajrasana and stay in it for a bit before you stand up. End this exercise with a few rounds of Tadasana.

Suryanamaskar with Variations

There are some variations to be made in your basic Suryanamaskar practice. These variations will help build your heart's capacity, increase concentration and awaken your body systems to the maximum.

Initially, to reap physical benefits, one may practise the dynamic version. The dynamic version simply means that you do the entire Suryanamaskar in fast mode. Initially, one may take time to do the twelve poses fast is maintaining the rhythm of breath and movement. As you get proficient, you can do the same fast and dynamically.

After you get comfortable with doing twenty dynamic rounds, you can incorporate breath retention into the practise.

In breath retention, inhale deeply and complete half a round with the twelve poses and exhale at the end of it. Then inhale again and complete the other half and exhale at the end of it. Thus, you complete twenty-four poses with internal breath retention. Practise five rounds of this.

Similarly, exhale in the prayer pose and complete half a round with the twelve poses and inhale after completion of this half round of Suryanamaskar. Then exhale again and finish the other half and inhale at the end of it. Thus, you complete twenty-four poses with external breath retention. Practise five rounds of this.

You can follow these up with another five rounds of regular Suryanamaskar practise with normal breathing if you don't feel tired after doing the breath retention Suryanamaskar practices.

Thus, you will have completed fifteen rounds of Suryanamaskar, five with internal breath retention, five wih external breath retention and five with normal breathing.

For spiritual practice, you can do a relaxed practice by holding each pose with the choice of doing one of the following:

1. Hold the pose and chant the Surya Mantra (see below) for that pose with awareness on the specific Chakra for that pose.
2. Hold the pose and with eyes closed and awareness at the eyebrow centre, chant one round of Gayatri mantra in each pose. Visualize a beautiful golden rising sun at the eyebrow centre.

The Surya Mantras:

1. Om Mitrayanamaha . . . Prayer pose
2. Om Ravenamah . . . Backward bending pose
3. Om Suryaynamaha . . . Forward bending pose
4. Om Bhanvenamaha . . . Horse riding pose
5. Om Khagayenamaha . . . Mountain pose
6. Om Pushnenamaha . . . Ashtanga Namaskar
7. Om Hiranyagarbhayanama . . . Cobra pose
8. Om Marichayenamaha . . . Mountain pose
9. Om Adityenamaha . . . Horse riding pose
10. Om Savitrenamaha . . . Forward bending
11. Om Arkayanamaha . . . Backward bending
12. Om Bhaskarayenamaha . . . Prayer pose

Practise Shavasana or Yoga Nidra for 5-30 mins respectively.

Pranayama Practise

Kapalbhati with Maha Bandha: The only difference from the Stage II practise is that with external breath retention, you will be practicing the Mool, Udiyana and Jalandhara bandhas together. (Check Pranayama insgructions in Section VII, Chapter 1)

Establish Jalandhara Bandha. Establish the Udiyana bandha by pulling in the abdominal area. Establish the Mool bandha by tightening your perineal area.

Thus, Mahabandha is performed with external breath retention.

Hold this position for as long as you can hold the Kumbhak and the Mahabandha. When you want to inhale or release the Mahabandha and Kumbhak, start by releasing the Mool bandha first, then the Uddiyana and finally the Jalandhara bandha. This makes one round. Do five rounds of this.

When you have become proficient in practising the Mahabandha, you should visualize the Apana Vayu rising from the Mooladhara Chakra and moving up to the Manipura Chakra to join with Prana Vayu and these vayus, along with the Samana Vayu, moving upwards to the Vishuddhi Chakra.

Bhastrika with Traces of Kaivalya Kumbhak: With consistent and regular practise, by now you would've become comfortable with the rapid inhale and exhale practise of Bhastrika. Every time after practising Bhastrika, just pause and stay in stillness and silence. You will experience the beginnings of what is called Kaivalya Kumbhak, or spontaneous suspension of breath. The movement of breath suspends as no air moves in or out of the body. However, it is not simply the suspension of breath but also a disassociation with everything on the outside as well as the inside. Your eyes remain closed but even the other senses seem to shut down. You experience Pratyahara. You connect with your internal world of watching and feeling everything inside you.

You experience this state of disconnect and dissociation due to the changes happening in your body at the physiological level. The functioning of body is regulated by the smooth flow of pranic energy within it.

The rapid breathing exercises affect the body in a number of ways. It charges the sleeping neurons and establishes new circuits within the two hemispheres of the brain. This in turn naturally affects the functioning of the central nervous system and the numerous neural pathways. These changes in your brain and body lead to the experience of this unusual state. Your body begins to synchronize with the vibrations and frequency of the universe. You realize that you are overcoming the limiting barriers of your body and its senses to cross over from this world of Maya to the world beyond, which is eternal and limitless.

With the practice of Bhastrika pranayama followed by Kumbhak, the physiological and subtle changes in the body and brain are deepened. Kumbhak practice, as mentioned earlier, begins to impact the movement of the vayus and raises up the Apana, Samana and Prana vayus towards the Vishuddhi Chakra.

Sit as usual in any of the meditational poses. Relax your whole body and gently close your eyes. Place your hands on your knees in Gyan or Chin mudra. Do fifty rounds of Bhastrika, then observe your normal flow of breath or of no breath, depending on the state of progress of your practise.

Anulom Vilom with Om Chanting and Kumbhak: The only addition to the Stage II alternate nostril breathing with breath retention is that in addition to counting to the rhythm of seconds, you have to chant Om. As you inhale through the left nostril, count three Oms, then hold and count twelve Oms, then as you exhale through the right nostril, count six Oms.

Then inhale through the right nostril for three Oms, then close both nostrils for sixteen Oms with awareness at the eyebrow centre, then exhale through left nostril for six Oms. This completes 1 round. Start with three and build it up to five rounds.

Throughout the practise, maintain awareness at the centre of the eyebrow and use your left hand's fingers to keep count. I use the lines on the inside of the fingers to keep count. If you have learnt to practise alternate nostril breathing mentally, without actually closing the nostrils, you can use the fingers of both hands to keep count.

This practice has been described by Swami Sivananda as Sukha Purva pranayama. He writes in 'Kundalini Yoga' that this practise removes all diseases, purifies the Nadis, steadies the wandering mind, improves digestion and circulation, helps Brahmacharya, and awakens Kundalini. All impurities are expelled from the body.

As mentioned earlier, these multi-tool practises of breath, mantra, mudra and visualization leave little space for thoughts, to push their way into your attempt to maintain one-pointed awareness of your practise.

Mudras

Unmani Mudra: The word Unmani means 'thoughtlessness' or 'mindlessness'. This is an important practice because it will be a part of many of the Kundalini Kriyas you will be doing in the higher practices.

n a subtle way, it involves training your faculties and mind to be simultaneously aware of the external and the internal. Normally, you close your eyes to internalize your awareness and block out the external world. However, in the final stages or even after full awakening of the Kundalini, you will be in a kind of dual world; both connected with the world around you and hitched on to the world beyond. Therefore, your later practises will include Unmani mudra to induce both states.

The steps are as follows:

- Sit in any of the meditational poses, with the back straight and whole body relaxed. Keep your eyes open.
- Take a deep breath. Although your eyes are open, do not focus on anything.
- As you inhale, take your awareness from Mooladhara to the Bindu Visarga while retaining the breath inside.
- As you exhale, feel the breath going down your spine, touching each of the Chakras starting from the Bindu to Ajna to Mooladhara and all the other Chakras in-between.

- As you approach the Mooladhara Chakra, the eyes should begin to close and at the Mooladhara Chakra, they should be firmly closed. This is one round. Start with five and build it up to ten rounds.

This kriya teaches you to have internal awareness even with the eyes open.

Khechari Mudra: This is an important practice for Kundalini awakening. Later on, it has to be practised in conjunction with other Kriyas for Chakra awakening.

This mudra holds a prime position in the practises for Kundalini awakening. It also happens to be one of my favourite practises. The great propagator of Hatha Yoga, Swami Swatmarama, devotes eighteen sutras (from sutra thirty-two to fifty-four, Chapter three) to Khechari mudra in the *Hatha Yoga Pradipika*.

Briefly, Khechari mudra involves curling up your tongue and touching the tip of the tongue on the upper palate. With repeated practise, the tongue is trained to reach inside or touch the opening to the nasal cavity. This is the location of the Lalana Chakra, where Amrit is ever dripping from the Bindu Visarga. Khechari mudra attempts to prevent this nectar from flowing downwards, where it will get destroyed by the sun at the Manipura Chakra. The steps are as follows:

- Sit in any meditational pose with the back straight, the body relaxed, the eyes closed and the hands in Gyan or Chin mudra on the knees.
- Take a deep breath, open your mouth and curl your tongue inside so that the underside of the tongue touches the upper palate, and its tip is pointed inside and reaches as far inside the mouth as possible.
- Once you've reached the final position, you can breathe normally, close your mouth and hold the inverted tongue position for as long as is comfortably possible.

- Slowly increase the time of holding the mudra along with pushing the tip of the tongue further and further inside the mouth until it touches the opening to the nasal cavity. This is an important practice with manifold effects, therefore further details of its spiritual and physiological effects and values have been elaborated earlier under the section on Mudras.

Focuses on: On the Lalana Chakra. On the tip of the tongue as it is stretched increasingly to reach the orifice. On the taste secreted inside the mouth, which indicates which Tattwa or element is active within your body.

Vipreeta Karani Mudra: You have reached that stage from where all your practices will be moving closer to Kundalini Kriyas.

The name of this mudra is self-explanatory. Vipareet means reverse and karni means to do. Let's understand the theory behind this practice.

Yoga devised the Vipreeta Karani mudra to reverse the flow of the nectar from Bindu and preserve it in the higher centres of our brain. Verse eighty-two of chapter three of the *Hatha Yoga Pradipika* states, 'After six months of this practise, all wrinkles and grey hair cannot be seen, and if practised for up to three hours, you conquer death.'

Kriya Yoga combines visualisation of the reverse flow of nectar to give further effect to the practise. Once you are established in the inverted position as detailed here, you visualize hot fluid being drawn up from the Manipura Chakra and collected at the Vishuddhi Chakra, the throat pit, where it is held and cooled and then taken to the Ajna then to the Bindu Visarga and finally to the Sahasrara Chakra at the crown of the head.

The steps are as follows:

- Get into Sarvangasana pose with a slight variation. In Vipreeta Karani mudra, the torso is slightly inclined to the floor at about forty-five degrees. The legs are vertical and the chin is not pressed against the chest as the mudra involves doing Ujjai pranayama as well.

- Lie down on the mat and relax your whole body.
- Place your hands next to your body, palms facing down.
- Keep the feet together. Slowly lift your legs and bring them over your head taking support of the palms, arms and shoulders.
- Once the legs are at ninety degrees, then turn the palms upward and rest the hips on the palms so that the body is at forty-five degrees to the floor as well as the legs. Become steady in this position.
- Once you are comfortable in the position, close your eyes and inhale with Ujjai pranayama.
- Fix your awareness at the Manipura Chakra and visualize that you are taking warm Amrut/nectar from the Manipura Chakra and pulling it up along the spine to the Vishuddhi Chakra, touching the Anahata Chakra along the way.
- Hold the nectar at the Vishuddhi Chakra and visualize it cooling down there. When you exhale with Ujjai pranayama, visualize and feel the breath and nectar moving up to the Ajna, the Bindu and finally to the Sahasrara Chakra.
- When you want to inhale, bring awareness back to the Manipura Chakra and repeat the whole practise. At the Sahasrara Chakra ends one round. Start with five and build it up to twenty-one rounds.

Focuses on: On the Chakras as you inhale and exhale and on the visualization of the warm nectar cooling at the Vishuddhi Chakra and going out through the Sahasrara Chakra.

Psychic Passages

As you progress towards more complex Kundalini practices, it becomes essential to know about the two psychic passages—The Arohan and Awrohan.

Arohan: This is the frontal passage of the Chakras from the Mooladhara to the Ajna Chakra. When you practise, you ascend along the frontal passage, touching awareness on each of the Chakras from the Mooladhara to the Ajna Chakra.

Awrohan: This is the passage through the spinal cord, your Sushumna Nadi, from the Ajna to the Mooladhara Chakra. When you practise Awrohan, you descend from the Ajna Chakra to the Mooladhara Chakra along the spinal cord with awareness of each Chakra in between.

Khechari Mudra with Shambhavi Mudra and Slow Breathing

Practise Khechari Mudra as described in Stage II. With consistent practise, you should be getting closer to the goal of touching the tip of your tongue to the opening of the nasal cavity. Once established in your final position, breathe normally but slowly, extending your breaths to five to eight per minute or even slower.

Khechari mudra, like pranayama, generates heat in the body so that the nectar turns liquid and flows from the Bindu Visarga, the moon within us. Awareness at the Ajna Chakra brings about the union of Ida and Pingala with Sushumna Nadi at the Ajna Chakra. Thus, it is known as Triveni, the meeting point of the three Nadis, just like the meeting of Ganga, Jamuna and Saraswati rivers at Prayag.

This union is converted into the union of five forces when you practise Khechari with Shambhavi mudra, that is, awareness at the Ajna Chakra. The five Nadis which converge at this cavity are Ida, Pingala, Sushumna, Gandhari and Hastijihva.

The attempt should be to focus on the three Chakras, the Ajna, the Lalana and the Bindu Visarga. Be aware of the sense of smell and taste as the nectar that flows from the Bindu Visarga. In sutra fifty, Chapter three of the *Hatha Yoga Pradipika*, Swami Swatmarama says, 'When you perform Khechari, the moon's nectar that flows has a saline, pungent and acidic flavour. It has the consistency of milk, ghee or honey. Fatal diseases and old age are warded off and from this, flows immortality and the eight powers, or siddhis.'

Kundalini Pranayama—Chakra Awareness

This is an important practise for Kundalini awakening. Swami Sivananda has called it the Kundalini Pranayama. It is important that you develop a mental and emotional attitude of gratitude towards your Gurus and reverence towards the Kundalini shakti. The steps are as follows:

- Sit comfortably in any of the meditational poses with your eyes closed, back straight and the whole body relaxed.
- In this pranayama, every inhale and exhale are practised deliberately with awareness moving from the Mooladhara to the Sahasrara Chakra as you inhale and back again from the Sahasrara to the Mooladhara Chakra as you exhale.
- Visualize your breath moving up through the Sushumna Nadi from the Mooladhara Chakra, touching each of the Chakras: Swadhisthan, Manipura, Anahata, Vishuddhi, Ajna, Bindu and finally, Sahasrara, then as you exhale visualize the breath moving down from the Sahasrara Chakra through the Sushumna Nadi back to the Mooladhara Chakra, touching each of the Chakras along the Sushumna Nadi. This is one round. Practise five to nine rounds of this.
- As you reach the Sahasrara Chakra, hold your awareness there. Visualize that your being is blessed with the light of Kundalini, dispelling the darkness around your soul and subsuming your whole being with light, power and wisdom.

It is helpful to have studied the physiology of your spine to visualize the spinal cord through which the Sushumna Nadi passes. As you practise, you can make your awareness more and more acute and try to sense the finer Nadis, the Chitra and Brahma Nadi, within the Sushumna Nadi.

It is a simple practise, but even as you practise it, you will not only deeply enjoy it but also find your mind fixating on the rhythmical feel of the breath travelling up and down with Chakra awareness.

Chakra Awareness through Frontal Passage and Lalana Chakra

This practise is similar to the one described above, except that the awareness, while ascending from the Mooladhara to the Sahasrara Chakra, moves through the frontal passage. The second difference is that while ascending, after the Vishuddhi Chakra, awareness is taken to the Lalana Chakra, at the opening of the orifice in the throat, then Nasikadrishti, which is nose-tip gazing, then the Ajna Chakra before proceeding to the Bindu Visarga and then finally the Sahasrara Chakra. The steps are as follows:

- Sit in padmasana or any meditational pose. Centre your awareness and relax your whole body. Close your eyes.
- Exhale completely and take your awareness to the Mooladhara Chakra and repeat, 'Mooladhara, Mooladhara, Mooladhara', mentally three times.
- Then as you inhale, ascend your awareness through each of the Chakras, while feeling each Chakra and mentally repeating their names—Swadhisthan, Manipura, Anahata, Vishuddhi, Lalana, Nasikadrishti, Ajna, Bindu and Sahasrara.
- Hold awareness at the Sahasrara Chakra for a few seconds.
- Then as you exhale, feel and mentally repeat the names of each Chakra as you descend to Bindu, Ajna, Vishuddhi, Anahata, Manipura, Swadhisthana and Mooladhara. This completes one round.
- Practise nine to twelve rounds of this. Hold awareness at the Mooladhara Chakra with exhalation, repeat 'Mooladhara' three times and start the next round.

Shanmukhi Pranayama

This is similar to Brahmari pranyama but is done with internal breath retention. It is a subtle practise of listening to the sounds within your brain. The steps are as follows:

- Sit in any of the meditational poses. Close your ears by pressing in the outer lobe of the ears with your thumbs.
- Place the forefingers on the eyes, the middle fingers on the nose tip, the ring fingers on the lips and the little fingers on the skin near the chin.
- Relax the whole body and keep the spine and head in a straight line.
- Close your ears, take a deep breath, close your nostrils with the middle fingers and hold the breath inside.
- Then listen to the sounds within your head. At first, you may hear some vague sounds or not anything at all.
- With practise, you will start to hear some sounds.
- Till that happens, try to focus on whatever sounds you can hear.
- Then after a few moments, some other sound may emerge. Focus your attention on this second sound. You go on progressing until you can hear subtler sounds.
- When you want to exhale, release the Kumbhak and breathe normally. This is one round. Do five rounds of this.
- Finally practise Bhramari pranayama for three to five rounds.
- End the practise by chanting Om thrice along with the Shanti Mantra.

4

STAGE IV

Kundalini Kriya

Khechari Mudra with Shambhavi Mudra and Slow Breathing

The steps are as follows:

- Sit in any meditation pose. Relax your whole body and centre yourself with breath awareness on the state of your being.
- Take a deep breath and curl your tongue to establish Khechari mudra, pushing the tongue as far inside the mouth as possible without discomfort.
- Then take your awareness to the eyebrow centre. The effort should make the skin at the centre of the brow feel puckered.
- Now close your eyes and maintain both the Khechari mudra and the internal Shambhavi mudra. Breathe normally.
- Try to extend each inhalation and exhalation so that you breathe about three to four times in one minute. Continue this for three to five minutes.
- When you are done, release Shambhavi mudra and then Khechari mudra. This is one round. Do five rounds of this.

Focuses on: This practice intensifies the awakening of the Ajna Chakra. In the practise of Khechari mudra, four Chakras are awakened and five Nadis converge at the Ajna Chakra. These manifest as changes in the functioning of the brain, the central nervous system which has transformational impact on the whole being of the person. By now it is all about your own awareness and experience.

Nada Sanchalana

The steps are as follows:

- Sit comfortably in any meditational pose. Relax your body and centre your awareness by watching the normal flow of breath. The eyes remain open in this practise in the beginning. You will close them in the second half of the practise with Unmani mudra.
- Exhale fully, drop your head forward without pressing your chin to the chest and with awareness on the Mooladhara Chakra, mentally repeat, 'Mooladhara, Mooladhara, Mooladhara.'
- As you inhale, raise your awareness through the frontal passage mentally repeating the name of each Chakra as you ascend from Swadhisthana to Manipura to Anahata, to Vishuddhi.
- At the Vishuddhi Chakra, tilt your head a little bit, say just about twenty degrees, with eyes open, internally take your awareness to the Bindu Visarga, mentally repeat, 'Bindu, Bindu, Bindu.'
- At the last of the Bindu sounds, say 'Om' loudly and let the three syllables A-O-M resound in you as you descend your awareness through the Awrohan passage with Unmani mudra.
- As you descend through the spinal passage, be conscious of the all the Chakras without repeating their names. As you reach the Mooladhara Chakra, open your eyes and drop your head.

- Mentally repeat, 'Mooladhara, Mooladhara, Mooladhara.' This completes one round. Start with seven rounds and gradually build it up to thirteen rounds. Each round should flow into the next.

Pawan Sanchalan

(Chakra Awareness with Khechari Mudra and Ujjai Pranayama)

In this practice, you maintain Khechari mudra throughout and every inhalation and exhalation is done with Ujjai pranayama. The steps are as follows:

- Sit in any of the meditational poses. Relax your whole body.
- As you inhale, lock your tongue in Khechari mudra.
- With open eyes, drop your head forward and exhale. Become conscious of the Mooladhara Chakra and mentally repeat, 'Mooladhara, Mooladhara, Mooladhara.'
- Then as you inhale with ujjai, say arohan mentally, ascend your awareness through the frontal passage, mentally repeating the name of each Chakra as you raise your head till you come to the Vishuddhi Chakra.
- At Vishuddhi, tilt your head back slightly, then with awareness on the Bindu Visarga, mentally repeat, 'Bindu, Bindu, Bindu.'
- Then mentally say Awrohan and let your awareness descend through the spinal column with exhalation in Ujjai, while mentally naming each Chakra, from Ajna to Swadhisthan.
- As you descend from the Bindu Visarga, you perform Unmani mudra and begin to move your head from the tilted position to again bending forward.
- When you reach the Mooladhara Chakra, close your eyes and complete the exhalation.
- Then open your eyes and with focus on the Mooladhara Chakra, repeat mentally, 'Mooladhara, Mooladhara, Mooladhara.'

- Start your next round immediately with inhalation as you ascend with arohan through the frontal passage. Practise fifteen to twenty rounds of this.

Shabdha Sanchalan

(Chakra Practise with awareness through frontal and spinal So Hum through Chakra)

This kriya is similar to Pawan Sanchalan but without the mental repetition of 'Mooladhara' and 'Bindu'. The mantra 'So Hum' (meaning 'I am That') is used instead; during ascent, 'So' and during descent, 'Hum'. Khechari and Unmani mudra are practised throughout as before. The steps are as follows:

- Sit in any meditational pose. Relax the whole body and centre your awareness. Keep your hands on the knees in Gyan or Chin mudra.
- Inhale and establish Khechari and maintain it till the end of the practise. Breathe in and out with Ujjai pranayama throughout the kriya.
- As in the earlier practises, exhale completely and drop your head forward with eyes open. Maintain internal awareness on the Mooladhara Chakra.
- As you inhale with Ujjai, internally say the mantra 'So' and ascend your consciousness through the frontal passage, becoming aware of the field of each Chakra from Mooladhara to Vishuddhi while simultaneously raising your head to the base position.
- At Vishuddhi, slightly tilt your head back, retain inhalation and become aware of Bindu for a few seconds. Then as you exhale, internally say the mantra 'Hum' and let the vibrations of the mantra descend along the spine from Ajna to Mooladhara with Unmani mudra.
- When you reach the Mooladhara Chakra, open your eyes. This makes one round. Initially start with ten rounds and slowly progress to twenty, then thirty and finally to fifty rounds.

- There is no perceptible break between the rounds. Each round flow into the next.

Maha Mudra with Uthanpadasana

For these practises, it is advisable for men to sit in Siddhasana and for women, the Siddha yoni asana, with the heel pressed into the Mooladhara Chakra. However, those who practise mostly in Padmasana and are not comfortable with the other two poses, may sit in Uthanpadasana. The steps are as follows:

- For Uthanpadasana, sit comfortably with both legs stretched out before you. This is the base position.
- Fold your left leg and place the heel firmly against the Mooladhara Chakra at the perineum. Place both hands on the right knee.
- Take a deep breath and establish Khechari mudra.
- Exhale fully, bend your head forward and become aware of the Mooladhara Chakra. Mentally repeat, 'Mooladhara, Mooladhara, Mooladhara.'
- As you inhale with Ujjai, begin to raise your head as you pass your awareness through the various Chakras through the frontal passage and come to the Vishuddhi Chakra.
- Then tilt your head up, with eyes open, become internally aware of the Bindu and while maintaining awareness there, repeat three times, 'Bindu, Bindu, Bindu.'
- Then bend forward and grasp the right big toe with both hands.
- Establish Moola bandha and Shambhavi mudra. Your eyes stay open. Mentally repeat, 'Shambhavi-Khechari-Moola', as many times as you can while holding the breath.
- As you repeat, your awareness must pass from Shambhavi to Khechari to Moola and then back to Shambhavi again. Initially, you may breathe normally while practising this.
- Start with repeating this at least three times in the beginning, gradually building it up to ten to twelve times with breath retention.

- Release Moola bandha and then Shambhavi. Maintaining Khechari, slide your awareness down the Awrohan passage with exhalation in Ujjai and Unmani mudra with awareness of each of the Chakras till you reach the Mooladhara Chakra.
- Bring your hands back to the knees.
- For the second half, repeat the same process but this time fold the right leg and grasp your left big toe as the left leg remains stretched out with its knee flat on the floor.
- Finally, it can be done with both legs stretched out. You can do three rounds, each with the legs in three different positions.

As you will notice, gradually your kriya has become complex enough so as to leave little room for the mind to do anything else other than the practice. Besides stilling the mind, it is affecting your body with the awakening of the Chakras, manipulating the energy flow with the mudras and redirecting the vayus with the bandhas. This is making changes down to the cellular level in the body and the neural level in the brain, resulting in transformation which is preparing you for transcendence.

Maha Bheda Mudra

As in Maha Mudra practice, this practise can be done in any of the meditational poses or in Uthanpadasana. I have described this practise in Uthanpadasana. The steps are as follows:

- As in Maha Mudra kriya, begin with your right leg stretched forward and your left leg folded and placed against your perineum.
- Inhale and perform Khechari mudra and keep it locked till the end of the practise. Drop your head forward with exhalation in ujjai and take awareness to the Mooladhara Chakra and chant 'Mooladhara, Mooladhara, Mooladhara' with full awareness.
- Then inhale in Ujjai through Arohan passage, ascending from the Mooladhara to the Vishuddhi Chakra with awareness on all

the Chakras in between, tilt your head and become aware of the Bindu Visarga and chant 'Bindu, Bindu, Bindu'.

- Then practise Unmani mudra with exhalation, let your awareness descend through the Awrohan passage, from Bindu down to Mooladhara. Then grasp your right big toe with both hands to get into Uthanpadasana.
- Then holding in exhalation, drop your chin to the chest and perform in a series, first Nasikagara Drishti, Uddiyana bandha and lastly Moola bandha. Your breath is still retained externally.
- Mentally repeat 'Nasika-Uddiyana-Moola', placing your awareness on each of these as you name them. To begin with, you can repeat it three to five times and build it up to fifteen times.
- When you are ready to release, start by releasing nasika drishti, then moola bandha and finally Uddiyana bandha. The eyes are open and Khechari is still in place. Bring your hands back on the knees and release Uthanpadasana.
- This is one round. Perform five rounds in the beginning and build it up to ten to twelve rounds.

Alternate Practise

The steps are as follows:

- Begin with establishing Khechari Mudra. Keep your eyes open.
- Then bend your head forward, internally look at the Mooladhara Chakra and mentally repeat 'Mooladhara' three times.
- Then inhale with Ujjai and pass through the frontal passage till you come to Vishuddhi.
- Tilt your head back as you pass from Vishuddhi to Bindu and mentally repeat 'Bindu' three times.
- With exhalation in Ujjai, while maintaining Khechari, take your awareness down the Awrohan passage, with awareness on each Chakra as you come down to the Mooladhara with Unmani mudra.

- Establish Mool bandha and Shambhavi mudra with breath still held externally and repeat 'Shambhavi-Khechari-Mool' with awareness moving from eyebrow centre to Khechari to the Mooladhara Chakra as you repeat each name. Do as many rounds as you can while holding your breath out.
- When you want to inhale, first release Shambhavi and then Mool.
- Then bring awareness back to Bindu and with exhalation, travel down through the Awrohan passage with awareness on each Chakra, from Bindu to Ajna to Mooladhara. This makes one round. Start with five rounds and build it up to twelve rounds.

Shakti Chalini

This practise intensifies your imagination of the Kundalini. The steps are as follows:

- Sit in a meditative pose. Inhale and curl the tongue in Khechari mudra. Your eyes remain closed throughout the practise.
- Exhale and lower the head. Internally locate the Mooladhara Chakra and mentally chant 'Mooladhara, Mooladhara, Mooladhara'.
- Inhale and raise your awareness, through the frontal passage, through all the Chakras to Vishuddhi, then tilt the head slightly as awareness goes straight to the Bindu Visarga from Vishuddhi.
- Holding the inhalation internally, practise Shanmukhi mudra, closing all the sense organs. Still holding the inhalation within, move your awareness down the Awrohan passage from Bindu to Mooladhara and then from Mooladhara to Bindu through Arohan passage in a continuous circle.
- Visualize this circular movement as a green snake with its tail at Bindu, its whole body sliding down and rising up the spine, its head coming up at Bindu and biting its own tail. Keep following this circular movement of the green snake till you feel like

exhaling. This is one round. Progress slowly with this practise.
Start with three rounds and build it up to nine rounds.

108 Mantra Chanting

You can pick any of the above-mentioned practises of mantra chanting
such as So-Hum with Nasika Drishti, Om with Shambhavi Mudra,
your Guru mantra or any other favourite mantra. The important
part is to do it 108 times. If you cannot fit this in with your morning
practice, you can practise it in the evening. Practise this for as long as
you want; maybe six months, one year or even longer. For me, it's a
daily practise of doing at least 3 rounds of a 108 bead of 3 different
mantras everyday. It may seem like a challenge but once you start on
these things, they are enjoyable and you can experience their benefits.

5

MEDITATION DHYANA

There are many methods of reaching a state of inner silence. I am listing and detailing some of these because we are prone to move towards certain practises depending on our disposition. Slowly but surely, meditation starts to become a large part of our practise.

The feeling of being taken over by a different state of being is out of this world. Through meditation, you get to experience states of being that are unlike anything else we have known.

While there is a whole world of meditation practises out there, I've detailed only two because these are more likely to align with the practises we've done for Kundalini Yoga. However, you are free to explore some other forms too, such as Mindfulness (inspired by Buddhist teachings), Transcendental Meditation and more.

Ajapa Japa: This is a simple and minimalist method of meditation practice. It makes use of a simple mantra chanted with synchronized breathing. This method is particularly suitable for emotional people.

Antar Mauna: Literally meaning 'inner silence', this is a method of alternatively watching, creating and disbanding thoughts. In this practise, you watch your mind by first watching your thoughts, then creating thoughts and finally blocking all thoughts. This method is particularly suitable for rational and logical thinkers.

Ajapa Japa Practise

At this stage of meditation, you are now poised at the last rung of the ladder to reach your final destination of the union of Kundalini Shakti with Supreme Consciousness at the Sahasrara Chakra at the crown of the head. You have also arrived at the most beautiful of all practises whatever you may call it. I find Ajapa Japa to be one of the simplest, most serene, transformational and transcendental practises.

In the Yogashiksha Upanishad, in Chapter six, Sutra fifty-four, it is said that the jiva (the individual soul) ever utters the mantra 'SoHum' with every exhale and inhale. One who practises this mantra with his every breath, becomes Enlightened.

Swami Satyananda has delineated the Ajapa Japa practice in six stages as one stage progressively leads to the next. I have put it here in my own words from the book Yoga and Kriya and from Swamiji's talk given at Cama Hall, Bombay, February, 1963, produced in Yoga Magazine of Bihar School of Yoga.

In the initial stages, you will find yourself alternating between introversion and extroversion. Introversion happens when these three components, the breath, the mantra and your focus on these, are present for an extended period of time. Extroversion happens when any of these components breaks away from your practise.

In the introverted state, breathing progresses from being minimal to long stretches of spontaneous suspension also called Kaivalya Kumbhak. The mantra also flows effortlessly and automatically. There is awareness of your state without the help of the senses or your mind.

Extroversion happens when your lungs do not have the capacity to keep up with the subtle pranic energy. Any disturbance in the breathing disturbs your mantra and awareness. Upon finding this weakness, the senses get extroverted and the mind jumps in to hijack your awareness.

Kundalini Kriya practice in the final stages when combined with meditational practices, like Ajapa Japa or Antar Mauna, act like a cushion against the explosive awakening of the Shakti at the Ajna Chakra. One of the problems people face after awakening Kundalini is the channelization of the energy released. This energy may prove to be too wild and unruly for some. However, this may not be the case for those who practise meditation. The mindfulness and awareness, wrought through the practice of meditation, create a homogenized and harmonized personality to constructively use the exponential energy released due to Kundalini practice. Swami Sivananda has instructed that we must channelize this energy into doing good for the people.

One can divide the two practises if time is a constraint. The Kundalini Kriya can be done in the morning; the meditational practises can be done in the evening. This also neatly divides your day into awakening energy at the start of the day and using it for the day's activities. The meditational practise in the evening helps reset any fragmentation or imbalance which may have set in during your extroverted state, as you went about your daily activities.

Preparation: Sit in your preferred meditation pose. A relaxed body is essential. Use the Shavasana technique of running your awareness from the tip of your toes to the top of your head, relaxing each part of your body.

The main components of this practice are breath, mantra and awareness.

Breath: You must be aware of each and every inhalation and exhalation. Not a single inhalation or exhalation should be missed. Ensure that your breathing is conscious instead of automatic throughout the day, even when you're asleep.

Mantra: The second aspect is of synchronizing the mantra with the breath. Introversion of the mind in watching the flow of breath makes your body feel light and relaxed and frees your mind of tension and stress, thus making it alert. At this stage, you introduce the mantra, 'SoHum'. 'So' is the natural vibration of your inhaled breath and 'Hum' is the natural vibration of your exhaled breath. You will hear this sound when you sit down quietly and listen to your own breathing.

Focuses on: This third aspect is usually the natural outcome of your successful unbroken watching of your conscious breathing and the synchronization of your mantra with it.

Stage I of Ajapa Japa

Sit comfortably in any meditational pose. As suggested earlier, relax the body and internalize awareness. Watch every single inhalation and exhalation. Practise this until there is no break in your awareness of watching the continuous flow of breath. When this state of unbroken awareness of breath is reached, then join the mantra 'SoHum' with your breathing. 'So' with every inhalation and 'Hum' with every exhalation. Continue till you reach an unbroken state of conscious breathing synchronized with SoHum.

In this state, visualize your breath as moving between your throat and your navel. With every inhalation, visualize your breath moving from the throat to the navel and from the navel to the throat with every exhalation; from Vishuddhi to Manipura and Manipura to Vishuddhi. The breath and mantra must flow continuously without a break. Attach the mantra So-hum to the descending and ascending breath.

Continue this practice till you feel that you have mastered it.

Stage II

In this stage, all remains the same except that you start with the exhaled breath with 'Hum' ascending from Manipura to Vishuddhi and then follow it up with inhalation with 'So' as you descend from Vishuddhi to Manipura. Instead of 'SoHum', the mantra will be 'HumSo'.

After some time, stop the ascension and descension of the breath. Take your awareness to the eyebrow centre or the heart centre. Maintain awareness there even as you continue to be fully aware of your breathing and the mantra. Those who are rational and need conviction of mind may focus on the eyebrow centre and those who are emotional and are led by their heart may focus on their heart centre.

Continue this practice until you have mastered it. Generally, it takes a month of practice to perfect it.

Stage III

At Stage III, Swami Satyananda Saraswati takes you to yet another state of awareness. Now, it is all about total awareness on the sound 'So' as you inhale and the sound 'Hum' as you exhale. Pause after every 'So' and 'Hum'; be aware only of the sound and vibrations of the mantra. After some time, you will spontaneously feel a mental vacuum form in your mind. You can also create this vacuum. Be aware of this vacuum: a state of nothingness. Resume the practice again.

Practise this until perfect or for one month.

Stage IV

In this stage, you start with focusing on the continuous flow of inhalation and exhalation. Just listen to the sound of your own breathing. Now inhale from the throat to the navel and exhale from the navel to the throat. After this is stabilized, feel the mantra 'So-hum' without saying it as the breath flows from inhale to exhale in one continuous motion; it should just be a continuous flow of 'SoHumSoHumSoHum'.

Then suspend your awareness and feel emptiness. Just be aware of this state. When it breaks, start the flow of 'SoHumSoHum' again with breath movement to-and-from the throat and the navel.

Practise this till you feel like moving on to the next stage.

Stage V

Stage V brings your Chakra awareness and your Ajapa Japa practise together. I don't know how to describe the actual experience of these practices. It is because there is nothing in our normal, day-to-day lives which even comes close to the experiences of meditational practices. All vocabulary and description are stultified. Do the practise and experience not only these wonderful states of being but also what they leave behind with you for the rest of the day.

Sit with your eyes closed in a meditational pose, relax your body, empty out the mind and centre yourself by observing the continuous flow of breath. When you feel yourself centred, take your awareness to your spinal passage and all the Chakras on it.

Inhale and move your awareness from the Ajna to the Mooladhara Chakra along the spinal column, touching awareness on all Chakras along the way without naming them or stopping on any. When you reach the Mooladhara, meditate on the Chakra and Kundalini for some time. Then exhale and raise back your awareness and breath to the Ajna, feeling each of the Chakras along the ascent. Deepen your spinal cord inhalation and exhalation with awareness of Chakras along the up-and-down passage.

With every inhalation, internally say the mantra 'So', piercing each of the Chakras as you descend to the Mooladhara. At the Mooladhara, meditate on the Kundalini and the Mooladhara Chakra. Meditate on the symbology of the Chakra.

As you exhale, ascend with the mantra 'Hum', touching each of the Chakras along the spinal column as you reach the Ajna Chakra. At Ajna, meditate on yourself; meditate on self-awareness.

You will surely feel immense peace, serenity and expansiveness. These become a part of you.

Stage VI

At this stage, Ajapa Japa is practised with Shanmukhi mudra. Once you have stabilized your breath with a relaxed body and internalized awareness, then do Shanmukhi mudra as explained earlier. Close your ears with the thumbs and the eyes with the forefingers, place middle fingers on the nostrils, ring fingers on the lips and little fingers on the skin below the lips.

Inhale deeply, close the nostrils with the middle fingers and hold the breath inside. Then run your consciousness from the Ajna to the Mooladhara Chakra with vibrations of mantra 'So' and back from the Mooladhara to the Ajna with the mantra 'Hum'. Release the breath. Lapse into mindfulness and self-awareness.

Then start the second round. After some days of practise, you can stop doing it with the Shanmukhi mudra. Merely practise each cycle of 'So' from Ajna to Mooladhara and back to Ajna from Mooladhara with 'Hum'. After each cycle, practise mindfulness and self-awareness.

The Ajapa Japa practice is widely prevalent in India, especially among senior citizens. You can observe older people who keep a rosary in a cloth bag that hangs from their wrists. They keep rotating the beads and chanting their mantras almost all through their waking hours. With their responsibilities over, they try to maintain contact with the Supreme through the unbroken repetition of the mantra.

Antar Mauna

All the higher practises of Kundalini Kriya and meditation techniques are systems whose purpose is to block the senses, still the mind, open dormant centres of the brain and central nervous system as well as practise awareness and transform the self at all levels. Finally equipped with this transformed self, you can transcend all the limitations of your senses, mind and brain-body consciousness to know the source of our creation, which is peerless, infinite and eternal.

Antar Mauna is a technique of overcoming the paradox of living in the world while remaining detached from it. It is a process of self-observation by alternately observing your thought process and also creating your own thoughts. It is a technique which slowly builds in you the ability to observe the workings of your own mind and also the capacity to create your own thoughts and at will, destroy them.

The thought process is normally a complex web over which we have no control. But through Antar Mauna, we can learn to make it flexible and controllable. This exercise is more challenging for people who are fully involved in worldly affairs and are trying to cross over to the other world, which is the controller of all that happens in this world and beyond.

When a person gets angry, they get completely submerged by the raging hot feeling of anger. Later on, the person finds it difficult to accept what they said or did when they were angry. Most of us are at this level of unawareness in our lives. But after sustained Antar Mauna practice, awareness of the functioning of your mind turns you into a witness of the approaching anger. The very act of watching your own anger dissolves it. Thus, in addition to lifting you to higher consciousness, meditational exercises benefit our daily lives in several ways.

Swami Satyananda Saraswati, in his phenomenal tome of over one thousand pages of 'Yoga and Kriya', has beautifully explained this practice. I have put it in my own words here to fit into the theme and format of this book. I have also taken from an article on Antar Mauna by Sannyasi Atmatattwananda, UK, published in Yoga Magazine.

There are six successive stages of Antar Mauna:

1. The first stage is cutting off the sense organs, which is the fifth stage in Patanjali's Ashtanga Yoga. It is, as you know by now, known as Pratyahara.
2. The second stage involves watching your spontaneous thought process. In this stage, you develop the witness attitude. The merging of the subject and object happens. Also, thoughts from the subconscious float into your consciousness.

3. In the third stage, you create your thoughts and then discard them at will. You are gaining control over your mind in the most crucial of all aspects of dharana and dhyana, that is, concentration and meditation. Also, in the process, some fears come to the surface and are simply discarded. Thus, it cleans your unconscious.

4. In the fourth stage, you let the thoughts be spontaneous but their disposal is done by you at will. You dive deeper into your subconscious and unconscious.

5. In the fifth stage, you enter thoughtless states. This generally happens only in deep sleep. Therefore, this state, where there is no content of mind but awareness is active, is called Laya, the Non-Conscious state.

6. The last stage is the state of being in a kind of deep sleep but without losing your awareness. This is the culmination of all yoga practice.

Stage I

The Practise: The steps are as follows:

- Sit in any meditational pose. Run your awareness throughout the body and relax every part.
- Imagine your body is light, loose and relaxed.
- Gently close your eyes. Stabilize yourself by watching the continuous flow of breath at the nose tip. This is the starting position and state of your being.
- Move your awareness to your ears. Listen to each and every sound that reaches your ears. Let your awareness jump from one sound to another; the far-away sound, the sound closest to you and all other sounds.
- Then focus on one sound. If you are in a time and place where there are no sounds, focus on the sound of your breath or maybe the whirring of a ceiling fan and other white noise.

- As you intensify your focus on the sound, slowly but surely only the sound remains. Now even you, the subject, is not there. Only the sound remains. There is no object or subject. Even the sense organs, in this case the ears, are separated from the sound. Only the experience remains.

- You may choose one sound or focus on a series of sounds. In the end, only the experience of the sounds remains.

The Theory: Withdrawal of the senses is of vital importance. Swami Satyananda cautions that the practise of dharana, concentration, is not simple. If you force concentration without first preparing the substratum of your mind, you will fall into an unconscious state. In one of his lectures Swamiji said that he once made a large gathering practise concentration. Many of them, he said, fell unconscious. Without first gaining mastery over the mind, concentration or dharana, cannot be achieved.

You may practise the withdrawal of senses, Pratyahara, by focussing on other sense organs too. Like the sense of smell or taste. Or even seeing what manifests behind closed eyes; you may see patterns, images, flashes of light or even a series of images like on a movie screen. You focus on your sense of smell by taking awareness to the nose. If there is no smell to focus on, you can focus on each and every feeling inside your nostrils: on the flow of the breath inside both nostrils; is the flow equal in both or is one nostril more active than the other? Is the breath sharp or soft, wet or dry, cool or warm? You intensify your senses inside the nostrils until only the experience remains.

With the continuous practice of Antar Mauna and disassociation of the senses, your mind becomes quiet. Thus, you have gained control over the wavering of your mind to some extent. But this is just the conscious layer of your mind which is the tip of the iceberg, so to speak. The rest of the subconscious and unconscious is in the depths of your being, which we will uncover systematically in the following stages.

Stage II

The Practise: After achieving Pratyahara, your mind becomes calmer and quieter. In this state, you begin to watch your own thoughts. The thoughts that will surface are without the support of an object. For example, if you see a school, then thoughts of studies, exams or such will pass through your mind. Such thoughts have a basis. But if suddenly the thought of a banana or something unconnected flashes in your mind, it becomes a spontaneous thought. It just pops up without any reason. Why and from where do these baseless thoughts spring from? According to psychologists, they come from your subconscious.

To avoid being judgmental, analytical or reactive towards your thoughts, repeat to yourself, 'I am watching my thoughts. I will not get entangled in them.' Despite this, you will find that you have started flowing with the thoughts. You are not aware of them. You are them. With a jolt, pull yourself away from the entanglement. Thus, you swing back and forth between self-awareness and self-dissolution. There will also be moments of absent-mindedness. In the initial stages, there will be flashes or short spans when there are no thoughts. That state of no-thought is a new experience for you. In deep sleep, there are no thoughts but then you are not aware of it. Now, you are conscious of this state.

With sustained practice, you will be finding yourself in spaces where there are no thoughts. You reach the paradox of an emptiness which is mindfulness. Emptiness and fullness exist together. This is an indication that you are in the process of cleaning your subconscious. You will find the past coming up to your conscious level and memories of you as a child or even an infant will come to you and surprise you. This is why Yogis are sometimes able to go back to their past lives.

Swamiji says that when you sit for Antar Mauna practise, you must prepare yourself to face unpleasant, negative, fearful thoughts and visions. You should not delude yourself by thinking that you are going to experience bliss, peace and beautiful light. This will happen eventually but not in the early stages of Antar Mauna.

Also, simply witnessing your thoughts is not good enough. You must try to understand them. You may even resort to writing them out or sharing them with your guide or a confidant. Exploration into your thoughts helps finally exhaust them. This is achieved through psychoanalysis too. But it's a painful process which takes years to wipe clean your slate of deep-seated fears and complexes.

When the emergence of thoughts from the subconscious increases, then it is time for you to step into the third stage of Antar Mauna. This is because, as Swamiji says, you cannot exhaust all your thoughts.

The Theory: After the Pratyahara practice, you will confront and encounter your own thought factory. Continue to sit still and with closed eyes, merely watch the procession of thoughts bubbling up of its own accord from within you. You have quietened the external stimulus to the mind with the withdrawal of your senses. The stimulus for the mind now comes from within you, from your accumulated memories and experiences.

In the beginning, the greater task is to not lose yourself in your thoughts. It is not in our nature or our conditioning to watch our thoughts. The most self-observation we do is limited to admiring ourselves in the mirror. Furthermore, 'I think, therefore, I am', was how Rene Descartes summed up our existence. But our Antar Mauna practice is all about distancing yourself from the belief that you are your thoughts to discover the true self that lies underneath. What we are trying to uncover is the Self which exists when all thoughts have been annihilated. How does one do this?

Stage II is the beginning of this process. The beauty of yoga is that if it claims that you are not your thoughts, then it gives you a tool, a technique to practise, to discover, know and experience this to verify these claims for yourself.

As you begin to watch your thoughts, you may be confounded by their randomness. It is a rare mind that does only systematic and organized thinking of something in particular. For most, there is little reference to the context of our thoughts. The worst part about this is when you're moments away from sleep, the flow of thoughts is like an endless jigsaw puzzle. But most of us remain unaware of this. Rarely in a moment of introversion do you realize the crazy torrent of thoughts.

Stage III

In Stage III, you do the opposite of what you did in Stage II. In this stage, both the witness attitude and spontaneous thoughts are replaced by creating thoughts at will and disbanding them at will as well. It is a logical follow up to Stage II.

So far you have tried to be a detached witness of the surge of thoughts bubbling up spontaneously. The third stage allows you to gain control over your thought process. At this stage, you will not allow any spontaneous thoughts to take over. You will destroy them and create your own thoughts.

The Practise: The steps are as follows:

- Sit in any meditative pose with your eyes closed. And let the mind games begin.
- Some thoughts crop up but you immediately finish them off.
- Then you create your own stream of thoughts. You have to select a theme and create a whole situation and its sequence of events. For example, you have spilt some milk. Follow this thought by answering questions like: how did the spill happen? Who will chastise you for spilling the milk? How would you reply to that person? And so on.
- Then end this chain of thoughts as quickly as you started them. This breaks the usual pattern of the mind having a mind of its own and deciding when, how and what you should think. We have brought this under control to some extent by the 'witness attitude' of watching your mind and the thoughts originating from it.

The ability to finish any thought process at will helps in either examining the thoughts or eliminating them. Swamiji says, if a thought or experience, especially a painful and unpleasant one, that has taken place in your life is not eliminated or at least immediately analysed, it will proceed directly to the subconscious. Once it gets there, it influences actions and reactions without you being able to understand, much less control them.

Therefore, it is advisable to think of something bad, unpleasant, troubling or painful and brood over it and become one with it. Then suddenly, without warming, you must destroy the thought. It will create an empty space for a while. Then you must start this process again and invite another destructive, disturbing thought. In one session, it is advisable not to have more than three thoughts. Do not repeat the thoughts. The mind has a tendency to brood and will try to generate the same thoughts. But if you have examined and destroyed these willingly, they will not recur.

Swamiji further counsels that the practice of these three stages will equip you in future planning too. This is because future planning depends on observation of the present. You must progress to each stage systematically. It is not advisable for people with a weak grip on their mind to attempt this practice. Generally speaking, if you have done all the practises so far, then most likely you have strengthened your psyche and developed mind control to some extent. This practice is not advisable for those who have neurosis or have not practised the various stages of yoga, especially Pratyahara, before attempting this meditation.

Stage IV

Stage IV of Antar Mauna opens the door to premonition, pre-cognitive and even prophetic thoughts. The challenge of this stage's practice is to not get entangled in them. You still have deeper levels to go to. The aim is not to get enamoured and stuck in them because they are obstacles in your progress.

In the fourth stage, when you begin to observe your mind and the thoughts emanating from it, you face a whirlwind of random thoughts. But slowly, in this riot and confusion of thoughts, arises one thought which is clearer and stronger than the rest. It comes from the subconscious and unconscious levels of your being. Our object is to clean the deeper levels of our consciousness to free and raise it to higher levels.

There will come a time when spontaneous thoughts stop. You experience a state of vacuum. In this state, sometimes you will become aware of some sounds or other stimuli around you and then they will disappear and you will lapse into the state of emptiness. It is much like the drowsy state that exists just before drifting off to sleep. You are intermittently aware of things around you and then you slip into sleep. This is the introversion and extroversion of your senses. In sleep, it happens involuntarily. In Antar Mauna, you are aware and you tell yourself that you are practising Antar Mauna.

When your mind is free of thoughts and there are traces of sense awareness, at this stage, Pratyahara is complete. After this you enter into Dharana.

Stage V

The practice of all the stages brings you to a stage wherein you have severed the link of spontaneous thoughts. You have also trained your mind to create and disband thoughts at will. You will now experience frequent thought-free states. You are sometimes aware of the external and sometimes of the 'SoHum' state. You remain in the unconscious for longer spells. Swamiji says that sometimes you will find that you have been unconscious for an hour. Then how do you come back at will?

This state of unconsciousness is called Jada Samadhi by Swamiji. It is an inert, lifeless state. To ensure that you do not enter into this jada state of Samadhi, you must practise the sixth stage.

Stage VI

The sixth stage is about developing awareness of the three states of consciousness, the conscious, subconscious and unconscious. It is an interesting stage that we are entering. We are now dealing with states that are not only unusual but also unknown to us.

When the senses are withdrawn, a thought-free state is reached when the mind has no anchor. One can say that it has no input and no output. It is in a state akin to sleep. Sleep is the only other state when the senses are withdrawn and the mind is free of any thoughts. At this stage, you have to tell yourself, 'I'm feeling sleepy, but I will not sleep'.

At this point, you can slip into the unconscious. It is like a man going down an abyss with a rope. If his hold on the rope is firm, he can come back to the top anytime. But if he slips, then he will fall into the deep, never to return.

At this stage, your consciousness, your awareness, is like the rope and your unconscious, the abyss. Loss of consciousness of your state is like losing your grip on the rope and this will take you into the deep abyss of your unconscious. Even if the loss of awareness lasts for but a moment, it will take fifteen to twenty minutes for you to come back to your senses.

For example, you may use a symbol or a mantra to maintain this grip on consciousness. But we also know that as sleep takes over, it is difficult to keep a firm grip on the symbol or the mantra. This is the test of Antar Mauna, inner silence. When this state is reached, you have to be aware of both states. You have to experience the sleep state and also be aware of it. So, it is sleep with awareness. Sleep and awareness of sleep happen simultaneously.

When sleep is about to take over your consciousness, it is important to have a symbol. This symbol must be a fixed one. In the sense, much earlier in your practise, you should have adopted a symbol and made it yours for practises like Shambhavi mudra. You cannot keep changing your symbol. You cannot hunt for the symbol when the sleep state is upon you because then your mental faculties will be weak. Your symbol should be like a beacon of light shining in the sleep state's darkness.

Swamiji describes it beautifully as the involution of your outer awareness and evolution of your inner consciousness.

Swamiji says that without a symbol, you will enter into a state of *laya*. *He cautions that the Laya Samadhi is a wonderful state.* You can be in it for hours. But your body metabolism will slow down. Your heart and lungs will slow down but when you come out of this state, you will remain the same in terms of transformation and transcendence. But as a result of being in the laya state, your heart and lungs will weaken and your body will accumulate toxins. These can cause suffering to the aspirant.

However, if the Laya Samadhi is skirted, then the aspirant enters Chaitanya Samadhi, which is a state of illumination. You will come out of this state transformed.

It is more than apparent that it is better to practise these under an experienced, realized soul.

End the practise with a heart full of gratitude towards the enlightened souls who form the shining path for all humans to experience their ultimate potential and destiny as human beings.

End of Practise with invocation

End the practise with Shanmukhi Mudra with internal retention and awareness of the sounds within your head. Practise this for five rounds.

Follow it up with five rounds of Bhramari pranayama.

Finally, end the practise with Om Chanting, Shanti Mantra and palming of eyes after rubbing both palms together.

Hari Om Tat Sat

BIBLIOGRAPHY

Axelrod, Julius. "The Pineal Gland and the 'Melatonin Hypothesis,' 1959-1974." Accessed on 22 April 2022. https://profiles.nlm. nih.gov/spotlight/hh/feature/pineal.

Ayyangar, T.R.Srinivasa. *The Yoga Upanishad's Sanskrit Text with The Commentary of Sri Upanishad-Brahmayogin.* 2019, 402. New Delhi: New Bhartiya Book Corporation.

Chapter 3. In *ShrimatBhagwat Purana: Vol I.* 51. Gorakhpur: Gita Press.

Clancy, Kelly. "Here's Why Your Brain Seems Mostly Dormant". Nautilus. 29 July 2015 https://nautilus.us/heres-why-your-brain-seems-mostly-dormant-3611/

Goyal, M., Singh, S., Sibinga, E. M., Gould, N. F., Rowland-Seymour, A., Sharma, R., Berger, Z., Sleicher, D., Maron, D. D., Shihab, H. M., Ranasinghe, P. D., Linn, S., Saha, S., Bass, E. B., and Haythornthwaite, J. A. (2014). "Meditation programs for psychological stress and well-being: a systematic review and meta-analysis." *JAMA internal medicine, 174*(3), 357–368. https://doi.org/10.1001/jamainternmed.2013.13018.

Jung, Carl. *The Psychology of Kundalini Yoga: Notes of the Seminar Given in 1932.* Oxford: Princeton University Press. 1996. DOI:10.1515/9781400821914.

Lazar, S. W., Kerr, C. E., Wasserman, R. H., Gray, J. R., Greve, D. N., Treadway, M. T., McGarvey, M., Quinn, B. T., Dusek, J. A., Benson, H., Rauch, S. L., Moore, C. I., & Fischl, B. (2005). "Meditation experience is associated with increased cortical thickness." *Neuroreport, 16*(17), 1893–1897. https://doi.org/10.1097/01.wnr.0000186598.66243.19

M, Sri and Dr N.K.Venkataramana. "The Unknown Dimensions of the Brain, Part I: Discussion between Sri M & Dr. N.K.Venkataramana." Accessed on 22 April 2022. https://www.youtube.com/watch?v=voSm4U5zjeM

McLeod, Dr Saul. "Carl Jung." 2018. https://www.simplypsychology.org/carl-jung.html.

Muktibodhananda, Swami. Chapter 2. In *Hatha Yoga Pradipika*. 270, 329. Ganga Darshan, Munger, Bihar: Yoga Publications Trust.

Popova, Maria. "The Science of Stress and How our emotions affect our susceptibility to burnout and disease." https://www.themarginalian.org/2015/07/20/Esther-sternberg-balance-within-stress-emotion/.

Pubmed. "Estimating brain age using high resolution pattern recognition: Younger brains in long-term meditation practitioners." HTTPS://pubmed.SSBI.not.nih.gov/27079530/.

Rooney, K. L., & Domar, A. D. (2018). "The relationship between stress and infertility." *Dialogues in clinical neuroscience, 20*(1), 41–47. https://doi.org/10.31887/DCNS.2018.20.1/klrooney.

Saraswati, Swami Satyananda. "Introduction." in *Kundalini Tantra*. xlv. Ganga Darshan,Munger, Bihar: Yoga Publications Trust.

Saraswati, Swami Satyananda. *Kundalini Tantra*. 13, 22, 31, 181, 189. Ganga Darshan, Munger, Bihar: Yoga Publications Trust.

Saraswati, Swami Satyananda. *Nine Principal Upanishads*. 55. Bihar: Yoga Publications.

Saraswati, Swami Satyananda. *Yoga and Kriya*. 582, 611, 641, 666, 688. Yoga Publications Trust.

Saraswati, Swami Satyasangananda. *Sri Vijnana Bhairava Tantra: The Ascent*. Ganga Darshan, Bihar: Yoga Publications Trust.

Saraswati, Swami Satyasangananda. *Sri Vijnana Bhairava Tantra: The Ascent*. 425–426. Ganga Darshan, Bihar: Yoga Publications Trust.

Sivananda, Swami. "Introduction." In *Kundalini Yoga*. Uttar Pradesh: Divine Life Society.

Sivananda, Sri Swami. *Kundalini Yoga*. Uttar Pradesh: Divine Life Society.

Sutter, Paul. "Is it a wave or a particle? It's Both Sort of..." 30 September 2019. https://www.space.com/wave-or-particle-ask-a-spaceman.html.

The Satsang Foundation. "Sri M-Unknown dimensions of the Brain Part-I." Accessed on 22 April 2022. https://m.facebook.com/TheSatsangFooundation.

Woodroffe, Sir John (Author Avalon). *Introduction to Tantra Sastra*. 40. New Delhi: Jyoti Enterprises.

Yale School of Medicine. "New Study find links between meditation and Brain functions." https://medicine.yale.edu/news/yale-medicine-magazine/article/new-study-finds-links-between-meditation-and-brain/.

Yoga Magazine. Accessed on 22 April 2022. http://www.yoga mag.net/archives/2000s/2005/0504/0504oaj.html.

SUGGESTED READINGS

1. Yoga Upanishads: Sanskrit Text with the Commentary of Sri Upanishad-Brahmayogin. English Translation by T. R. Srinivasa Ayyangar. It covers all the types of Yoga and practises.
2. Kundalini Yoga: By Swami Sivananda Saraswati, A Divine Life Society Publication, Terri Garhwal, UP.
3. Kundalini Tantra: by Swami Satyananda Saraswati, Yoga Publications Trust, Munger, Bihar.
4. Hatha Yoga Pradipika: by Swami Muktibodhananda, Yoga Publications Trust, Munger, Bihar.
5. Bhagwat Gita: Gita Press
6. Shiva Samhita: Published by Kaivalya Dham, Lonavala.
7. Mandukya Upanishad Wisdom of the Rishis: The Three Upanishads by Shri M published by Magenta Press, 2012
8. Asana Pranayama Mudra Bandha: by Swami Satyananda Saraswati, Yoga Publication Trust, Munger, Bihar.
9. Sri Vijnana Bhairava Tantra: The Ascent: by Swami Satyasangananda Saraswati
10. Yoga Sutras of Patanjali: The Four Chapters on Freedom by Swami Satyananda Saraswati

11. Kriya & Yoga: Swami Satyananda Saraswati, Yoga Publication Trust, Munger, Bihar.

12. The Gospels of Ramakrishna Paramhansa: Two Volumes by Mahendranath Gupta

13. Yoga Darshan: Swami Swami Niranjanananda Saraswati, Yoga Publication Trust, Munger, Bihar.

14. Stalking the Wild Pendulum: by Bentov, I, Fontana, Great Britain, 1979.

15. Karma and Reincarnation: Dr. Hiroshi Motoyama, Avon Books

16. Theories of the Chakras: Bridge to Higher Consciousness, Hiroshi Motoyama, New Age Books.

17. Kashmir Shaivism: by Dr Kamalakar Mishra, Indica Books

18. Tattwa Shuddhi: The Tantric practise of inner purification: by Swami Satyasangananda, Yoga Publication Trust, Munger, Bihar.

19. Swara Yoga: The Tantric Science of Brain Breathing: by Swami Muktibodhananda, Yoga Publication Trust, Munger, Bihar.

20. Prana and Pranayama: by Swami Niranjanaanda Saraswati, Yoga Publication Trust, Munger, Bihar

21. Bhagwat Puran Two Volumes: Gita Press

22. Autobiography of a Yoga: by Paramhansa Yogananda, Yogaratna Satsangadha Society of India.

23. A Search In Secret India: by Paul Brunton, (please check publisher etc.)

24. Prana Vidya, Swami Satyananda Saraswati, Swami Niranjanananda Saraswati, Yoga Publication Trust, Ganga Darshan, Munger, Bihar, India.

YouTube, Symposiums and Lectures:

1. The Emerging Science Foundation: Kundalini Living with an inner revolution/ Bonnie Greenwell, Ph.D., Kundalini Symposium-2013.

2. Dimensions of the Brain, Part I, II, III: Shri M in conversation with Dr Venkataramana N.K. You Tube.
3. Swami Satyananda: Awakening of Kundalini, YouTube
4. Swami Satyasangananda: On Ambition of Kundalini Rise.
5. Evolution of Consciousness: Swami Satyananda Saraswati
6. Consciousness and Matter: Swami Satyananda Saraswati

NOTES

Shavasana

This is a relaxation practise which most people love.

The steps are as follows:

- Lie down on your yoga mat on your back. See that your body is straight, with the spine and head aligned.
- Keep your feet about a foot apart, flopping to the side in relaxation and hands a little away from the body with palms turned upwards with fingers curled in relaxation.
- Adjust your clothing and position to ensure that you are comfortable. Relax your whole body.

Breath Awareness

The steps are as follows:

- Gently close your eyes and keep them closed till the end of the practice.
- Internalize your awareness and observe your natural breathing.

- After a few rounds of watching your breath, take your awareness to your navel centre.
- Watch the upward-downward movement of the navel centre as you inhale and exhale.
- Watch it go up with every inhalation and down with every exhalation.
- Counting one upward-downward movement as one round, count from eleven backwards to zero without missing any count in between.
- Then move your awareness away from your navel centre and become aware of your whole body.
- As you inhale, feel relaxation spreading to all parts of the body and as you exhale, feel all stress, tension and negativity flowing out of the body.

Body part awareness with relaxation

In the next stage of Shavasana, you rotate your awareness throughout your body starting from the right side of the body. The steps are as follows:

- Move awareness to the right arm, from the tip of the fingers to the shoulder and relax the whole right arm;
- Then move your awareness to the right side of the body from the shoulder joint to the hip joint and relax it;
- Then become aware of the whole right leg from the hip joint to tip of the toes and relax it;
- Then rotate awareness from fingertips to the toes of the right side of the body and feel the whole right side of the body completely relaxed.
- Similarly, run your awareness through the left side body, starting with the left arm, the left side of the body, the left leg and finally to the whole left side body.

- After relaxing both sides of the body, take your awareness to the back of your body and relax the whole back and the whole spine. Finally, relax your entire face.
- Then once again, run your awareness throughout your body and feel complete relaxation in the whole body. Mentally repeat, 'My whole body is relaxed', three times while running awareness throughout the body.
- Then become aware of your breathing from the nose tip to the lungs and the lungs to the nose tip. Practise this for at least eleven rounds.
- End your practice by gently moving your fingers and toes and finally opening your eyes.

Yoga Nidra

I would highly recommend that you go through the book, *Yoga Nidra* by Swami Satyananda Saraswati to get a complete package of the scientific, physiological and spiritual aspects of Yoga Nidra. This is an awesome practise without which, I would say that no yoga practise is complete. It may not be a part of your daily practise. However, for some time, it is good to make it a part of your regular practise. You may even combine it with your evening meditation, mantra and japa practice.

The book also has many sample Yoga Nidra practises, both long form and short form. There are also Swami Satyananda and Swami Nityananda's recorded Yoga Nidra practises on YouTube.